Experiencing Other Minds in the Courtroom

Experiencing Other Minds in the Courtroom

NEAL FEIGENSON

The University of Chicago Press Chicago and London

The University of Chicago Press, Chicago 60637
The University of Chicago Press, Ltd., London

Printed in the United States of America

25 24 23 22 21 20 19 18 17 16   1 2 3 4 5

ISBN-13: 978-0-226-41373-0 (cloth)
ISBN-13: 978-0-226-41387-7 (e-book)
DOI: 10.7208/chicago/9780226413877.001.0001

Library of Congress Cataloging-in-Publication Data

Names: Feigenson, Neal, author.
Title: Experiencing other minds in the courtroom / Neal Feigenson.
Description: Chicago ; London : The University of Chicago Press, 2016. | Includes bibliographical references and index.
Identifiers: LCCN 2016014737| ISBN 9780226413730 (cloth : alk. paper) | ISBN 9780226413877 (e-book)
Subjects: LCSH: Evidence (Law) | Judicial process. | Examination of witnesses.
Classification: LCC K2261 .F457 2016 | DDC 347/.064—dc23 LC record available at https://lccn.loc.gov/2016014737

♾ This paper meets the requirements of ANSI/NISO Z39.48–1992 (Permanence of Paper).

Contents

1 Simulating Subjectivity 1

2 Knowing Other Minds, Simulating Worlds 6

3 Simulations as Evidence: Conceptual and Legal Overview 21

4 "That's What I See!" 32

5 The Science of Subjectivity 67

6 Ex Machina 101

7 Judging the Person 115

8 The Future of Simulations 146

Acknowledgments 155 *Notes 159*
References 197 *Index 219*

ONE

Simulating Subjectivity

To decide cases justly, judges and juries must, among other things, determine the facts. From the evidence presented in court—eyewitnesses' testimony about what they saw or heard, supplemented by documentary or forensic evidence, expert testimony, and sometimes photos, videos, or audio recordings—they try to build coherent accounts of what happened.

But what if the disputed fact is a perceptual experience known only to the person who experienced it?[1] What a litigant hears or sees (or heard or saw) may be critical, not as evidence of some event in the external world, but as the fact of the matter itself. A plaintiff who suffers from tinnitus as a result of an accident says he now constantly hears a very loud buzzing sound that no one else can hear, limiting his sleep and fraying his nerves. Another plaintiff contends that malpractice in the performance of LASIK surgery has left his vision blurred and doubled, making it very difficult for him to work. Yet another claims that the negligently delayed diagnosis of a condition known as idiopathic intracranial hypertension, which causes pressure on the optic nerve, has reduced her field of vision to a small fraction of what it once was. And a defendant in a criminal case, a police officer, alleges that he fired his gun in justified self-defense because, in the heat of the moment, he *thought* he saw the victim driving his car straight at him, even though a dashboard camera video from a trailing police cruiser shows that the victim's vehicle was not headed toward the officer at all.

The outcomes of cases like these may depend on whether jurors believe that the litigants' verbal reports capture their actual sensory experiences. The police officer may go to prison if jurors do not credit his testimony about what he thought he saw. The civil plaintiffs may recover damages in any event, but jurors who think they really understand what it's like to experience the plaintiffs' impaired vision or hearing may award them hundreds of thousands or even millions of dollars more.

How do litigants like these *prove* that their subjective experiences are (or were) what they claim them to be? Typically, they tell us and trust that we'll both believe them and appreciate what their words mean. After all, who would know better what their experiences are or have been? Other witnesses may corroborate their reports. Wives describe their husbands' changed behaviors. Doctors explain how they've carefully measured their patients' hearing or vision and confirm the nature and extent of the claimed impairments.

In a handful of cases, lawyers, litigants, and expert witnesses have gone further. They have created photos, videos, animations, and sound files that purport to *recreate* the litigants' sensations. In the tinnitus case, for instance, jurors put on headphones and listened to sounds that, according to the plaintiff and his audiologist, corresponded to the loud buzzing the plaintiff was hearing inside his head. In the LASIK case, the jury saw photographs of the plaintiff's workplace as it appeared to him, Photoshopped to match his blurred and distorted vision. During settlement negotiations in the idiopathic intracranial hypertension case, the plaintiff's lawyer played for opposing counsel a video that displayed scenes from the plaintiff's daily life, first as they would appear to someone with normal vision and then as they appeared to the plaintiff with her severely constricted vision. And in the shooting case, the defense lawyer showed jurors a computer animation of what the critical events looked like to the defendant officer, from his point of view. These sorts of visual or auditory exhibits—what the law calls *demonstrative evidence*—purport to let jurors *know*, and not merely know *about*, what it's like to be inside the litigant's mind.[2]

But how is that possible? How can anyone really know what it's like to have another person's sensory experiences, when only that person has direct access to them? How can we ever experience another person's *qualia*, the phenomenal qualities of his mental life?

More to the point, why should courts ever admit visual or auditory evidence that purports to convey what another person's consciousness is like? Of course trial advocates may be as creatively persuasive as the judge, the rules of evidence, and their resources allow. And, to be sure, methods of proof have sometimes run ahead of their scientific warrants. But should jurors be allowed to consider photos or videos that, according to their proponents, recreate a person's subjective reality?

Courts ought to be skeptical. Judges and jurors care, and should care, about getting the facts right, whether those facts have to do with external reality or a litigant's state of mind. In the generation since the US Supreme Court's landmark decision in *Daubert v. Merrell Dow Pharmaceuticals* (1993), courts have been increasingly focused on the need to ensure that scientific evidence in particular is trustworthy. And the public's faith in the law depends in part on its confidence that verdicts are sufficiently tethered to the truth. The very audacity of purporting to simulate another person's private mental experience for all to see or hear should make judges suspicious.

Yet in the handful of cases in which these simulations have been offered, courts have routinely admitted them. Simulations have also, as noted, played a role in settlement negotiations. Only once, to the best of my knowledge, has a simulation of subjectivity been excluded.[3]

In a world in which computer technology seems nearly omnipotent, and neuroscientists and bioengineers have penetrated the mind so far as to enable people to control cursors on screens and robotic arms just by thinking, maybe it's not that hard to believe that conscious experience could be uncovered, measured, and digitally recreated. Considering the wide range of contexts in which litigants' subjective experiences may be at issue—from disability claimants seeking benefits for impaired vision or hearing and sexual harassment victims alleging hostile work environments to prosecutors trying to prove a victim's fear as an element of extortion (see Kolber 2011)—we can imagine many opportunities for simulating subjectivity in the courtroom. Where might it end? If simulations of tinnitus or blurred vision are allowed, what about simulating the hallucinations that schizophrenics experience? Might jurors be invited to experience, if briefly, a plaintiff's physical pain? Might it be possible someday to scan a person's brain to extract her memories and display them on a courtroom screen? And even if it ever becomes possible, would it be a good idea to allow it?

Simulations of subjectivity are made possible, and plausible, by a combination of digital technology, clinical science, creative lawyering, trial practice, the law of evidence, and popular culture. Who thinks this sort of evidence up, how is it made, and how is it presented in court? Do judges and lawyers treat these simulations in a way that illuminates or obscures the very different sorts of claims they make to provide reliable knowledge about litigants' subjective experiences? How do jurors respond to the vicarious experience of being inside a litigant's mind? What does admitting this sort of evidence of subjective states tell us about what the law is willing to recognize as a fact? And given that all fact-finding at trial is part of a fundamentally normative enterprise—deciding how much compensation a personal injury plaintiff *deserves* for her pain and suffering, or whether a defendant in a criminal case *ought* to be punished for the harm he caused—how might simulations affect the justice that judges and jurors dispense?

This book addresses these questions. Seeing or hearing what purports to be someone else's sensations can be a far more powerful way to learn what those sensations are like than merely being told about them. Seeing, or hearing, is believing.[4] Whether a simulation of subjectivity actually provides reliable knowledge about the other person's inner experience, however, depends on the strength of our grounds for believing in it. And that depends largely on how the simulation was made. Some are backed by scientific authority and offer knowledge of litigants' sensations at least as trustworthy as, say, the knowledge of external events that computer-animated re-creations of accidents or crimes, commonly admitted as expert evidence, provide. Other simulations rest only on the litigant's say-so: "That's what I see (or hear)." How reliably each type of exhibit can recreate another person's sensations—and how each may mislead—are questions of philosophical and general interest, as well as a concern for the law.

Lawyers and judges have not always clearly distinguished among the different knowledge claims made on behalf of different types of simulations. Sometimes jurors have been invited to believe that a re-creation provided better evidence of the litigant's subjective experience than it possibly could have. Some scientifically based simulations, on the other hand, may be given *less* weight than they deserve if the principles and methods used to create them aren't made clear. By more carefully appraising each exhibit's evidentiary support, judges, lawyers, and jurors can promote the wiser use of this powerful new form of evidence.

Simulations of subjectivity have been used most often in personal injury cases, to support plaintiffs' claims for pain and suffering damages. In these cases, simulations can profoundly change the way justice is done. They can anchor what jurors think about plaintiffs' impairments and reshape jurors' responses to plaintiffs' testimony about their suffering. Perhaps most significantly, experiencing a simulation puts jurors in the plaintiff's shoes as no other evidence can, giving them unparalleled insight into the plaintiff's condition, but also threatening to bias their judgments. As more litigants in more kinds of cases seek to recreate their subjective perceptions in court, understanding these simulations and their effects on legal decision making will become ever more important.

Chapter 2, "Knowing Other Minds, Simulating Worlds," places the simulation of subjectivity in broader contexts. How should we think in general about the claim that people's sensations can be digitally recreated for others to share? The chapter briefly surveys the conflicting philosophical and psychological views about how far we can know other minds—specifically, others' sensory experiences. It also argues that, as a society, we are deeply ambivalent about digital simulations of reality and especially of personhood. Chapter 3, "Simulations as Evidence: Conceptual and Legal Overview," then sets out two frameworks for understanding how the law approaches simulations of subjective experience. The first is epistemological. I distinguish three types of simulations, each of which makes a very different kind of claim to provide reliable knowledge of the perceptual experience it purports to recreate. The second is doctrinal. I summarize the law of demonstrative evidence and explain why it leaves judges and jurors much room to misconstrue these exhibits' probative value.

The next three chapters present case studies of the types of simulation. I examine the simulations in detail, describing how they were made and used in litigation and analyzing the sort of knowledge of the litigant's sensations that each offered. Chapter 4, "That's What I See!," discusses "artist's sketch" simulations; chapter 5, "The Science of Subjectivity," simulations based on psychophysical testing; and chapter 6, "Ex Machina," those based on physical measurements of the litigant's perceptual apparatus. The persuasive effects of every simulation, however, go beyond its epistemological value. I draw on cognitive psychology and visual and media studies, among other disciplines, to discuss how each simulation may (or may not) have convinced its audiences that they could vicariously experience and thus really know what it was like to see or hear as the litigant did.

As already noted, simulations have mostly been used in personal injury cases to support plaintiffs' claims for pain and suffering damages. Chapter 7, "Judging the Person," explores how jurors' responses to simulations may interact with their reactions to the plaintiffs' testimony, reshaping their judgments about the damages these plaintiffs deserve. Finally, chapter 8, "The Future of Simulations," offers a glimpse of the next generation of evidentiary re-creations of subjectivity.

TWO

Knowing Other Minds, Simulating Worlds

Most of this book is about the legal life of simulations of subjective experience: how they are created for use in litigation, how lawyers argue for or against their admissibility at trial, how judges decide whether to admit them, what litigants and expert witnesses say about them on the stand, and how jurors are likely to think about them. But quite apart from how these simulations may fare as courtroom evidence, the very idea that people's sensations can be digitally recreated for others to experience vicariously is fascinating and problematic.

This chapter offers two broad perspectives on the simulation of subjective experience. The first addresses the basic philosophical question of how far we can really know what another person's conscious experiences are like. On one hand, some philosophers contend that we can't know what those experiences are like for the person who has them because phenomenal experience is always experience from a first-person perspective, which no one else can share. On the other, the physics and physiology of perception, everyday "mind reading," the science of mirror neurons, and various philosophical arguments, including phenomenology's understanding of perceptual experience, suggest that we can know well enough what others' subjective experiences are like even if we can't have those experiences ourselves. These debates may help us to plumb our own conflicted responses to the prospect of simulating subjectivity in the courtroom.

The second perspective is cultural. As a society we are

deeply ambivalent about digital simulations in general. We crave the knowledge they make possible, but we're nagged by doubts about the reality of what we're seeing and hearing. And we are especially anxious about the digitization of what we prize as human consciousness. When judges and jurors encounter simulations of subjectivity in court, what they take to be their common-sense responses may well be shaped by these anxieties, whether they acknowledge them or not.

I begin with a few clarifications. The "other minds" in this book's title is at once too broad and too narrow. It's too broad because, first, our concern is not with the entirety of litigants' mental lives, but only with the relatively small portion (e.g., Wilson 2002) constituted by conscious experience. Second, we're not concerned with the entirety of conscious experience, but only with *phenomenal* experience—perceptions and "feels."[1] Throughout the book I use various phrases interchangeably to identify the sought-after object of knowledge and the goal of courtroom simulations: *perception*, *subjective perception*, *experience*, *sensation*, *inner reality*, and so on. What I mean in every instance is how things look or sound to the litigant. The philosophers' word for these sorts of phenomenal qualities is *qualia* (Robinson 2008).[2]

"Other minds" is also too narrow, because subjective perception doesn't take place just in the mind (or the brain). "Perception . . . is not a process in the brain, but a kind of skillful activity on the part of the animal as a whole" (Noë 2004, 2; see also Gibson 1979). As neuroscientist Jan Lauwereyns has written, sense perception is *sensorimotor* perception. "We have to explore and construct our subjectivity," associating actions and perceptions: "'This is what it looks like when I do this' and 'This is what I get if I do that'" (2012, 205). Subjective experience is not only embodied, but is a function of being a person acting in the world. Some would argue, moreover, that sensory perception is not just an individual matter: "Just as meanings are shared, so are sensory experiences" (Howes 2005, 4). Perception itself, cultural anthropologists contend, cannot be fully understood in a psychology lab, because it is also shaped by culture and history (Classen 2012; Howes 2005).

Let's put these complications to the side for now. We'll begin by assuming there is something intelligible called phenomenal (or perceptual or sensory) experience, apart from whatever it may be an experience *of*, whatever the person may be doing or trying to do when having that experience, and whatever influence the person's culture may exert on that experience.

And we'll assume the general feature of the phenomenal experiences in which we are interested is that they have "distinctive subjective *feels*"—that there is something it is *like* to have those experiences (Carruthers 2000, 13; see also Block 1995). Given that, we can ask, Can anyone really know what it's like for another person to have the phenomenal experiences that person does?[3]

One intuitively compelling answer is, No, we can't really know what it's like for another person to have the phenomenal experiences he or she does. The fundamental reason we can't is that to know what it's like to have those experiences, you just have to have them—those particular experiences, those qualia, or ones very similar—and having any particular qualia is a uniquely first-person sort of thing, which in principle isn't available to anyone else.[4]

Let's spell this out. Simply by introspection, we seem to know the qualia that help to make up *our own* conscious experience more immediately and more certainly than we can know anything else. For instance, although I may be mistaken about the source of a pain, I can't be mistaken about whether I'm having the feeling that I'm calling pain (I may, of course, be uncertain about whether to call it pain), and although I may have trouble putting the feeling into words, I can't be mistaken about what that feeling feels like.[5] But no one else has that same first-person access to my conscious, phenomenal experience, nor I to theirs. So no one's conscious experience is directly available to anyone else (see generally Güzeldere 1997).[6]

That is, when it comes to others' qualia, there seems to be a threshold we can't cross. As William James put it long ago in *The Principles of Psychology*: "A blind man may know all *about* the sky's blueness, and I may know all *about* your toothache, conceptually . . . but so long as he has not felt the blueness, nor I the toothache, our knowledge . . . of these realities will be hollow and inadequate" (James [1890] 1950, 2:7). More recently, philosopher Frank Jackson (1986) posed the case of Mary, who is confined to a black-and-white room and, through black-and-white books and television programs, learns everything there is to know about the physical nature of the world and, in particular, color vision. If Mary is let out of the room on a sunny day or given a color television, will she learn anything new? Of course she will: she will now know *what it's like* (for her) to see whatever colors she sees. This knowledge could not be conveyed by however many propositional lessons Mary read or heard. She simply had to experience it for herself. She had to acquire this knowledge by acquaintance, not merely by description.

James's and Jackson's general point is to distinguish conceptual knowledge from direct sensory experience, and in that respect, the inaccessibility of others' qualia is similar to that of any other phenomenal experience we are physically incapable of having. But while a normally sighted person can know the sky's blueness by looking at the sky, many philosophers contend that there is no equivalent way for anyone else, ever, to know *your* toothache—that is to say, to know *what it's like* to experience that particular toothache, the one you're experiencing.

That's because, according to philosopher John Searle (1992) and others, the pain (or any other phenomenal experience) has a subjective, first-person character, which cannot be reduced to its third-person, objective, physical features, such as the pattern of neuronal firings that, based on the best available neuroscientific information, cause the experience. Even if we are someday able to explain how consciousness arises from brain activity or to give a satisfactory functionalist account of the role of consciousness, no objective description of the causes or correlates of consciousness can ever capture its distinctively first-person features: what the pain feels like to the person experiencing it. "Every mental state has to be *somebody's* mental state. Mental states only exist as subjective, first-person phenomena" (70). That is to say, the first-person experience is *ontologically* different from third-person reality. And this ontological difference "has obvious epistemic consequences: my knowledge that I am in pain has a different sort of basis than my knowledge that you are in pain" (118).

The philosopher Thomas Nagel, in his classic essay "What Is It Like to Be a Bat?" (1974), similarly posits that *experience*—what it is like for a bat to be a bat or, for that matter, a person to be that person—has a fundamentally subjective character in that it is "essentially connected with a single point of view." When we try to understand any other aspect of reality, we do so "by reducing our dependence on individual or species-specific points of view toward the object of investigation. We describe it not in terms of the impressions it makes on our senses, but in terms of its more general effects and of properties detectable by means other than the human senses. The less it depends on a specifically human viewpoint, the more *objective* is our description" (444), and hence the better our understanding. But, Nagel continues,

> experience itself . . . does not seem to fit the pattern. The idea of moving from appearance to reality seems to make no sense here. What is the analogue in this case to pursuing a more objective understanding of the same phenomena by abandoning

> the initial subjective viewpoint toward them in favour of another that is more objective but concerns the same thing? . . . If the subjective character of experience is fully comprehensible only from one point of view, then any shift to greater objectivity—that is, less attachment to a specific viewpoint—does not take us nearer to the real nature of the phenomenon: It takes us farther away from it. (444–45)

Searle argues that whatever I can know about your pain, it can't be the same as what I can know about mine, because my knowledge of *my* pain is infused with my first-person experience of it, whereas my knowledge of *your* pain lacks your first-person experience of it. Nagel concludes that we can't grasp the subjective character of others' experiences in anything like the way we achieve knowledge of anything else, because those methods lead to knowledge by leaving the subjective behind—precisely the point of view that's essential to knowing what conscious experience is like.[7] In sum, no matter what neuroscience and other disciplines may uncover about the nature, causes, and functions of conscious experience, we cannot, in principle, know what it's like for others to have those experiences, because those experiences are essentially subjective and hence cognitively inaccessible to us (van Gulick 1997, 559).

In David Lodge's novel *Thinks . . .* , Ralph the neuroscientist remarks to his friend Helen: "That's the problem of consciousness in a nutshell: How to give an objective, third-person account of a subjective, first-person phenomenon." Helen replies, "Oh, . . . but novelists have been doing that for the last two hundred years" (Lodge 2002, 42). Novelists have the considerable advantage of creating the characters whose consciousness they evoke. But even a skilled novelist's powers of description, it would seem, can do no more than evoke, suggest, give some idea of; we can't, merely on the basis of verbal description, *really know* what it's like for another person to have the phenomenal experiences she or he does. Some philosophers, psychologists, and neuroscientists would argue, however, that it *is* possible to know what another person's phenomenal experience is like, at least with the degree of reliability and confidence that suffices for our knowledge of other kinds of facts, without having done what others contend is impossible: having had the experience in question from the other person's subjective, first-person perspective. I'll identify several arguments, as well as counterarguments to them.

First, start with some fairly straightforward inferences from physics and physiology. Assume that all mental phenomena, including all qualia, are caused by something physical, namely, physiological, including neurophysiological, states (sometimes called *supervenience*; e.g., Searle 1992),[8] so that any two identical physiological states must correspond to the identical mental state. Then if your normally functioning eyes, visual cortex, and related brain areas are identical for all practical purposes to mine, and given that the receptivity of the cones in the retina to the various electromagnetic wavelengths that produce sensations of color and the way the brain processes those electromagnetic signals to yield sensations of color are themselves matters of objective physical fact, you and I can be pretty sure that when we're looking at the same thing under the same lighting conditions, our qualia are more or less the same. It's *logically* possible that what you subjectively experience when you see what everyone calls red is the same as what I subjectively experience when I see what everyone calls green (the *inverted spectrum* or *inverted qualia* hypothetical well-known in the philosophy of mind and perception literature since Locke; see Byrne 2014). If, however, the color you subjectively experience when looking at something everyone calls red is *not at all* what I subjectively experience when looking at the same thing, there should be some observable physical and/or behavioral differences between us (Churchland 2002; see also Palmer 1999).[9] In the absence of any such evidence, it is reasonable to infer that our subjective visual experiences, our color qualia, are the same.

This argument, if valid,[10] shows that *ordinarily*, we can confidently infer that others' qualia in response to similar stimuli are very similar if not identical to our own. Sometimes, though, those confident inferences will be wrong. That dramatically aberrant subjective perceptions, such as inverted color qualia, are in principle physically or behaviorally detectable does not ensure that, as a *practical* matter, they will be, and that caveat applies a fortiori to less dramatic differences in qualia.

More importantly, the argument's basic logic does not justify the inference that we can know what it's like for others to have the sorts of subjective experiences we'll be studying in this book. For one thing, some of those experiences don't reflect responses to external stimuli at all. The plaintiff who suffers from subjective tinnitus, for example, experiences a kind of auditory hallucination. Physics and physiology, at least in the current state of those sciences, offer no basis for inferring what such hallucinations may be like.

Here's a more fundamental difficulty. The argument from physics and physiology includes these points: (1) We assume, in the absence of contrary evidence, that your visual apparatus (including eyes, visual pathway, visual cortex, and so on) is similar in all relevant respects to mine. (2) If two people who have more or less identical sets of visual apparatus look at the same thing under the same viewing conditions, they'll have (more or less) the same qualia. (3) Therefore, if we're looking at the same thing under the same viewing conditions, your qualia must be (more or less) the same as mine—which is to say, I can know what it's like for you to have that visual experience because I know what it's like for me to have it.

In the cases discussed in this book, however, the other person's qualia (when looking at the same thing as we are, under the same conditions) *differ* from ours; at least, the other person knows that her qualia are different from what they were before her accident or illness. Assuming the truth of (2) above (and holding viewing conditions and so on constant), it follows that her visual apparatus must differ from ours. So the inferential chain starting with (1) never gets going, and, therefore, the argument from physics and physiology seems to be largely beside the point.

Second, folk psychology supports the claim that we can know what others' inner experiences are like. For most people, "solving th[e] other minds problem seems to be no problem at all" (Epley and Waytz 2010, 498), because we naturally and intuitively make inferences about other people's specific, individual mental states—their beliefs, preferences, needs, and so on—all the time.[11] Our ability to reason about other minds "forms the backbone of all cooperative social life" (Epley 2014, xvii). And if these habits of mind perception weren't accurate enough often enough, presumably they would not have evolved to become our common sense habits.[12] If I am at a baseball game, for instance, and I watch the home team come from behind to win in the bottom of the ninth, I may leap out of my seat, cheering. At that moment I know what *I'm* subjectively experiencing. At the same moment, I see and hear (and feel, through the vibrations in the stadium) that most of the fans around me are doing the same. Isn't it reasonable for me to conclude that I know, more or less, that those who are behaving the same way I am are thinking and feeling what I'm thinking and feeling?[13]

This plausible argument gets us only so far, however. It smacks of naive realism (e.g., Gilovich and Griffin 2010), the idea that there's an objective world out there that everyone sees the same way, provided that they're not blind or irrational (Robinson et al. 1995). Naive realists tend not to recognize how their own idiosyncratic perspectives shape their perceptions, attitudes, and conduct, and to take for granted that others will share their perceptions and beliefs, unless those others are biased (Pronin 2008; Pronin, Gilovich, and Ross 2004). I assume the people around me are thinking and feeling what I'm thinking and feeling because there's an objective event to which everyone responding similarly assigns the same meaning.[14] I tend to ignore the possibility that others may be cheering because they've won a bet on the game, or because their fantasy league player has come through, or simply because everyone around them is cheering. In addition, while appreciating or empathizing with another person's mental state may enable us to understand something, perhaps a good deal, *about* it, we cannot directly experience what she or he feels, and so what we think we know about that person's phenomenal experience is likely to be less sensorially intense than what she or he is actually experiencing (Epley and Waytz 2010).

A *third* argument is that we can know other minds because we're wired to create simulations of others' minds in our own (Goldman 2006). Mimicking another person's facial expressions and bodily posture is both an effect and a cause of recognizing the other's mental states associated with those behaviors (Epley and Waytz 2010; Iacoboni 2009). Neuroscience has traced empathic mimicry to the brain: specifically, the *mirror neuron* system (Iacoboni 2009; Rizzolati and Craighero 2004). Visuomotor mirror neurons in monkeys, for instance, "discharge both when [a] monkey does a particular action and when it observes another individual (monkey or human) doing a similar action" (Rizzolati and Craighero 2004, 169). Mirror neuron activity is not limited to watching others perform actions. Studies have shown, for instance, that many of the same brain regions are activated when one experiences a painful stimulus and when one observes one's significant other receiving a similar stimulus (Singer et al. 2004) and that watching someone being touched activates some of the same brain regions as being touched oneself (Keysers et al. 2004). One researcher claims that studies of mirror neurons suggest that "our brains are capable of mirroring the deepest aspects of the minds of others" (Iacoboni 2009, 7).

The theory that we can know other minds by simulating them in our own is subject to various criticisms, including that it is prone to the same egocentric biases as the intuitive "mind reading" just discussed (Gallagher and Zahavi 2012). What we know about mirror neurons, moreover, much like what we know about mind reading, doesn't entitle us to conclude that, in the cases studied in this book, we can know what it's like for another person to have the sensory experiences that he or she does. For instance, the brain areas activated when observing a loved one in pain comprise only part of one's own "pain matrix." Activity increases in the areas associated with affective processing of the other's pain, that is, with appreciating its significance to the person suffering the pain, but it does *not* increase in the areas associated with the pain's sensory qualities—what the pain feels like (Singer et al. 2004).[15]

Perhaps most importantly, in the cases with which we are concerned, there is simply nothing to observe that would trigger any mirror neuron system that matters. The judge and the jurors can't see a litigant's distorted vision; they can't hear his tinnitus. So the mirror neuron research falls well short of indicating that judges and jurors can know what it's like for the litigants in our cases to have the perceptual experiences they have.

A *fourth* argument is philosophical. It rejects the contention that we can't know what others' phenomenal experiences are like simply because we haven't had those experiences ourselves. Philosopher Lawrence Nemirow explains that to know what it's like to have an experience is to know how to *imagine* having it (Nemirow 2006; see also Carruthers 2000).[16] That's plausible: if we ourselves have had a particular phenomenal experience, we think we are justified in saying at some later time, when we are no longer having that experience, that we know what it's like to have it. But it turns out that having had a particular experience is not a prerequisite for being able to imagine it. As David Hume ([1739] 1896) argued nearly three centuries ago, we can imaginatively extrapolate from experiences we have had to similar experiences we haven't.[17] And in this regard, there's no difference between other people's experiences (which, in principle, we can never have, according to the philosophical argument set out earlier) and experiences we just happen not to have had yet ourselves.

The catch is that the target experience cannot be very far removed from what we have experienced ourselves.[18] So this argument, like the one from physiology and physics above, may founder when it comes up against the aberrant perceptual experiences of the litigants in our cases. We should hesitate before concluding that a judge or a juror who has never lived with tinnitus or the halos and starbursts following some LASIK surgeries, or who has perhaps experienced only very mild versions of either of these impairments, can really imagine what it's like for others to endure their far more severe versions of the same conditions.

Fifth, the philosophical tradition of *phenomenology* presents a set of responses to the claim that we can't really know what others' inner experiences are like because those experiences are inherently private and therefore inaccessible to us. Phenomenology is the study of "the structures of experience, or consciousness . . . as experienced from the subjective or first-person point of view" (Smith 2013), and it claims to generate knowledge of important aspects, if not the entirety, of conscious experience.

For phenomenologists, conscious experience transcends the merely subjective in several ways. Edmund Husserl, for instance, maintained that perceptual and other conscious states are *intentional* in the sense of always being *of* something, oriented toward "intentional objects" (Kersten 1997), thus identifying perception's significance in how it locates the perceiver in the world beyond the person's private consciousness. More to our purposes, phenomenologists have argued that we can apprehend the conscious experiences of another person intersubjectively through *empathy*, which Husserl conceived of as "an immediately felt correspondence between the kinesthetically perceived intentional movements of [one's own] body . . . and the outwardly perceived movements and positions of an external body" (Kern 1997, 358). You don't come to know my feelings (as suggested by the folk psychological model of mind reading sketched above) by first introspecting your own feelings and then deliberately inferring that if I am behaving similarly to you under conditions similar to yours, I must be feeling the same way. Rather, according to philosopher Max Scheler and others, your encounter with my person acquaints you directly (i.e., noninferentially) with my feelings because we are both intentional beings with bodily presences in the world, with which we naturally express our psychological states (Scheler [1912] 1970; see Zahavi 2005). Research phenomenologists, meanwhile, presume that intersubjective knowledge about consciousness can be generated through systematic first-person reports (e.g., Price and Barrell 2012). Indeed, it could be argued that insofar as consciousness is available to introspection and then to being communicated to others, it is *already* intersubjective because the concepts we employ to reflect on our inner experiences are shaped by language and hence by shared culture.[19]

These phenomenological strategies for knowing others' subjective experiences, however, don't seem to speak to our main concern, which is the "feel" of particular sensory experiences. The focus of many philosophical phenomenologists on the *types* and *structures* of conscious experience indicates that their goal is to develop systematic conceptual knowledge (e.g., Goodman 1966) rather than particularized knowledge of what it's like for some individual person to have the phenomenal experiences she or he does.[20] The methodological presumption that first-person experience can be made known through language, moreover, entails that what is being made known is propositional content (specifically, verbal conceptualizations of experience, filtered through the chosen protocols for observing and reporting) rather than the experience's phenomenal character. But it's precisely that character we want to know about when we ask whether others can know what it's like for a litigant to have his or her sensory experiences. And even if we can empathically intuit the other's experience—a questionable prospect in the case of the perceptual impairments at issue in our cases, since they present few if any bodily signs we can recognize—it's not the case that "we can experience the other in precisely the same way as she herself does, nor that the other's consciousness is accessible to us in precisely the same way that our own is" (Gallagher and Zahavi 2012, 204). The very fact that intersubjectivity is possible indicates that "there must exist a bridge between my self-acquaintance and my acquaintance with others" (206), yet the other's experience remains at a distance just when we most want to reach it.

In sum, we find two general strategies for responding to the claims of some philosophers that we can never really know what other people's subjective experiences are like for them. One is that we can because the similar constitution of our bodies and brains and our common participation in social life enable us to infer it, if not to know it even more directly (as per the simulation theory of mind and phenomenological empathy). The other is that the skeptics are looking for the wrong sort of answer to our basic question. If *knowledge* of *what it's like* is what we're after, then what we seek is necessarily conceptual (in addition to whatever else it may be), and the same concepts we use to grasp what it's like for *us* to experience what we do bring *others'* experiences within reach of our understanding.[21]

But everyone seems to agree that we can't directly observe another person's conscious experience and that we don't yet have a satisfactory causal account of how observable (and measurable) brain states give rise to conscious experience. We therefore can't generate third-person, objective representations of subjective experience that are epistemologically equivalent to *recordings* of external phenomena or reconstructions based on accurate measurement of those phenomena. A simulation, then, is a second-best epistemological option, capable of enhancing our knowledge of what the other's phenomenal experience is like—to the extent that it accurately and reliably reproduces (essential features of) that experience. Can it do this?

How disposed judges and jurors are to trust evidentiary simulations as accurate re-creations of litigants' perceptual experiences may be shaped by popular attitudes toward computer simulation in general. Those attitudes are themselves conflicted. One tension is epistemological; the second, existential.

As a society, we depend on and greatly value the knowledge that computer simulations provide. From architecture and industrial design to meteorology, biology, physics, and economics, from planning wars to preparing for natural disasters, as well as in news, education, and entertainment, simulations have come to occupy an increasingly important role in the sciences, the professions, and everyday life. Architects and engineers test multiple versions of designs for buildings and bridges and learn how each will perform under different conditions. Chemists, biologists, and physicists discover and study the structure of complex objects and events by generating and processing vastly greater amounts of relevant data than they could if constrained by physical tools (e.g., Galison 1996; Turkle 2009). Automotive safety experts crash-test cars without the cost of wrecking actual vehicles (Wolf 1999); nuclear physicists simulate the effects of atomic weapons without creating radioactive fallout (Turkle 2009).

Educators and others deploy simulations to visualize aspects of reality too small, too large, too ephemeral, or too complex to see, or where no camera was around to record what we want to see (e.g., "Inner Life of a Cell" 2006).[22] And computer-generated re-creations of external events and devices have become commonplace in the law (e.g., Schofield and Mason 2012).

Yet we can't help but wonder: to the extent that we turn to simulations to provide knowledge about reality, how can we depend on them to do that, given that everything we see in a simulation is *made up* by the program from the data people have chosen to enter into it?

We can think about this doubt in various ways. If we consider the simulation as a representation or an image of reality, it's clear that its veridicality is never entirely separable from its *subjunctive* nature (Wolf 1999). A simulation always potentially shows what could be or would be or might have been. How confident can we be that we're looking at the actual and not just at one of many possibles? The manipulability of the simulation contrasts with the presumptive veridicality of the ordinary photo or video. In place of the *indexical* relation of a photo or video to the reality it depicts, based on the causal connection between the image and the reality before the lens,[23] users and consumers of computer simulations must ask how accurately and completely the program models the world being simulated, which, especially in the case of scientific simulations, can be a complicated, subtle, and contested question (see Galison 1996; Winsberg 2010).[24]

In a world of increased reliance on computer simulations, as communications scholar Mark Wolf writes, "there is a greater willingness to trade close indexical linkage for new knowledge that would otherwise be unattainable within the stricter requirements of indexical linkage that were once needed to validate knowledge empirically" (Wolf 1999, 274). Against the doubts arising from subjunctivity, then, we place a confidence born out of the enormous explanatory and predictive successes of scientific and engineering simulations. We *want* to believe that digital imagining can lead to knowledge that's as reliable as what we're accustomed to finding in more familiar and presumptively trustworthy sorts of representations, because the promise of having that knowledge is so enticing.

Nor is the lack of indexicality the only reason why viewers may be anxious about the knowledge of the real that simulations purport to offer. To borrow another term from semiotics, the *iconicity* of simulations—their *resemblance* to what they purport to represent—can itself seduce viewers into believing that they faithfully recreate reality.[25] Ever-increasing computational power enables immersive simulations to come closer and closer to providing the "essential copy" of reality that artists and technologists have sought for millennia (Biocca, Kim, and Levy 1995, 7).[26] "Screen versions of reality may come to seem like reality itself" (Turkle 2009, 17), a self-deception to which those who work with simulations as models may be especially prone. Their professional and personal investment in simulations' capabilities feeds their trust that what they and their colleagues have created is valid, despite their intimate knowledge of the manipulability of those very images.

One more epistemological concern is worth mentioning. As just noted, even the scientists who work with simulations to model reality can be drawn in by the "pretty pictures" that result. In part, these clear, precise, finished digital images can persuade, and sometimes mislead, by appearing to *eliminate uncertainty*. They may look like what historian of science Peter Galison calls the "the 'golden event': the single picture of such clarity and distinctness that it commands acceptance" as proof of the existence of what is depicted (Galison 1997, 22), but they often represent the fruits of research in progress, subject to statistical margins of error (Turkle 2009). Simulations don't show the error bars. As a result, they can lure even those who should know better into thinking they can know more, and more confidently, than the evidence warrants.

The second source of anxiety about simulations of subjectivity is existential. Specifically, we're anxious about the digitization of personhood. We marvel at Deep Blue, the IBM computer that defeated chess champion Garry Kasparov in 1997, and at Watson, the more advanced IBM computer that won first prize playing *Jeopardy* in 2011. But we worry about what, if anything, will remain uniquely human as more and more capacities once thought distinctively human are digitized (Hamilton 2009).

Consider how increasingly plausible it is to believe that what we may need to know about other people's selves can be digitized. We've become used to algorithms that "know" our preferences and suggest items for us to purchase based on our previous purchases, our Internet surfing habits, or even our "private" e-mails. Companies may soon engage in "predictive shopping," using predictions based on our past digital and other behaviors "to enroll [us] in special programs in which [we] receive goods and services, and are asked to pay for them, before [we] have actually chosen them" (Sunstein 2014). Bots perform an ever-wider range of online tasks—choosing, sorting, even entering into contracts, exhibiting a kind of agency once associated exclusively with actual humans (see Hamilton 2009). If people's desires can be emulated by computer programs, why can't another aspect of their inner lives, their phenomenal experiences, be translated into bits and then converted into tangible form, so that we can know what they're like by experiencing them ourselves?

That this is not just a fantasy is suggested by multiple lines of research that use digital tools to reconnect minds to the world after the usual connections between the two have been severed. Neurophysiologists and neuroengineers have created brain-machine interfaces that allow paralyzed patients to control robotic arms with their thoughts (Regalado 2014). Meanwhile, neuroscientists, through the digital mediation of functional MRI, report eliciting communicative thoughts from patients diagnosed as vegetative (Monti et al. 2010). Closer to the focus of this book, researchers have been able to recreate from scans of people's brains the images at which the people were looking when scanned (e.g., Cowen, Chun, and Kuhl 2014). An article in a leading neuroscience journal has proclaimed: "Reconstruction of the subjective contents of human perception may soon be a reality" (Kay and Gallant 2009, 246). In short, technological and scientific progress seems to be making digital simulations of subjectivity possible at the same time as the cultural ubiquity of digital mediation makes them credible.

Skeptics of the digital life have responded in two ways. The first has been to voice concerns about the threats to the self that increasingly digitized knowledge of persons presents, and about the growing dependence on digital mediation in place of face-to-face encounters with other people. Art historian Barbara Maria Stafford describes modern medical brain imaging as a continuation of older medical illustrations' fetishizing of single organs and body parts, separating the physical body from the animating spirit: "The specter of desubstantialization and decontextualization haunts the neurosciences" (1996, 140). Sociologist of science Sherry Turkle (2011) worries that the ubiquity of Internet-enabled devices and social networking has accustomed people to diminished interactions with others. Computer scientist Jaron Lanier (2011) similarly complains that Facebook's templates require users to build constricted online presences; these reduced selves then become the standard by which others are known to us.

The second response has been to insist that consciousness will, after all, remain the last redoubt against the sweep of digitization. Postmodernists may worry that the self itself may be "completely catalogued and analyzed and then artificially revived as though real" (Baudrillard 1983). Turkle (2011), however, maintains that ultimately it isn't possible to recreate digitally what our perceptions and preferences really feel like, because bits and algorithms don't have bodies, histories, or subconsciouses, all of which are essential parts of our lived and felt lives (see also Carr 2010). An artificial intelligence may pass some version of the Turing test, but it won't have a self. Subjective experience, even the small slice of selfhood represented by impaired vision or a ringing in the ears, can't really be replicated.[27]

All this societal ambivalence, both epistemological and existential, is triggered when lawyers introduce demonstrative evidence of subjective experience in settlement negotiations or trials. Litigators, of course, aren't doing epistemology, or cultural studies for that matter, at least not consciously. They're trying to win cases. But simulations of subjective perception would be expected to help them win only when the trier of fact (or, in a settlement negotiation, opposing counsel anticipating what the trier will think) finds the simulations believable enough as illustrations or proof of those perceptions.[28] And jurors' thoughts and feelings about that are likely to be influenced by the conflicting attitudes toward the digitization of personhood circulating in the culture at large.

THREE

Simulations as Evidence: Conceptual and Legal Overview

To understand the legal life of simulations, we need to know more about the kind of knowledge they are capable of providing and the rules judges use to evaluate them. This chapter begins by addressing these exhibits' epistemological status. I distinguish three types of simulations, each of which makes a very different sort of knowledge claim about the subjective experience it purports to recreate. I then address simulations' evidentiary status, briefly overviewing the law of demonstrative evidence. As we'll see, the rules governing admissibility, as is perhaps to be expected, only loosely constrain what judges and, more importantly, jurors think simulations can teach them about litigants' subjective states.

The three basic types of simulations are the *artist's sketch*, the *psychophysical*, and the *machine readout*. Each is based on a different source of information about the litigant's perceptual experience; each is also fashioned from that information by a different method. As a consequence, the three types differ in the quality of knowledge they can offer about the litigant's sensations.

To analyze knowledge claims in this way is to identify epistemological value with probative value, and probative value with reliability. The more reliable the information about the litigant's subjective experience on which an exhibit is based and the more trustworthy the method by which that information is converted into the exhibit, the more we can count on the exhibit as proof of the facts it purports to show, and hence the stronger the knowledge claim it makes. This generalization oversimplifies the evidentiary analysis a bit but, I believe, acceptably for our purposes.[1] The distinctions I draw are intended to be easy to grasp, in that they rely on concepts that are familiar in the law of evidence and, I hope, common sense.[2]

The Artist's Sketch

The artist's sketch simulation is produced when the litigant collaborates with someone who has expertise in fashioning digital images or sounds. Much as an eyewitness to a crime might collaborate with a police investigator wielding an Identikit to work up a sketch of a suspect, so here the litigant and someone adept at manipulating photographic data or digital sound files go back and forth until the litigant says the picture or sound corresponds to what he sees or hears. The person working with the litigant to create the exhibit need not have any scientific expertise relevant to the litigant's clinical condition, only the tools and skills to translate the litigant's self-reported experience into visual or auditory form. The claim that the resulting picture or sound file accurately simulates the litigant's sensory experience thus rests entirely on the litigant's say-so. Visual examples of this kind of simulation include Photoshopped pictures of the kind used in the LASIK malpractice case mentioned in chapter 1 (*Devadas v. Niksarli* 2009) and the computer animation used in the police shooting case mentioned in the same chapter (*State v. Murtha* 2006). Auditory examples include tinnitus sound files, generic or litigant-specific, whose accuracy is verified only by the person's claim that the sound matches what he hears in his head.[3]

The Psychophysical Simulation

A second type of simulation purports to translate into tangible form the litigant's perceptual capacities as measured by psychophysical testing: by optometrists or ophthalmologists in the case of visual impairments or audiologists in the case of tinnitus. Here the authority for the trustworthiness of the simulation is derived not just from the plaintiff's claim that it accurately reproduces what she sees or hears, but also from the reliability and validity of the underlying clinical measurements, based on the scientific principles and methodology used in the field. The process of measuring the litigant's sensations always remains partly subjective, because the data depend on her conscious responses to test stimuli (whether in the form of verbal responses, button pushes, dial adjustments, or what have you). But in contrast to the introspective descriptions on which artist's sketch simulations are based, the psychophysical data are not *entirely* subjective, because they are grounded in professionally disciplined, quantitative measurement. The conversion of the data into pictures or sounds, moreover, may be at least partly automated. The tinnitus case mentioned in chapter 1 (*Janson* 2011) is an example of a psychophysical simulation: the sound files were based on the audiologist's psychoacoustic data obtained from his clinical tests of the plaintiff's hearing. A visual example is the video simulation in the case of the woman suffering from idiopathic intracranial hypertension, also mentioned in that chapter (*Smith v. Jones* 2012).[4]

The Machine Readout

A third type of simulation is derived entirely from physical measurements of the patient himself. For instance, ophthalmologists may use *wavefront technology* to measure the eye's optics, specifically, aberrations in the patterns of light reaching the retina (e.g., Williams, Applegate, and Thibos 2004). By processing the resulting optical data using complex algorithms, wavefront analysis can generate an *image simulation* representing the patient's visual perception of any given object (to be precise, the patient's retinal image of that object)—blurred, doubled, or otherwise deformed or degraded in precisely the way the patient's corneal or other defects indicate (e.g., Mattioli and Tripoli 2006; Roorda 2004). The resulting picture of what the world looks like to a person with a precisely measured corneal condition is thus more fully objective than the psychophysical simulation in that it bypasses entirely the person's conscious expression of his own internal experience. An example of this third type of simulation is an exhibit introduced in another LASIK malpractice suit, in which the plaintiff claimed that the surgery exacerbated a prior corneal condition and should not have been performed. The plaintiff offered, and the court admitted, a wavefront study done by another ophthalmologist who treated the plaintiff a few years later. That study included an image simulation of how an "E" on a standard eye chart looked to the plaintiff at that time, given the further degeneration of his cornea (*Schiffer v. Speaker* 2005).

To recap, here are the three types of simulations:[5]

Type of Simulation	Source Information about Litigant's Experience	Example
Artist's sketch	Litigant's introspection	*Devadas, Murtha*
Psychophysical	Clinical testing	*Smith, Janson*
Machine readout	Physical measurement	*Schiffer*

Simulations may, of course, vary in many ways besides their different kinds of evidentiary warrant. Re-creations of subjective hearing, for instance, may have different psychological effects, and different effects on judgment, from re-creations of subjective vision. The particular form of a demonstrative exhibit and the manner in which it is presented in court may raise distinct evidentiary issues. These sorts of differences are pursued in more detail in chapters 4 through 6. The taxonomy offered here is intended only to identify and elucidate broad distinctions among the simulations' epistemological bases.

We can make four general observations about these simulations. *First*, they can be a very powerful form of evidence. Verbal self-reports, whatever their other rhetorical virtues, tend to offer only a rather imprecise sense of what it's like to see or hear what the speaker claims to be seeing or hearing. That's just the nature of words; they're both ambiguous and vague as tools for denoting such rich and complex phenomena as perceived experience.[6] Verbal reports also depend on the speaker's ability to describe her experience to others, an ability that varies enormously from one person to the next. Simulations are different. Unlike the spoken words of testimony, simulations are in the same perceptual modality as the sensations they purport to recreate. Because they *resemble* that reality, we intuitively believe that the sound files in *Janson*, the photographs in *Devadas*, and the video in *Smith* put us in touch with the respective plaintiffs' subjective reality in a way that words alone cannot.[7] As a consequence, they share the persuasive force of photo, video, and sound recordings of external reality, as well as of "real" evidence (the law's term for the actual things involved in the litigated events, e.g., the murder weapon). They seem to give us direct, immediate access to the fact of the matter, which comports with the principle implicit in the law of evidence that the best evidence is that which is closest in time and space to the events at issue (the "Ground Zero" theory of evidence; Scheppele 1998).

By providing judge and jurors with the vicarious *experience* of the litigant's subjective perception, moreover, simulations offer a richness of knowledge and a level of confidence in that knowledge beyond anything mere verbal description can provide. The person who has had the experience of *x* can remember and imagine *x* in ways that someone lacking that experience cannot (Lewis 1997). Jurors will draw on those memories and mental images when they go to the jury room to deliberate.

One more feature that adds to the persuasive force of these simulations is that they purport to recreate the *individual litigant's* particular sensations, rather than to depict more generically a certain kind of distorted vision or tinnitus sound. We can imagine, for instance, a LASIK malpractice plaintiff testifying that, before the onset of his condition, he used to see at his ophthalmologist's office posters of impaired eyesight, and that now his vision is just like what one of the posters shows.[8] A judge might well allow the poster as demonstrative evidence, based on the plaintiff's authentication of it as a "fair and accurate representation" of what he now sees. Comparable generic simulations of tinnitus, such as the "Sounds of Tinnitus" available online at the American Tinnitus Association website,[9] have reportedly been used in some cases.[10] These exhibits can certainly help illustrate the plaintiff's verbal description of his plight. But an exhibit that purports to recreate the litigant's unique sensations, and a fortiori one that has been derived from clinical measurements of the litigant's behavior or perceptual apparatus itself, would seem to stake an even stronger claim to establish what it's like *for him* to experience what he does.

Second, and crucially, the different types of simulations make very different sorts of claims to provide reliable, justified knowledge about what it's like to experience the subjective states they purport to recreate. The artist's sketch simulation is based entirely on the litigant's self-reported introspective access to his own perceptions. The litigant's report could well be accurate, if imprecise; as observed earlier, no one would know better than she what her subjective experience is like. But what sort of *probative value* does the artist's sketch have? Arguably none. According to textbook evidence law, an item of evidence has probative value if it "affects the probability that a fact is as a party claims it to be" (Cleary 1984, 542). Given the litigant's verbal description of her subjective experience, this type of simulation doesn't make it any more likely that the litigant's subjective experience is as she claims it to be.

The counterargument is that the artist's sketch does have *some* probative value. Because it conveys *more information* than the litigant's words alone do about what it's like to see or hear as she does,[11] the artist's sketch tends to make the whole fact of the matter—what the litigant's experience is like for her, in all its sensory detail (or at least what can be captured in a tangible exhibit)—more probably the case than it would be if jurors were given only a much less complete (because solely verbal) description of that fact.[12] Still, it seems clear that the artist's sketch simulation does not have any probative value *independent* of the litigant's claim that it corresponds to her experience. Whatever epistemological value this type of simulation has depends entirely on the litigant's say-so.

In contrast, the psychophysical simulation augments the purely first-person account with the additional source of knowledge of sensory functioning that valid clinical science, reliably applied, can provide. This type of exhibit remains inherently subjective because the clinical data depend on the person's responses to test stimuli. And yet it's not merely subjective, because the clinical methods and measurements, at least in principle, imbue those responses with greater objectivity and precision than an introspective report alone can yield. Like the artist's sketch, the images or sounds of the psychophysical exhibit itself don't offer independent evidence, over and above the underlying data, that the litigant's experience really is as the exhibit represents it; they just give visible or audible form to the data. But the nature of these data, as well as the particular processes by which they are converted into images or sounds, mean that psychophysical simulations can offer better warranted evidence than the artist's sketch can of what the litigant's sensations are really like.

The third type of simulation, the machine readout, avoids self-report entirely *and* automatically registers the reality it depicts. In both respects, this type of simulation is capable of offering more objective knowledge of the litigant's subjective experience than either of the other two types. The machine readout can't provide direct access to that subjective experience; wavefront technology takes us as far as the retina but not into the visual cortex, much less to wherever consciousness resides. How important a caveat that is depends in part on how much people's visual experiences are influenced by their expectations, desires, and other "top-down" cognitive and emotional processes, and not just the "bottom-up" information their retinas receive. This technology has the potential, however, to put jurors' and judges' knowledge of what it's like for the litigant to see or hear as he does on a more solid evidentiary footing, comparable to the basis of our technologically mediated knowledge of much of external reality—for instance, the computer-generated simulations of accidents or crimes commonly admitted as substantive proof at trial.

This is not to say that any given scientifically based simulation is necessarily more accurate than an artist's sketch. Artist's sketch simulations, based only on the litigant's say-so (and the consultant's digital design skills), may represent the litigant's phenomenal experience as accurately as we could reasonably wish (although there are many reasons to question this claimed accuracy, as I explain in chapter 4). At the same time, scientifically based simulations may be inaccurate for any number of reasons: dubious or unsettled clinical principles and methods, errors or biases in their implementation, and distortions introduced in the process of generating the image or sound file. (I explore these and other concerns in chapters 5 and 6.) The issue, rather, is how we know what we think we know; or, to put it another way, by what authority a simulation purports to display the litigant's subjective experience accurately; or, in terms of the standard conception of knowledge as *justified* true belief (Chisholm 1957), how well justified is each type of simulation's claim to let us know what it's like for the litigant to perceive as she does.

Third, it's worth emphasizing (again) that however precise and trustworthy the knowledge of litigants' sensations that simulations provide, none of them *record* those conscious states themselves in the way that a standard photo or video records external reality. Even the more objective, scientifically based types of simulations are limited to what can be measured—behaviors under clinical test conditions or physical features of the eye's optics. They can't get behind those observables to the conscious experiences that (we have good reason to presume) correspond to them. Yet because of their persuasive power, judges and jurors may think simulations tell them more about litigants' subjective states than they actually do. As a result, decision makers may be *overconfident* in the inferences they draw from their experiences of the simulations (see Feigenson 2014), tending to discount any reasons to believe that these exhibits may be less reliable than their proponents contend, as well as any contrary evidence about the extent of the litigants' sensory impairments.

Fourth, simulations of subjective perception do not ordinarily wear their epistemological warrants on their sleeves. We often can't tell just by looking at or listening to one of these exhibits how it was derived and therefore what sort of knowledge it's offering. A photo simulation of blurry vision, for example, may look the same whether it is derived from wavefront data, the results of a clinical exam, or nothing more than the litigant's assertion, "That's what I see." As a result, judges and especially jurors may not always be as mindful as they should be of how strong a knowledge claim the simulation they encounter is actually capable of making.

Evidentiary law and practice can guide, at least to some extent, how far simulations contribute to jurors' knowledge of litigants' perceptual states. A trial judge may exclude a proffered exhibit, so that it plays no role at all, or admit it with instructions that jurors consider it only for a limited purpose, which may constrain their use of it. To understand how judges have responded to proffers of simulated subjectivity—as noted in chapter 1, they've allowed them in every case but one—and whether their responses have illuminated or obscured the simulations' epistemological value, a brief overview of the law of demonstrative evidence is needed.

That law, unfortunately, is confused in several respects. Courts and legal academics disagree even about what the phrase *demonstrative evidence* means. Although most would agree that it refers to a tangible display that is "not the actual thing, but represents the actual thing" (Mauet and Wolfson 2012, 315), some older sources extend the category to cover anything "from which the trier of fact may derive a relevant firsthand sense impression" (Cleary 1984, 664), including real evidence. The law is especially in disarray with regard to our central concern: how to categorize the degree of probative value a given item may have. Some sources differentiate "demonstrative" from "substantive" evidence; under this view, demonstratives "do not have independent probative value for determining the substantive issues in the case" (Broun 2006, 374). Such demonstrative "aids" are allowed in court only to *illustrate* other evidence (typically testimony) and thus to help the trier of fact understand that other evidence.[13] A common example is an anatomical chart a doctor may use to explain his testimony (Mauet and Wolfson 2012). Other sources assert that the category of demonstrative evidence includes items like photos or videos of the scene of the litigated events, which may be admitted as substantive evidence, that is, as having independent probative force (Mueller and Kirkpatrick 2012). Under this view, a demonstrative exhibit may be illustrative (like the anatomical chart) *or* substantive (like the photo or the video). And some authorities go so far as to say that "demonstrative evidence . . . is just as much substantive evidence of the facts it depicts or portrays as is real or testimonial evidence" (*State v. Swinton* 2004, 802n20).

Perhaps this incoherence persists because often, not much of practical significance rides on characterizing a demonstrative as only an illustrative aid (that is, not independently probative) or as a substantive exhibit (that is, independently probative). For many sorts of demonstratives—graphs, photos, or videos, for instance—the same sort of testimony suffices to lay the foundation for and thus authenticate the exhibit for admission: the statement of a qualified witness that the exhibit fairly and accurately represents what its proponent claims it represents (Mueller and Kirkpatrick 2012).[14] (Other kinds of exhibits, including surveillance videos that no eyewitness can say fairly and accurately represent what the witness recalls having seen, as well as more complex kinds of computer-generated imagery, require a more elaborate foundation.[15]) Then, assuming the demonstrative is admitted, what the lawyers may care about most is whether the jurors will be permitted to see (or hear) it only during the evidentiary phase of trial and perhaps during closing argument, or whether they will also be allowed to review it during deliberations. Distinctions between illustrative and substantive admission often don't matter here, either, because judges have discretion to allow even purely illustrative, nonprobative items to go to the jury room (Mauet and Wolfson 2012).

In any event, the muddled doctrinal framework allows, and possibly even invites, judges to admit different kinds of simulations in ways that fail to make clear their epistemological differences. Begin with artist's sketch simulations. Judges inclined to admit them merely as nonprobative *illustrations* of the litigant's testimony about his or her perceptual experience can find doctrinal support, as we've seen. The judge in *Murtha*, the police shooting case, admitted the video animation as just this sort of illustrative aid. This approach, however, elides the sense in which artist's sketch simulations arguably *do* add probative value by enabling jurors to know more about what the litigant's perceptual experience is like, additional knowledge that may be no more but also no less trustworthy than the litigant's own testimony. Judges inclined to admit artist's sketch simulations as *substantive* exhibits can also find authority on which to rely. Some, including the judge in *Devadas*, appear to have taken this approach. But admitting these simulations as substantive, without more, tends to obscure the fact that they have no probative force *independent* of the litigant's attestation. The difficulty, in terms of the illustrative-substantive distinction, is that artist's sketch simulations are *both* illustrative and substantive.

The point is not that artist's sketch simulations should never be admitted. Backed by the litigant's own eyewitness (or earwitness) testimony that the sketch fairly and accurately represents what the litigant sees (or hears), they would appear to rest on as firm a basis as, say, other evidence offered by a lone eyewitness. The point is that a complacent judicial attitude toward their admission may *mislead* jurors as to their actual probative value. And as explained in chapter 4, jurors may well be inclined to believe that artist's sketch simulations are more reliable, and more probative, than they can possibly be.

Scientifically based simulations, whether psychophysical or machine readout, are a different story. The law of evidence insists that if a substantive exhibit is the product of scientific or other expertise, it should be admitted only if the expert responsible for the exhibit has relied on valid principles and methods and has implemented those principles and methods in a reliable fashion both to generate the underlying information and to produce the exhibit itself (Federal Rules of Evidence 2014, 702, 901(b)(9)).[16] Judges have so far properly tended to treat scientifically based simulations as substantive evidence and have asked for at least some showing that the expertise justifying their admission meets the jurisdiction's standards for expert evidence. Judicial scrutiny, however, has been insufficient, as discussed in more detail in chapters 5 and 6. This leaves jurors more room to make epistemological errors—in either direction—especially if opposing counsel is not up to the task of effectively cross-examining the proponent's expert witness. As with the artist's sketch simulation, jurors may give a scientifically based simulation *more* weight than it deserves as proof that the litigant's subjective experience actually is as the simulation presents it. Inadequate vetting can also result in the opposite problem: if the lawyers and expert witness(es) fail to articulate thoroughly the knowledge claims that a scientifically based simulation makes, jurors may give it too *little* weight, failing to understand that this type of simulation can provide quite reliable knowledge of the litigant's subjective experience.

Probative value is not the only requirement for the admission of evidence. The law also allows judges to exclude an item of evidence if its probative value is substantially outweighed by any risk that it will mislead jurors, confuse the issues, cause unfair prejudice, or impair good decision making in other ways (Federal Rule of Evidence 2014, 403). The risk that jurors will misconstrue and, in particular, overestimate the probative value of an artist's sketch simulation, noted above, raises concerns under this rule. The failure of some judges to instruct jurors adequately on the simulation's probative value exacerbates that risk. Simulations can also mislead or confuse jurors or unfairly prejudice them in other ways. For instance, they can prompt strong emotional responses, which (according to the law) should not influence legal judgments. And in personal injury cases, experiencing for themselves what the plaintiff sees or hears may induce jurors to gauge how much the plaintiff is suffering by reflecting on how bad it would be for *them* to have to live with those impairments—a fundamental confusion that the law's rule against "Golden Rule" arguments tries to avoid. Judges so far appear to have devoted little if any attention to evaluating these risks.

Trials are about more than determining facts. The courtroom provides a forum for the pursuit of knowledge in order to enable judges and jurors to decide cases justly. The conduct of trials reflects norms of fair process as well as extrinsic policy concerns, and for jurors, truth-seeking is bound up with moral evaluation. Still, we want legal judgments to be as closely tethered to the fact of the matter as these other considerations allow. How reliable is the knowledge of other minds that lawyers, consultants, experts, and litigants construct in court by means of simulations?[17] The following chapters explore how the knowledge claims made on behalf of the different types of simulations have been put forward and contested in five actual cases.

FOUR

"That's What I See!"

Legal facts are often established through eyewitness evidence. Eyewitnesses' perceptions and memories may be flawed; their testimony may be self-interested, unclear, or inconsistent; the testimony of one eyewitness may conflict with that of another, or with documentary, forensic, or other evidence. But often, eyewitness testimony is enough to persuade decision makers that the facts probably, or even beyond a reasonable doubt, are as the proponent alleges them to be. And sometimes the testimony of a single witness is treated as sufficient proof.

If the testimony of a single eyewitness can be enough to prove that an *external* event happened as the witness describes it, is there anything fundamentally different about relying on the sole eyewitness (or earwitness) to an *internal* event, especially one that is ongoing? We might think that a litigant's firsthand account of her present sensory experience would be at least as reliable as an eyewitness account of a past external event, since it's immune to what the law calls the "testimonial infirmities" of misperception and faulty memory. The witness may not be able to describe her sensations precisely, but she can't be mistaken about whether she's experiencing those perceptions or what they're like to her as she's experiencing them. And if she's experiencing them now, any flaws in her memory are beside the point.[1]

But even if jurors would be justified in relying on the litigant's testimony in forming their beliefs about what her sensory impairment is like, she and her lawyer may rightly be concerned that jurors will fail to appreciate fully what her experience is *really* like. Mere words cannot convey the sensory richness of visual or auditory phenomena. Mere description, however detailed and evocative, is no substitute for the experience itself. If the litigant and her lawyer are *not* concerned about this, they're ignoring a basic social psychological insight: the *illusion of transparency* (Gilovich, Savitsky, and Medvec 1998). Specifically, when one person communicates with another, she tends to assume the other person will understand the intentions behind the communication and the other features of the communicator's conscious mental state as well as the communicator herself does. Failing to recognize this egocentric bias in her judgment, the communicator overestimates how well she will be understood (e.g., Epley and Caruso 2009).

The following experiment brilliantly illustrates the point (Newton 1990; see also discussion in Griffin and Ross 1991). Participants were given a list of well-known songs and asked to choose one and tap out the rhythm to another person sitting nearby. The tapper was also asked to estimate the likelihood that the listener would correctly identify the song. The listener was asked to try to identify the song and then to estimate the proportion of other listeners who would succeed in the same task. On average, tappers estimated the probability of correct identifications as 50%. The actual rate was just 2.5%—as the listeners themselves accurately estimated.[2] Why did the tappers so greatly overestimate the probability that their listeners would name the song being tapped? Consider the tapper's subjective experience: as he taps, he imagines, even hears in his mind, the tune, the words, perhaps the full orchestration. The listener, of course, hears only the taps. The tapper fails to make allowance for the fact that his subjective experience of the song is much more richly elaborated than the listener's, and so he thinks the listener's task of identifying the song is much easier than it really is.

When a personal injury plaintiff tries to describe her impaired perceptual experience to the judge and the jurors, she knows exactly what that experience is like. Its salience to her, and the importance of conveying it to her audience, may lead her to expect that the judge and the jurors will understand her words just as she does. She may think her words will evoke in them what they represent for her. Instead, she may find that her words are distressingly like the finger taps. Her full perceptual experience is like a song she, but not others, can hear.

In this chapter we examine two cases in which litigants used demonstrative displays to *illustrate* their words and thus let judges and jurors see what only the litigant directly experienced. In *Devadas*, the plaintiff displayed Photoshopped pictures of what the world now looked like to him, after the LASIK surgery he claimed should never have been performed:

objects blurred and doubled, headlights and streetlights at night turned into distracting "starbursts." In *Murtha*, a police officer, charged with using excessive force when he fired his gun at a fleeing suspect, claimed self-defense and played for jurors a computer animation that showed them what he *thought* he saw in the critical moment: the suspect's car headed straight at him. In each instance, the litigant worked with a visual consultant who adjusted the pixels until the litigant said, in effect, "That's what it's like." And in each case, the litigant swore on the stand, according to the prescribed legal formula, that the images "fairly and accurately represented" his visual experience.

We'll explore the reasons why each of these "artist's sketch" simulations may or may not have accurately depicted the respective litigants' subjective experience. More importantly, given our concern throughout with simulations' epistemological value, jurors may well have thought the exhibits in these cases did more than just illustrate the litigants' testimony; they may have instead treated the simulations as *independent proof* of the litigants' sensory experience. We'll see how the form and content of the images, the media used to make them, the words used in court to describe them, and the jurors' own habits of thought may have inclined them to misconstrue the simulations' probative value and hence the kind of knowledge the exhibits were capable of offering.

For each case, we'll also ask how the structure and presentation of each visual display served each lawyer's rhetorical goals—increasing the award of pain and suffering damages in the first case; obtaining a judgment of acquittal and possibly saving the client from prison in the second. In *Devadas*, the content and sequence of the exhibits constituted an implicit visual argument that emphasized how far the plaintiff's vision deviated from an objective norm. In *Murtha*, the animation portion of the exhibit reconstructed the defendant's subjective perception as a cinematic narrative that helped jurors to identify with the defendant and to justify his violent behavior.

Devadas v. Niksarli

Johnson Devadas was a pharmacist who lived and worked in Queens, New York. In March 2004 he accompanied his wife, Sara, to the offices of Dr. Kevin Niksarli, a LASIK surgeon. Sara's eyesight was poor and she was considering LASIK surgery to correct her vision. While there, Johnson thought about having the corrective surgery himself. Dr. Niksarli and his technicians conducted the standard optometrical screens, including pachymetry (measuring the thickness of the patient's corneas), and determined that Devadas was a suitable candidate for LASIK surgery.

As it turned out, he wasn't. According to the trial testimony of one of Devadas's medical experts, Devadas had a contraindication to LASIK surgery, *forme fruste keratoconus*. Keratoconus is a cone-shaped distortion of the cornea; form fruste keratoconus is a subclinical condition that is sometimes an early stage of keratoconus. The expert opined that Devadas's condition was a stable or abortive form of keratoconus that probably would not have progressed without the LASIK surgery. The surgery, however, led to ectasia, a progressive thinning of the cornea. Ectasia causes problems with visual quality, including blurriness, halos, double vision, glare, contrast sensitivity, starbursts, and a host of related phenomena involving the distortion of light as it passes through the diseased cornea.

Devadas and his wife sued Dr. Niksarli and his LASIK surgery business in May 2007. They alleged that Dr. Niksarli had committed malpractice by performing the surgery when a reasonable surgeon would not have, owing to Devadas's prior condition, and by not fully disclosing the potential risks and side effects of the procedure, thus failing to obtain Devadas's informed consent. The case went to trial two years later. Devadas and his wife testified about the events leading up to the surgery and the impaired and deteriorating vision that followed. Medical experts testified for both sides.[3] Devadas also described at length how his visual impairments affected his work at the pharmacy and his family life. Ultimately the jury of six returned a verdict for the plaintiffs of $5.6 million, including $3.1 million for pain and suffering damages (*Devadas v. Niksarli* 2009; LASIK Newswire 2009).

Devadas's lawyer, Todd J. Krouner of Chappaqua, New York, specializes in LASIK malpractice litigation. A few years before, in *Schiffer v. Speaker* (2005), Krouner had obtained for another client what was then the largest LASIK malpractice verdict, a $7.25 million award.[4] In cases like this, Krouner says, he faces the challenge of persuading jurors how bad impaired vision can be, given that his clients aren't physically disabled in any obvious way.[5] Pictures can help him convey this.

To create visual aids for the *Devadas* trial, Krouner had the plaintiff work with Dr. Roger Davis of Vision Simulations. Davis is a clinical psychologist who himself suffers from complications from LASIK surgery that he underwent in 1998. He has since campaigned to raise public awareness of the risks of LASIK, including depression and even suicide (Davis 2008). On his Vision Simulations website, Davis described how he creates simulations for people like Devadas, starting with an ordinary photograph: "We work back and forth across the internet, refining the simulations again and again until the patient says 'That's what I see!' The final simulations are printed as high resolution 8 x 10s (which can be blown up to poster size for the courtroom) and look just like real photographs."[6] Visitors to the website can see for themselves, using a slider, how ordinary photos can be adjusted for different degrees of blurriness, halos, starbursting, and other impairments.

Devadas and Davis collaborated to create several series of photos and photo simulations. As Devadas later testified: "After e-mailing [Davis] the picture, I talked it over [on] the telephone in describing how I see and the halos that I see, the double visions that I see, and I described to him how far apart that they are. And we went back and forth and we corrected it as we went. And . . . the image that we ended up with . . . best depicted the way that I see" (*Devadas* 2009, trial transcript, May 20, 2009, 216). Of the several sets of photos, Krouner selected two for use at trial: a series of six pictures showing bottles of medications on Devadas's pharmacy shelves and a series of five pictures of an intersection on his nighttime commute home. Each series begins with a digital photo that Sara Devadas took using a typical consumer digital camera set to auto-focus, followed by photo simulations adjusted to depict what Devadas claimed to see through each eye, uncorrected or corrected with contact lenses.

On the first day of trial, just before Judge Doris Ling-Cohan welcomed the jurors into the courtroom, defense counsel Neil Ekblom, of the firm of Clausen Miller PC in New York City, objected to the photo simulations on the ground that they were misleading and inaccurate as depictions of the plaintiff's eyesight. He also objected to having Dr. Davis take the stand, arguing that any testimony by him that the pictures represented what Johnson Devadas could see would be medical testimony, which Davis, as a psychologist but not a medical doctor, was not competent to give. After a bit of skirmishing and an off-the-record discussion, the lawyers agreed that the photos would be admitted into evidence but that Davis would not need to testify about them and would not be identified by name when Devadas took the stand to explain how the photos had been made.

As each photo simulation was introduced, Devadas affirmed that it was "a fair and accurate representation of what [his] vision [was] like [that day]" in that eye, with or without corrective lenses as the picture indicated. Otherwise he did not attempt to explain what the pictures depicted, preferring to let them "speak for themselves." Although the plaintiff's own testimony provided the evidentiary foundation for admitting the photo simulations, attorney Krouner also had other witnesses bolster jurors' faith in them. For instance, he showed several of the photo simulations (the last three from the pharmacy sequence and the first from the nighttime inter-

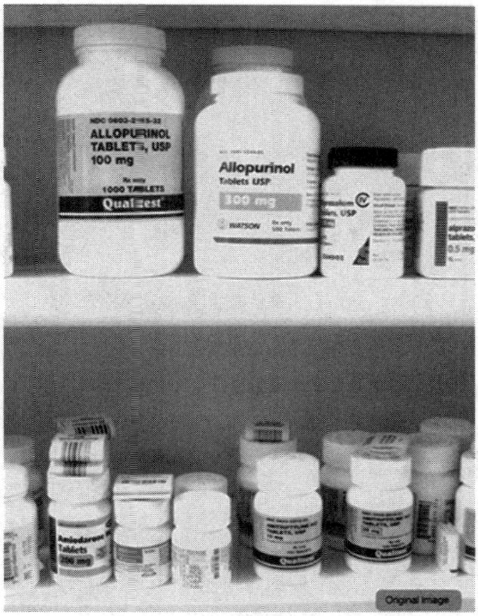

Figure 4.1. *Devadas*: photo of pharmacy shelf. Courtesy of Todd Krouner.

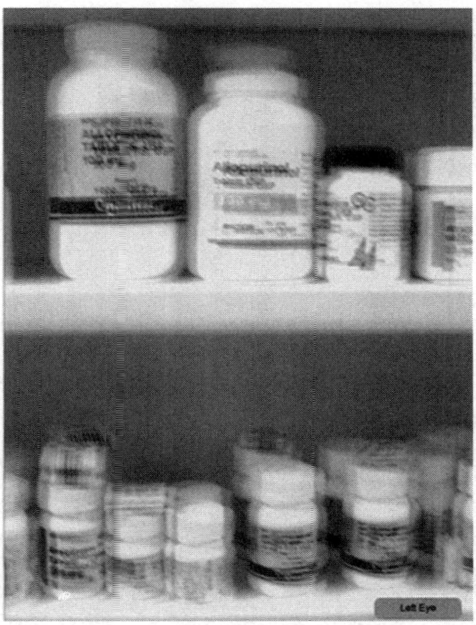

Figure 4.2. Photo simulation of view of pharmacy shelf as plaintiff sees it through his left eye. Courtesy of Todd Krouner.

Figure 4.3. Photo of intersection at night. Courtesy of Todd Krouner.

Figure 4.4. Photo simulation of view of intersection as plaintiff sees it through his left eye. Courtesy of Todd Krouner.

section set) to his expert ophthalmological witness, Dr. Paul Donzis, who testified that, to "a reasonable degree of medical certainty," based on his own wavefront studies of Devadas's optical capacities, each was a "fair and accurate depiction" of what Devadas was able to see (*Devadas* transcript, May 26, 2009, 609–13). Finally, in his closing argument, Krouner asked jurors to imagine themselves driving at night or working in a pharmacy with the plaintiff's impaired vision; as he said this, he displayed the corresponding photo simulations on the screen, thus implying that the photos accurately showed jurors what it was like to see as Johnson Devadas did (*Devadas* transcript, June 8, 2009, 2347).

Artist's sketch simulations of subjective experience raise epistemological (not to mention jurisprudential) concerns if jurors mistakenly treat them as independent sources of proof of what litigants' experiences are actually like. But could the jurors in *Devadas* really have thought the photo simulations provided independent proof of Johnson Devadas's visual experience? After all, Devadas *told* the jury how he and Roger Davis, the visual consultant, had created the photo simulations. His testimony makes it quite clear that the simulations were the equivalent of sketches—Photoshopped illustrations of what the plaintiff *said* he experienced—and that their claim to depict how he actually saw rested solely on his assertion that they did.

In fact, there are many reasons why jurors may well have thought the photo simulations themselves provided an independent—and reliable—source of proof of what it was like for Devadas to see with his visual impairments. To begin with, at no time did Judge Ling-Cohan explicitly instruct jurors whether to treat the photo simulations as merely illustrative (nonprobative) or as substantive (probative) exhibits. Rather, the simulations appear to have been treated as full evidentiary exhibits, on a par with every other trial exhibit. In her charge to the jury, the judge read the form instructions limiting jurors to consideration of the exhibits and the testimony in the case, but she did not differentiate among exhibits (*Devadas* transcript, June 8, 2009).[7] In the absence of clear guidance from the court, jurors were left to draw their own inferences from the photo simulations. So how might they have thought about these pictures? Can jurors discern the difference between pictures with and without independent probative value, when the pictures look the same—"just like real photographs"?

A simple example will help us get started. The cover of the June 17, 1986, issue of the tabloid *New York Post* blared, "Khadafy Goes Daffy." Inside was a story with the headline "Madman Moammar Now a Druggie Drag Queen." The story featured a clumsily retouched picture with the caption "Dressed in drag, Libyan leader Moammar Khadafy might look like this." Plainly the picture does not in any way *prove* that Khadafy looked as depicted. For "proof" of that, we must turn to the words of the story (or the sources on which the story purports to rely). The picture merely illustrates the words.

It should be equally obvious to any juror that *some* items of demonstrative evidence merely illustrate a witness's words, adding no probative value to those words. When an expert in a medical malpractice case, say, uses an anatomical chart or draws on a whiteboard a schematic of part of the body to show the location of an injury, incision, or implanted device, it's plain that the chart or drawing does not itself prove the location of any of those things. Rather, the expert's use of the chart or drawing simply helps the jury to understand his or her testimony.

Did the photo simulations in *Devadas* have any greater evidentiary warrant than the medical expert's drawing, or, for that matter, the *Post*'s retouched photograph of Khadafy? The answer is not entirely clear. The plaintiff himself testified that the simulations were based entirely on what *he claimed* he was able to see. In that sense, they no more proved the existence of what they purported to show—what it was like to see as he did—than the picture in the *Post* proved how Khadafy looked. On the other hand, the photo simulations provided much more phenomenal detail about the plaintiff's claimed visual experience than his words alone did. In that sense, to the extent that jurors believed Devadas when he told them, "That's what I see," the simulations did tend to prove what his subjective experience was like. This is different from the medical expert's use of a drawing, which is not offered to prove the phenomenal facts of what a perceptual experience is like; it's also different from the Khadafy picture, which for all we can tell lacks anyone in Devadas's position who can compare the picture to direct perception and swear that the one fairly and accurately represents the other. Thus, as explained in chapter 3, the photo simulations were *both* illustrative and substantive. What is clear, though, is that these pictures did not provide jurors with any *independent* evidentiary warrant for believing they accurately depicted what it was like to see as Devadas did.

Yet jurors may well have thought the photo simulations did exactly this. Just seeing them may have made the jurors more likely to believe that Devadas's visual experience really was as the simulations depicted it. Here are eight reasons why this could have happened.

First, in the very act of seeing the pictures and understanding what they appeared to show (e.g., a blurry and doubled view of a pharmacy shelf), jurors would intuitively believe that what they were seeing was true—that the pictures truthfully depicted what they purported to depict. To understand is to believe; "comprehension includes acceptance of that which is comprehended" (Gilbert 1991, 107). Critical thoughts about the simulation's truthfulness and reliability are literally "off screen" and would occur to jurors only later, if at all.

Second, equally if not more importantly, the photo simulations themselves, because they gave the appearance of being normal photographs, were likely to be taken up as offering reliable knowledge of what it was like to see as Johnson Devadas did. "In general, people appear to accept photos as veridical recordings of what happened, the photo's existence acting as evidence that the event occurred as depicted" (Henkel 2012, 774). The simple fact that photos *look like* what they claim to represent makes them intuitively credible. This resemblance enables the naive viewer to "look through" the photo to what it depicts and to imagine that the photo is offering that depicted reality more or less directly, and therefore reliably (Feigenson and Spiesel 2009; see Gilovich and Griffin 2010). Compare this to the more obvious instances of purely illustrative evidence, such as the medical chart or drawing mentioned above, which plainly don't look like what a person with ordinary vision would see if gazing (perhaps through a surgical incision) at the actual body part or object the drawing depicts. The whole point of the photo simulations in *Devadas,* in contrast, was to look exactly like what they supposedly depicted: the plaintiff's subjective visual experience.

Third, and relatedly, the photo simulations would likely be regarded as probative evidence of Devadas's visual experience because they seemed to be *objective.* Hearing only a verbal description of what his impaired vision was like, jurors would probably be aware that whatever they conceived his visual experience to be was in part a product of their own imaginations. But when they saw photos purporting to represent that vision accurately, they would attribute what they knew not to their own imagining, but to the photos themselves (the *aboutness* principle; Higgins 1998). This would have underscored their belief that the photos provided knowledge of the plaintiff's subjective state that was "objective" (and therefore more reliable) in the sense of *arising from the object* of their own perceptions.

To expand on this: research on *reality monitoring* indicates that people sometimes find it hard to distinguish among the various sources of what they think they know—what they have personally experienced, what they've been told, what they've read or seen in the media, or even what they've merely imagined (Johnson 1998; Johnson and Raye 1981). For example, showing participants photographs of what the researchers present as scenes from the participants' childhood can induce them to form "memories" of the events those scenes depict, even though the participants never actually experienced those events (e.g., Garry and Gerrie 2005). And when people read a story from which a particular conclusion can be inferred, seeing a photo depicting the conclusion of the story leads them to recall that they read that conclusion as well, even though the story itself does not contain it (Henkel 2012). That is, the distinct sources of what one thinks one has experienced fade; what remains is the memory, which is intuitively believed to track reality. It follows that when the *Devadas* jurors were deliberating, they may well have found it hard to recall that the photo simulations owed their claim to represent the plaintiff's subjective reality faithfully entirely to his say-so. Rather, the jurors would have been inclined simply to remember the simulation itself as the source of their presumptively accurate knowledge of that reality.

Fourth, having first heard Devadas's description of his perceptual impairments, the jurors may have been inclined to treat the photo simulations as additional, independent evidence for their initial belief in the truthfulness of what he had described. That is, they may have interpreted the photo simulations as *pseudoevidence* (Newman et al. 2012). Pursuant to the well-known *confirmation bias* (Nickerson 1998), people tend to construe new information in a way that supports their prior beliefs. Accordingly, "people may selectively interpret information gleaned from a photo or description as consistent with their hypothesis and/or they may use such information to cue the mental generation of thoughts and images consistent with their hypothesis" (Newman et al. 2012, 973). As we've seen, the photo simulations didn't actually provide any independent evidence that Devadas's perceptual experience was as the simulations depicted it. But because the simulations were introduced after his description of his experience, the jurors may have construed them as supporting, or confirming, evidence of that description.

Fifth, the jurors were likely to believe the photo simulations truly represented what they purported to—the plaintiff's subjective experience—because of the ease and immediacy with which viewers ordinarily understand the gist of what they see in a photo. According to cognitive psychological research on *processing fluency*, the easier it is for people to perceive or otherwise mentally process something, the more they tend to like it (Winkielman et al. 2003) and the more they are inclined to believe it's true (Reber and Schwarz 1999; for a review, see Oppenheimer 2008). The photo simulations surely made it much easier for the jurors to imagine what Devadas's visual experience was like than his verbal descriptions of "blurriness" and "starbursts" did. It takes time to listen to and process words, but viewers can get the gist of a picture in one-third of a second or less (Loftus, Nelson, and Kallmann 1983). Jurors who listened to Devadas's verbal description of blurriness and starbursts had to try to resolve those words' inherent vagueness through effortful imagination, as they decided just how blurry "blurry" was. No such effort was required to understand the picture: *that's* how blurry it is. In addition, experiencing simulations enables jurors to form richer mental representations of the internal reality the simulations purport to depict, which further enhances processing fluency and makes them *more confident* they now know what that reality is really like (Gill, Swann, and Silvera 1998).

Sixth, when the jurors looked at the photo simulations on the courtroom screen, Devadas's visual experience became *their* experience. As noted in chapter 2, *experiencing* something provides a kind of knowledge that is not reducible to what one can glean from a verbal or other description (e.g., Jackson 1986). This becomes obvious when one compares the photo simulations to Devadas's testimonial description of his eyesight. He mentioned "blurriness," "double vision," "halos," and "starbursts"—all accurate enough terms, as far as we can tell, but none of them offering anything like the richness, the saturation of the sensory field, that the photographs do.[8] Experiencing something also gives the experiencer *abilities* she or he would not otherwise have: it allows a person to remember and imagine what she or he has experienced in ways that someone who has not had the experience cannot (Lewis 1997). Experiencing the photo simulations would thus have given the jurors a richer sense than the plaintiff's words alone could that they could really *know* what his visual experience was like (cf. Nemirow 2006).

Seventh, consider how the photo simulations were *verbally framed* in court. In contrast to the zaniness of the *Post*'s claim about Khadafy and the photo caption's explicit use of the modal "might," Devadas's description of his impaired vision was inherently credible: the words of a believable plaintiff, supported by the expert testimony of a qualified ophthalmologist. And, as we've seen, the foundation that attorney Todd Krouner had Devadas recite for the photo simulations during the trial (repeated in a slightly different context during the expert's testimony), that each was "a fair and accurate representation" of the state of the plaintiff's vision, encouraged jurors to believe the photos *did* look like the plaintiff's subjective reality. In short, the exhibits were verbally framed as trustworthy evidence of his sensations.

Eighth, even had the jurors been more clearly advised that the photo simulations were "only illustrative" in the sense of being an *approximation* rather than an exact replication of Devadas's vision, they might well have given them too much weight in forming their beliefs about what his visual experience was really like. In the absence of any other tangible, comparably vivid display of what it was like to see as Devadas did, the rich mental representations that the jurors derived from the simulations would have tended to occupy their understanding of Devadas's perceptions. The simulations would have *anchored* their thoughts about what his perceptions were like (see Gilovich and Griffin 2010)—all the more so because the jurors would have had no reason to adjust that anchor in any particular direction (e.g., to think the actual blurriness was less rather than more pronounced) or to any particular extent.

That said, we might ask at this point: if the litigant testifies that the simulation fairly and accurately represents what it's like to have his perceptual experience, *and we believe him*, what's the problem? Johnson Devadas may well have been telling the truth to the best of his ability when he swore the photo simulations "best depicted the way" that he saw. On that basis alone, wouldn't the photo simulations have provided jurors with useful visual information to supplement their understanding of his words? Given Devadas's affirmation of the pictures' accuracy, wouldn't the simulations therefore have had probative value, and hence have added to jurors' justified belief about what it was like for him to see as he did?

By way of comparison, one might think it's impossible for someone who hasn't experienced "locked-in syndrome," in which a person is fully conscious but largely or entirely unable to move, to imagine what it's like to suffer from that condition. Yet anyone who has seen *The Diving Bell and the Butterfly* (Schnabel 2007), the story of French journalist Jean-Dominique Bauby, who found himself in this condition after a stroke, comes away with a vivid and memorable impression of what that experience is like. We have every reason to believe that Bauby, on whose memoir (written by blinking his left eyelid in response to letters shown by an assistant) the movie is based, and Julian Schnabel, the director, accurately reported and visualized the experience of locked-in syndrome.

Why not equally believe Devadas and be equally persuaded that the photo simulations can let us know what his visual experience is like? Recall that no one else had more direct access to Devadas's visual experience than Devadas himself did. Indeed, no one else had direct access at all. Consider also that drawings of visual experiences have long been regarded as a reputable *scientific* technique for making the participant-observer's sensations available to others.[9] Why don't these visual precedents tend to validate further the accuracy of the photo simulations—with perhaps the difference that digital image editing software allowed these photo simulations to replicate Devadas's subjective experience *more faithfully* than the ink or pastel drawings made by scientific research subjects?

One problem, of course, is that jurors shouldn't uncritically accept a personal injury plaintiff's account of how bad his impairments are, given the plaintiff's incentive to exaggerate their severity. He is not a disinterested scientific investigator or experimental subject. Yet even if Devadas was honestly expressing his belief that the simulations corresponded to what he knew through introspection, his sincere belief in that correspondence did not make it so, and jurors had no way to know how far their courtroom experience of the simulation might have varied from the plaintiff's own sensations. Here are six reasons not to take the plaintiff's "That's what I see!" at face value. It is important to remember that these observations apply to a litigant's authentication of *any type* of simulation as a "fair and accurate representation" of his sensations, since that attestation is always based on the litigant's comparison of the exhibit with what he knows through introspection. The observations are especially critical with regard to artist's sketch simulations, however, because the litigant's authentication is the *only* warrant for their accuracy.

First, there is another difference between Devadas's observations of his perceptions and those reported in the scientific literature: Devadas is not a systematic, trained observer of his own phenomenal experience (see Price and Barrell 2012; Varela and Shear 1999). This doesn't discredit what he reported, but it does suggest that his descriptions of his experience, and his ability to judge whether Roger Davis's photo simulations corresponded to his self-observations, may have been less precise than those of a disciplined researcher.[10]

Second, Devadas's own perceptual judgments, even if accurate to the best of his abilities, may have been less precise than the jurors' own. That is, his threshold for discriminating a *just noticeable difference* between percepts may have been higher.[11] Consequently, Devadas may have believed and honestly testified that some feature of the simulation matched the corresponding feature of his visual experience, when other people, including the judge and the jurors, would (if only they had direct access to his percepts) have observed a difference. The divergence could be in either direction—the simulation might have overstated or understated the actual degree of impairment—but the judge and the jurors would have had no way of determining which.

Third, and more importantly, in at least some instances, the plaintiff may not be in a position to say whether a simulation matches his subjective experience because the impairment itself prevents the plaintiff from seeing or hearing the simulation as a person without that impairment does. Consider the usual witness who authenticates an ordinary photograph by asserting that it "fairly and accurately represents" what the witness recalls having seen. The witness claims to have matched the photo to his remembered perceptions and found that the one corresponds well enough to the other. Now consider Johnson Devadas. His vision, he told the court, was blurred and doubled. When he looked around his pharmacy, he saw shelves and bottles blurred and doubled. The image that would match that perception *for him* would be an *ordinary* photograph of the shelves and bottles, not the photo simulation, altered so as to appear blurred and doubled to someone with unimpaired vision. The altered photo would have appeared to Devadas to be even blurrier and more doubled, because his impairment affected his experience of *everything* he saw. The simulation may or may not have replicated for a person with *normal* vision what Devadas saw when he looked out at the world[12]—but, without more, it would seem that Devadas himself could not say the simulation fairly and accurately represented what he perceived.

Indeed, in the one case in which an artist's sketch simulation was excluded from evidence, the trial judge seems to have concluded that the plaintiff's visual impairments prevented him from being able to testify that the altered photos fairly and accurately represented his impaired vision. *Wilke v. Dudley* was another LASIK malpractice case in which Todd Krouner, representing the plaintiff, sought to introduce photo simulations created by Roger Davis and the plaintiff. At the hearing on defendants' motion in limine to exclude the simulations, attorney Mark Budzinski, representing the defendant, argued:

> The inherent problem is Mr. Wilke, who at least by his own testimony does not have normal vision, cannot establish the foundation for how a normal person sees those photographs. He may be able to do that if he were able to, if he had 20/20 uncorrected vision or if he had—if he could look at these simulations with glasses and say, you know, that's how I see without my glasses. His testimony is that his vision is not correctable with . . . Intacs, glasses, or contacts. So he cannot, by his own admission, establish the foundation and the authenticity for a jury with respect to those simulations. . . . He's trying to lay the foundation for halos through vision wherein he experiences halos. He's trying to lay the foundation for the accurate depiction of glare where he, by his testimony at least, experiences glare.

THE COURT: My concern was just said at the end. How does Mr. Wilke know what 20/20 vision sees to be able to say this is what it looks like for me? (*Wilke v. Dudley* 2011, hearing transcript, December 12, 2013, n.p.).

The difficulty parallels the "El Greco fallacy" (Firestone 2013; Rock 1966). The Spanish Renaissance painter El Greco is famous for his paintings of unnaturally elongated figures. Why did he depict his subjects that way? A popular theory, originated by an ophthalmologist early in the twentieth century, is that El Greco suffered from an astigmatism that distorted his vision. "If El Greco experienced a stretched-out world, it was reasoned, then perhaps he simply painted what he saw. . . . Of course, reflection on this theory reveals a confusion: If El Greco truly experienced a stretched-out world, then he also would have experienced a stretched-out *canvas*—and so any real-world distortions experienced by an astigmatic El Greco would never have transferred to his reproductions" (Firestone 2013, 672). Instead, El Greco's elongated figures must have been due to a stylistic choice, as art historians have long recognized.

Like an astigmatic artist, Johnson Devadas saw both reality and its representations through his impairment. As he perceived things, the undistorted photo, not the distorted simulation, more closely matched his visual experience of the world.[13] How, then, could a plaintiff like Devadas, with pervasive perceptual impairments, attest that the *simulation* fairly and accurately represented what he saw? To be clear: The argument is *not* that Devadas's vision was not really distorted in the way he described, any more than that El Greco's figures are not really elongated. The argument is that the plaintiff himself could not, solely on the basis of his visual comparison of the simulation to his visual experience, justifiably claim that the simulation corresponded to his experience. The situation is even more problematic for certain other litigants. For instance, a person with the same tinnitus sound in both ears cannot directly confirm that a sound file accurately replicates the sound he hears in his head, because if the sound file perfectly matched the internal sound in loudness, pitch, and tone, the tinnitus would completely mask the external sound and prevent the person from hearing it, and thus from attesting that it matches the sound in his head.[14]

Are there ways around this difficulty? In principle and potentially in practice, yes. For example, a person with a vision problem in only one eye can confirm the accuracy of the simulation by using his contralateral eye. A person whose visual defect (such as myopia) is completely correctable with eyeglasses or contact lenses can confirm the simulation's accuracy by viewing it while wearing corrective lenses (Barsky 2004). Corrective lenses cannot, however, adjust for visual impairments caused by higher-order corneal aberrations of the sort Johnson Devadas had (*Devadas* transcript, May 26, 2009, 605).

Todd Krouner had his client explain how he was able to confirm that some of the photo simulations corresponded to his visual experience. For instance, with regard to the photo of what his pharmacy shelf looked like when viewed through his left eye, Devadas testified: "I wore the contacts in my right eye and I covered my right eye and looked through the left eye. And by comparing the images, because I have the best corrected vision in my right eye, I was able to describe what I saw with my left" (*Devadas* transcript, May 20, 2009, 217). In principle, the corrective lens converts Devadas's right eye into one with something close to "normal" vision, giving him approximately the same baseline as the judge and the jurors would be presumed to have. In principle, he would then be able to compare the view of the ordinary photo through his left eye with the view of the gradually adjusted Photoshopped photo through his right eye, and determine when the two matched. It's an imperfect method, though, because Devadas's corrected vision in his right eye was not ideal (as we can infer from the simulation of his vision in that eye, which differs from the digital photo with the camera set to auto-focus), and so his partly impaired vision with the contact lens would have affected whatever judgments he made using that eye. As for the simulations of uncorrected vision in his right eye, Devadas explained: "With my right eye I have to wear my contacts to see how it looked, and then from memory I would have to take off my contacts and I had to compare the images of how it looked with my contacts in versus how it looked without my contacts which I will then see. So I had to use my memory to see how I saw it with my contacts in" (218). This compounds the difficulty of ascertaining whether the simulation matched Devadas's subjective vision because his judgment was based on a comparison of a *remembered* image (the Photoshopped picture as seen through his right eye, with contacts) with a currently viewed image (the unaltered photo seen without contacts).[15]

This may not seem very different from the usual case of the authentication of an ordinary photograph, in which a witness who observed events many months or years before trial attests that the photo fairly and accurately represents what he or she remembers having seen. There is, however, a crucial difference, having to do with the nature of photographic evidence. And from this difference, we can infer that even if Devadas had been in a position to state that the simulations matched his subjective experience, jurors might still have been misled in believing, on the basis of his say-so alone, that the simulations provided photographically reliable evidence of his experience.

Ordinary photos, although typically authenticated by an eyewitness to the depicted scene, are presumed to be accurate not solely because, according to the witness, they represent reality *iconically*—that is, because they look like what they purport to represent. They are also presumed accurate because they are generally thought to represent what they depict *indexically*. Ordinary photos and videos are typically considered indexical signifiers of what they depict (Sebeok 1994) because we understand them to be physically caused by their objects (more precisely, by the reflection of light off the surfaces of those objects and the capture of that light by the camera). Photos and videos are indexical, moreover, in that the very fact they were taken or shot "points to an event in the world, as a form of designation that draws reality into the image field" (Green and Lowry 2003, 48). For both reasons, photos and videos are able to provide evidence that what they depict *was there*, in front of the lens at the time the photo or video was taken (Barthes 1981).

To be sure, the indexicality of photos and other images is more problematic than this.[16] But assuming the notion of photographic indexicality has some meaningful content, its main implication for law is this: the trustworthiness of ordinary photographic evidence is generally understood to rest on sources *independent* of the authenticating witness's say-so, namely, its indexicality and technological objectivity. In contrast, the photo simulations that Johnson Devadas testified fairly and accurately represented his subjective visual sensations might have matched those sensations iconically (we have to take his word for that, since we have no direct access to his subjective experience), *but they could not possibly have done so indexically*. These simulations use the visual vocabulary of photography (recall the claim on Roger Davis's website: they "look just like real photographs"), but they're not photos in the usual sense. What the visual simulations showed was a function of what Devadas *told* Davis they *should* show. To interpret the simulations as reliable evidence of Devadas's subjective vision on the same terms as ordinary photos are understood to be reliable evidence of the external reality they depict, and to accept Devadas's word alone as sufficient to authenticate them for this purpose, is to smuggle in an implicit claim about their accuracy and trustworthiness that their mere (supposed) resemblance to his subjective state does not justify.[17]

Fourth, the last two points—that Devadas's ability to discriminate between different visual stimuli may have diverged from the audience's and that Devadas might not have been in a position to say conclusively that the simulation matched his experience—are instances of a more general constraint on how far simulations can let people know what it's like to experience another person's subjective perceptions. Triers of fact cannot help but see the simulations through *their own* eyes, and their visual capacities may vary not only from the plaintiff's, which the simulation purports to recreate, but also from each other's. For this reason alone, it's highly unlikely that any simulation can precisely replicate for all audiences the phenomenal character of the litigant's subjective state. The more that differences in degree (e.g., the blurriness of a simulation of visual defocus) matter to jurors' judgments about the severity of the plaintiff's injuries, the more important these divergences would be.

Fifth, the back-and-forth process of creating an artist's sketch simulation, as Johnson Devadas described it, allows the litigant's introspective judgments about his phenomenal experience to be influenced by the picture the visual consultant is generating. I have already mentioned research indicating that people's memories for events from their personal lives can be altered by seeing photos that purport to depict those events but contain details that never actually occurred (Garry and Gerrie 2005). One might expect that present perceptions would be less malleable than long-term memories and thus less prone to these sorts of biasing effects. Still, the suggestive force of the picture-in-progress might well lead a litigant to exclaim, "That's what I see!," not entirely because the picture matches what the litigant independently introspects his experience to be, but rather because he has, at least in part, molded his conscious sense of his experience to match the picture.

Sixth and finally, the litigant's claim that the simulation fairly and accurately represents his subjective experience may be subject to *demand characteristics*: the litigant knows that his lawyer, and possibly the expert with whom the litigant collaborates in producing the exhibit, want that to be his judgment. The litigant may not be simply fabricating his testimony, but demand characteristics may lead him to gloss over at least some differences between the simulation and his experience that he might, in other circumstances, be capable of discerning. Even assuming the litigant is honestly and diligently exercising his perceptual abilities to determine whether the photo simulation "fairly and accurately represents" his phenomenal experience, we cannot know exactly what his necessarily subjective standard may be for concluding, "That's what I see." For instance, the litigant may be prepared to sign off on a degree of correspondence between simulation and subjective experience that includes artifacts of the image creation process—consider what appears to be the use of the clone tool to create the impression of the halos in the simulation of Devadas's nighttime commute—that may not faithfully represent the facts of his experience.

In short, if we care about whether simulations can provide justified true belief about what it's like for a litigant to experience what she or he does, an exhibit authenticated only by the litigant's honest claim "That's what I see," even if it meets the permissive threshold for being shown in court, should leave jurors with considerable doubt. Jurors are likely to mistake a simulation whose knowledge claim rests entirely on the litigant's say-so for independent substantive evidence of the litigant's subjective state. Needless to say, the litigant's words are not enough to transform the former into the latter. Moreover, jurors have no way to penetrate the assertion "That's what I see," to determine how far the courtroom exhibit may vary from what the litigant is actually experiencing—as it almost surely does, for any one or more of the reasons just given.

It may be countered that neither of these concerns should trouble judges or jurors very much Since jurors may properly use an artist's sketch simulation to help them better understand the litigant's description of his perceptual experience, some might argue that there is no *practical* difference between believing what Devadas says and then using the photo simulation as illustrative evidence, on the one hand, and using it as independent substantive proof of his perceptual experience, on the other. Yet mistaking the simulation's evidentiary warrant would still be a significant *epistemological* confusion. And any inaccuracies in how the photo simulations represent the litigant's actual visual experience (say, in how blurry his vision is, or how glaring the "starbursts" are) could well have practical effects, because the judgment to which they ultimately pertain, the award of pain and suffering damages, is a continuous variable (dollars) rather than a dichotomous one (e.g., liability), and thus more sensitive to small changes in inputs.

So far I have relied heavily on cognitive and perceptual psychology to explain how jurors may respond to artist's sketch simulations like the Photoshopped photos in *Devadas*, and to describe the gap between what jurors are likely to believe and what they are justified in believing about the knowledge these simulations provide. To appreciate more fully how the simulations in *Devadas* may have induced jurors to believe they could experience his visual impairments for themselves, we turn from psychology to media studies and visual rhetoric.

Understanding the impact on jurors of the photo simulations in *Devadas* (and that of similar exhibits in other cases) requires us to examine how photography mediated what jurors may have believed they could know about Devadas's subjective experience. The claim that the photo simulations reliably represented Devadas's vision borrowed credibility from the widespread cultural faith in the objectivity and reliability of ordinary digital photography. And while evidentiary simulations purport to recreate *facts* (in this case, the facts of the plaintiff's visual experience), they, like any other evidence, are also always shaped by rhetorical purpose. The purpose in this case was to persuade jurors that Johnson Devadas's vision diverged significantly from that of normally sighted people and that, as a consequence, he deserved substantial damages for his pain and suffering. We will therefore explore the *visual rhetoric* of the photo simulations and their courtroom display.

Begin with the use of photography itself. People still tend to presume, as the earliest makers and consumers of photographs did, that a photo accurately depicts whatever was in front of the lens when the picture was taken—the photo as "pencil of nature" (Fox Talbot [1844] 2011), the "mirror with a memory" (Holmes 1859).[18] This presumption is supported by the widespread belief in the indexicality of photographs, as explained above: photos stand in an indexical relation to what they depict because the photographic image has been *physically caused by* what it depicts and because the act of taking the photo deictically *points to* the reality in front of the camera when the photo was taken (Green and Lowry 2003). We intuitively tend to believe that the photo presents (albeit incompletely) the appearance of that reality and therefore that it provides independent evidence of that reality as of the time the picture was taken. These beliefs persist as our default response to photos in the digital age, when the indexicality of the photo has become ever more problematic (see Dzenko 2009).[19]

The initial or "reference" photo in each sequence of images in *Devadas* raises none of the concerns that might unsettle our default belief in its veridicality. Each photo anchored viewers in a presumptively accurate representation of external reality. In his testimony, Johnson Devadas assured the court that, despite his visual impairments, he knew the photos were "genuine" because he was with his wife when she took them, using the camera's auto-focus feature (*Devadas* transcript, May 20, 2009, 215). That is to say, the judge and the jurors were given to believe that the camera automatically, and therefore objectively (see Daston and Galison 2007), recorded what was in front of it at the time, and that these reference photos were not deliberately altered later.

The photo simulations followed, one after the other, in what appeared to viewers to be the same medium and format as the initial, reference photograph. Devadas told the jurors that he and "a colleague who was savvy with the computer" edited or "corrected" the initial photo to create the simulations (*Devadas* transcript, May 20, 2009, 216).[20] Yet what the jurors *saw* when they looked at the simulations were images resembling the initial, unedited photos in visual density and color, as well as size, format, distance, and point of view. The simulations, that is, were placed on *the same order of representation* as ordinary digital photographs. And just as viewers adopt the point of view of the camera's lens and regard ordinary photos as a trustworthy and accurate record of the external reality in front of the lens, so the photo simulations encouraged the jurors to believe they were occupying Devadas's *subjective* position in the world and seeing an equally trustworthy record of what it was like for him to see as he did.

Of course, a photograph, while every bit the mechanical wonder Oliver Wendell Holmes Sr. effusively described in 1859, does not simply copy visible reality. It's a two-dimensional representation of a three-dimensional scene, demarcated and removed from the sensory surround. The photo offers a visual access to reality that is mediated in several ways: by the technology built into the camera; by the many choices, intentional or subconscious, on the part of the person taking the photo as to what, when, and how to photograph; and, not least, by the interpretive habits viewers bring to the "reading" of the photo.[21] Yet since, as noted above, people are accustomed to "looking through" photos and conflating them with what the photos depict, it also seems natural to conflate the *visual experience* of the photo with the *visual experience* of what the photo depicts. Hence, the *Devadas* jurors may well have believed the photo simulations enabled them to experience what the plaintiff did.

They couldn't, not only because a photo isn't the same as what it depicts, but also because vision doesn't work the same way as photography. The distinctions between the two have often been emphasized (e.g., Battye 2014; Gregory 1997; Lauwereyns 2012; Noë 2004; Palmer 1999). Perception is *active*, both "overtly" (through eye and other physical movements) and "covertly" (through attentional focus and other cognitive processing independent of movements of the eye, head, or body) (Lauwereyns 2012), whereas a photo represents a single moment in time (actually, the typically short duration of the shutter speed) as a fixed image. Visual experience may omit (e.g., because of inattentional blindness) what a photo would record as being in the visual field. Acute vision is limited to the center of the visual field, whereas the photo (depending on the lens and depth of field) may represent a constant level of resolution throughout. We can't perceive colors on the margins of our visual field; a typical color photo is colored in its entirety. The light and color depicted in the photo, moreover, are not the same as what we would see if looking at the actual scene (regardless of lighting conditions), but are in part a function of what the digital camera's hardware and software are capable of producing, including the type of color filtering the camera employs.[22] The intensity of colors as they appear to our eyes, but not as captured by a camera, depends on variations in illumination. After-effects of bodily motion can affect visual perception but not what the camera records. And our visual experience is affected by our purposes, motives, transient affect, and other "top-down" cognitive influences (e.g., Balcetis and Lassiter 2010; Barrett and Bar 2009; but see Firestone and Scholl 2014);[23] what the camera captures is not. So while "there are important similarities between eyes and cameras in terms of optical phenomena . . . , there are no similarities whatever in terms of *perceptual* phenomena" (Palmer 1999, 5).

Photographic simulations may *understate* the severity of a plaintiff's impairments to the extent that those impairments affect his vision in ways photography cannot capture. They may *overstate* the severity of his impairments by failing to reflect how the plaintiff compensates for his impaired vision—by adjusting his focus, moving his eyes, head, or body to get additional and better views, relying more on his other senses, or simply habituating to his sensory inputs. But in any event, photo simulations *cannot replicate* the plaintiff's subjective experience. They can only model it. Yet because these simulations embody a "rhetoric of the real" (Feigenson and Spiesel 2009), according to which photographic images provide direct and dependable access to what they depict, jurors may well have believed the simulations gave them more reliable knowledge of the plaintiff's subjective experience than they possibly could have.

The photo simulations in *Devadas* were rhetorical in still more specific ways. In each sequence, the initial reference photo, followed by the simulations, implicitly furthered the plaintiff's argumentative goal, which, as noted earlier, was to enable the jurors to appreciate how far his perceptual experience diverged from the norm. All things being equal, the more his subjective experience differed from that of most people, the more severe his impairments were, and hence the larger the damage award needed to compensate him fairly for his suffering.[24] The conceptual structure underlying the sequence in which the images were displayed was crucial to this rhetorical aim. The reference photo equated "normal" vision, to which Devadas's subjective experience was to be contrasted, with a *digital photograph*. Devadas's subjectivity was then constructed by the *divergence* between the Photoshopped photos and the reference photo. The implicit logic is an analogy: Devadas's visual experience differed from the norm as the edited photos differed from the unedited one.

That may seem obvious. The subjectivity of phenomenal perception is, aside from afterimages, dreams, hallucinations, and the like, typically understood in relation to the *object* of perception.[25] Our perceptions are ordinarily *of* something. So any difference between my perceptual experience and yours must usually be illustrated with reference to something that we are both attending to: I see or hear it one way; you see or hear it differently (or not at all).[26] In the case of visual perception, therefore, it may seem entirely unexceptional to posit the photograph in place of the perceived object and then to represent one person's subjective visual experience as a divergence from that photographic baseline.

This implicit analogical argument, however, has several problematic features. *First*, equating normal vision with the single standard of what can be seen in a digital photograph, as the reference photos in *Devadas* did, collapses the variance in the population's visual capacities into a single level of visual ability. In fact, people's sensory capacities, visual and other, vary in a host of ways, many of which do not rise to the level of significant impairment. For instance, 20/20 vision is often understood as "normal" acuity, but "20/20 does not represent a watershed value that cleanly differentiates normal results from abnormal. . . . Normal visual acuity varies between wide limits, just as . . . most other measurable properties and functions of humans do." Visual acuity in typical populations follows a Gaussian distribution (Frisén 1990, 29). The implicit positing of a single visual norm resembles the construct of the *statistically normal* person as a unitary entity (a concept that dates to the first half of the nineteenth century; see Boring 1950; Hacking 1990). This greatly simplifies the comparison between the plaintiff's vision and the "norm." Rather than placing his impairments on a field consisting of varying visual abilities, the judgment of how bad it is to see as he does is reduced to a single contrast (or series of contrasts).

Second, equating normal vision with a reference photograph reifies normal vision as *objective* vision. Photos, as explained above, are presumed to be truthful read-offs from reality, period. It's necessary to identify normal vision as the objective vision symbolized by the reference photo in order to make the analogical argument work: the plaintiff's vision differs from the norm as the photo simulations differ from the reference photo. But just as we have reasons to doubt the claimed equivalence between Devadas's subjective vision and the photo simulations, we also have good reason to question the implicit linkage of "normal" vision to the unedited reference photo. The presumed objectivity of the latter, transposed to the former, elides the fact that *everyone's* vision is necessarily subjective in the sense of *not* offering transparent, perfectly veridical access to reality.[27] It erases the Baconian principle of the fallibility of perception (see Gilbert 1998). Indeed, equating normal vision with the photo's presumptively objective vision changed the question the jurors were asked to consider from "How far does Johnson Devadas's visual experience differ from that of people with 'normal' vision?" to "How far does Johnson Devadas's visual experience differ from seeing things *as they are*?" This marked Devadas's visual experience as *distinctively* subjective—"normal" eyesight, represented by the reference photo, is by implication not subjectively limited at all—and thus amplified the divergence of his experience from the standard.

Third, the visual analogical argument changed the question at hand in an even more troublesome way. The legal issue was how much worse Devadas's vision was as a result of the defendant's negligence; Dr. Niksarli was legally responsible only for damages attributable to his negligence. The proper comparison, therefore, should have been between Devadas's vision before and after the LASIK surgery. His vision was imperfect before the surgery; otherwise he would not have considered himself a candidate for the corrective procedure in the first place. Using an ordinary, presumptively veridical photo to represent the *status quo ante* implied that his vision was unimpaired before, thus further stretching the gap between his current visual experience and the jurors' baseline for gauging how severely he had been harmed.[28]

The photo simulations were also designed to reconstruct Johnson Devadas's subjective experience as a sequence of *rhetorically significant* moments. According to the practice he follows in cases like this, attorney Todd Krouner had no hand in the taking or editing of the pictures, but he choreographed the subject matter by advising the client to follow a "template" that includes photographs of three sorts of scenes: a domestic or family scene, a scene from the workplace, and a night vision picture.[29] The logic is clear. The first sort of scene humanizes the plaintiff and shows the effect his impairments have on his relations with his loved ones, implicitly appealing to the viewers' sympathies.[30] The nighttime scene dramatizes some of the most significant impairments that LASIK can cause, including the halos and starbursts. Krouner advises clients to take a photo of a major intersection that local jurors might recognize, ideally a scene including street signs, street lights, traffic lights, and signs of businesses, so that consultant Roger Davis will have adequate "latitude" to show the effects of the plaintiff's condition on his night vision.[31] And in this case, the workplace scene—the close-up of the pharmacy shelf, followed by the simulations depicting Devadas's double vision—was especially powerful evidence because of what Krouner described as Devadas's "riveting" testimony of how his double vision led him to take the wrong drug off the shelf:

> The most recent near miss, as I call it, was between two drugs. There is a hydralazine and hydroxyzine. [Hydralazine] is a medication used to treat high blood pressure, and the other medication, hydroxyzine, . . . is an antihistamine type of drug to treat allergic reactions. [B]oth of them are situated on the same shelf near the same proximity and they are made by the same manufacturer. . . . I typed the medication correctly, the label came out. . . . I had pulled hydroxyzine off the shelf instead of the hydralazine. [When the assisting technician counted the pills], she said, "John, you pulled the wrong drug," and this is what causes my anxiety at work. . . . I'm always anticipating something that may go wrong due to my vision (*Devadas* transcript, June 1, 2009, 1272–73).

Tragedy was averted, but the Photoshopped picture of the shelf enabled the jurors to visualize how easy it must have been for Devadas to mix up the two similarly named drugs, and thus to empathize with the anxiety that such mistakes, and the prospect of more, caused him. (Indeed, their response may have been mixed with anxiety about suffering the consequences of such a mistake themselves.)

Taken together, the workplace and nighttime drive scenes at least hinted at a *narrative* of Devadas's daily life as a visually impaired person. Two still photos were hardly enough to tell the story of Devadas's everyday life, or even to enable the jurors to see how any particular sequence of events unfolded.[32] But they did suggest Devadas's routine by a kind of synecdoche and thus evoked for the jurors, as they vicariously experienced his visual impairments, something of the character he and his attorney hoped to present in court: a hard-working professional, laboring to do his responsible job (at which he impliedly worked such long hours that he drove home in the dark) under significant visual handicap. To the extent that the simulations contributed to a portrait of Devadas as a sympathetic and deserving person, they enhanced his prospects for a favorable liability judgment and increased damages.[33]

We don't know why the jurors thought Devadas's impairments were so severe as to be worth $3 million in future pain and suffering damages, or indeed whether they might not have sought to use this part of their compensatory award to punish Dr. Niksarli for any misconduct they believed to be particularly egregious or offensive (punitive damages being unavailable in a malpractice case). And it is impossible to know how large a role the photo simulations played in persuading the jurors that Johnson Devadas's visual impairments were as debilitating as they believed them to be, despite the defendant's evidence to the contrary. It seems plausible to infer, though, that by making his visual experience seem *more real* to them, the simulations helped the jurors to resist or reconcile ostensibly inconsistent evidence (and to dismiss as a quibble the defense expert's claim that the simulations may have exaggerated the plaintiff's loss of acuity).[34] Above all, it seems reasonable to suggest that by offering the jurors what they understood to be an objectively accurate and reliable impression of Devadas's subjective experience, the simulations inclined them to believe they could know what it was like for Devadas to have to live with those impairments, and thus to empathize with him. Finally, by helping to portray Devadas as a deserving person, the simulations may well have encouraged the jurors to translate that empathy into a substantial pain and suffering award.

State v. Murtha

The video animation in *Murtha*, the excessive force case, differs in many ways from the others in this book. This was a criminal case, not a personal injury lawsuit; the simulation addressed not damages but liability; and what was at stake was not additional dollars in compensation but whether Officer Murtha would be sent to prison or walk out of the courtroom a free man. The lawyer in this case—unlike the other cases—deployed the simulation in response to a very convincing demonstrative that his opponent, the prosecutor, had already shown: a dashboard camera video that offered apparently conclusive visual evidence of how the critical events had transpired. And the exhibit was offered to show what the defendant, Murtha, claimed to have perceived at a crucial past moment, not what he continued to experience in the present.[35]

Perhaps most importantly, the animation component of the display in *Murtha*, unlike the other demonstrative exhibits discussed in this and the following chapters, did not attempt to recreate a litigant's subjective sensory experience (or even part of it) with phenomenal verisimilitude. It was a kind of cartoon, easily distinguishable in form, color, level of detail, and apparent texture from what the defendant (or any of us) would see if looking out at the same scene in reality. Its aim, therefore, was *not* to enable jurors to experience for themselves what the defendant claimed to have seen in quite the same way as the other exhibits examined in this book. Its aim was to persuade jurors that, despite the contrary evidence of the dashcam video, Officer Murtha *could honestly have believed* that the suspect was momentarily headed straight for him and therefore that he was facing an imminent threat to his life, justifying his use of deadly force in response. The defendant's credibility, rather than the adequacy of his verbal testimony to describe and explain his mental experience, was on the line.

Despite these differences, it's worth studying the video animation in *Murtha* because doing so will broaden our understanding of how re-creations of subjective perception are being deployed in the law. Specifically, by constructing Murtha's subjectivity in the crucial moment as a *cinematic narrative*, the video animation furthered the rhetorical goal of convincing the jurors not only that Murtha was telling the truth about what he misperceived, but also that his misperception and thus his use of deadly force were reasonable.

In October 2006, Hartford, Connecticut, police officer Robert Murtha was acquitted on charges including first-degree assault arising from his January 2003 shooting of a suspect attempting to flee in a stolen car (*State v. Murtha* 2006).[36] Murtha had chased the driver in his police cruiser until the driver stopped his car in a snowbank on the side of the road. As Murtha got out of his cruiser and approached the other car, the suspect pulled back onto the road and sped away. Murtha fired several shots at the driver's side window, striking and injuring the driver.

In his original incident report, Murtha asserted that the suspect's car had hit him before pulling away, prompting him to shoot in self-defense. But Murtha changed his story when he became aware that a dashboard camera video from another police cruiser following the chase showed not only that the other car had not hit Murtha, but that Murtha had run after the car and fired at the driver as the car sped away. At trial, Murtha claimed that in the stress of the moment, he *thought* the car was headed straight toward him when the driver first pulled back onto the road. His reasonable (albeit mistaken) perception that the suspect was using or about to use deadly physical force against him or was about to inflict great bodily harm would be a complete justification to the shooting (Connecticut General Statutes 2015, §53a-19).

The prosecution showed the jury the video from the other police cruiser, depicting the chase and the shooting. Now that the jurors were being invited to rely on visual media for their reconstruction of the critical events, Murtha's attorney Hugh Keefe, of the New Haven firm of Lynch, Traub, Keefe and Errante, realized he could not cede the visual field entirely to the state. He needed something visual to counter this compelling state's evidence—something to show the incident from what Murtha claimed was his perspective.

Legal visual consultant Jeffrey Taylor had worked on other cases involving police defendants accused of using excessive force. He had created computer animations to depict the events *as they appeared to the officers*, to enable the judge and jurors to understand how an officer suffering from "tunnel vision" in the stress of the moment might see the world differently than others would. Taylor read an article about the *Murtha* case, contacted Keefe, and told him about his firm's capabilities. Keefe was "fascinated" by the idea of helping the jurors see, and not merely hear from Murtha's testimony, what Murtha thought he saw—his subjective visual perception of the events in question.[37] The animation would show not what actually happened, but rather what Officer Murtha (reasonably) *believed* had happened.

Keefe described the scenario, including the existence of the dashcam video, to Taylor. Taylor then began working closely with Robert Murtha. "I work like a doctor," Taylor says. "I ask specific questions about what happened. I get the witness's perspective of what he saw. I have them reenact the whole situation. From this I get a scene in my mind of what it looks like." Taylor and his staff then matched the envisioned sequence to the physical evidence, drew a storyboard, and created a draft animation. Taylor then presented the draft to Murtha for his "authentication." Murtha agreed with some aspects and suggested changes to others, indicating, "This is not what I saw." Taylor revised the animation accordingly. Once the animation was "substantially similar" to what Murtha said he remembered, Taylor considered it ready for use as a demonstrative exhibit.[38]

The visual display begins with a portion of the dashcam video of the pursuit of the suspect's car. The video runs for about half a minute until the camera approaches to within twenty feet of Murtha's cruiser, which is stopped in the roadway with its lights flashing, near the suspect's car, itself stopped in the snow on the side of the road. As the suspect begins to pull back onto the road, the action "freezes" momentarily and the video turns into an animation. (It was also Taylor's idea to couple the animation to the dashcam video in this way.) The "camera's eye" changes from being the output from a dashboard camera mounted on the following police cruiser to that of a "virtual camera" internal to the computer. This virtual camera's (and our) point of view rises up and rotates to the left around Murtha's cruiser, coming to rest behind a digital Officer Murtha as he stands, outstretched arm holding his gun, confronting the car. The viewer is now just behind Murtha, sharing his point of view in the crucial moment: the bright headlights of the suspect's car flash in our eyes, the left front headlight seemingly only a few feet away. The car could, for all that appears, be headed right at us, and the animation holds the shot for almost two seconds. Then the virtual camera pulls away, up, back, and around again to the point of view from the dashboard camera; all the while the scene remains frozen, the suspect's car still facing Murtha. Finally the suspect's car continues down the road, away from us, while Murtha, walking (not running alongside the car as seen in the dashcam video) fires three shots.

Prosecutor James Thomas objected to the animation, contending (out of the jury's hearing) that the animation was argumentative, inaccurate, and not a fair representation of reality as indicated by the video (*State v. Murtha*, trial transcript, October 16, 2006). Judge Christine Keller reviewed the animation-plus-video several times. Based on Murtha's testimony that the animation fairly and accurately depicted what he thought he saw, Judge Keller found that the animation satisfied the test used in previous cases involving day-in-the-life movies and video reenactments of accidents. She also found that it did not reflect any exaggeration or "artistic embellishment" (ibid., 7, 9). Accordingly, the judge allowed the jurors to see the entire display, instructing them that the video animation was "not purporting or presented . . . to be an exact, precise reenactment of the incident, but it [was] offered into evidence for the limited purpose of helping to illustrate . . . what Mr. Murtha claim[ed] he honestly believed was happening at the time the incident occurred" (ibid., 10–11).

The judge got this much right. The animation plainly did not constitute independent proof of what Murtha thought he saw. Whether the animation simulated Murtha's subjective perception in the moment accurately enough depended on the credibility of Murtha's testimony. The animation was not tethered to external reality in the indexical way that photos or videos are usually presumed to be, nor was it tethered to the defendant's internal reality by the kind of psychophysical tests or physical measurements used in the cases discussed in the next two chapters. What linked it to Murtha's belief about what he saw was that Murtha said it was linked, period. This is clearly an example of an artist's sketch demonstrative, and the judge recognized it as such.

But this begs the question: why would an illustration of Murtha's words be *helpful* to the jurors (which, as explained in chapter 3, is the minimum requirement for an illustrative exhibit to be admissible)? Earlier, in a sidebar with the lawyers, Judge Keller had determined, "This demonstrative evidence will, in fact, assist the jury in understanding one of the key issues in the justification defense; that is, whether or not Mr. Murtha could have honestly believed at the time of the incident that the car was heading toward him and that he was facing imminent deadly threat. I find it's more probative than prejudicial on that point" (*State v. Murtha* transcript, October 16, 2006, 9). Asserting that the animation had *probative* value, however, muddied the waters that the judge seemed to clarify in the instruction quoted earlier. If the animation itself had probative value, then it would have been capable of proving something, over and above its illustrative function. This animation did not have probative value.

That point aside, what *specifically* about the animation might have helped the jurors decide whether Murtha could have honestly believed that he saw what he claimed to have seen? If it would have been difficult for the jurors to imagine, based on Murtha's testimony alone, what he meant by saying that he saw the suspect's car headed toward him, the animation might have helped them to visualize and hence understand his claim. Some studies of computer-generated re-creations of events support the hypothesis that these exhibits can help jurors visualize unfamiliar scenarios and thus understand better what happened (e.g., Dunn, Salovey, and Feigenson 2006). But Murtha's testimony wasn't difficult to comprehend in this sense. It's not that the jurors would have had a hard time imagining what it would be for a stopped car to pull back onto the road and momentarily face the officer. The issue, rather, was whether the jurors should have believed Murtha when he testified that that is what he thought he saw.

Conceivably, the animation might have assisted the jurors with that judgment by showing that Murtha's claimed misperception was not too far removed from a correct perception of the scene, as best as that could be inferred from the video evidence. Murtha did not say, for instance, that he recalled having seen the suspect's car approach him from behind or come at him at sixty miles per hour. He simply misjudged, for a moment, the angle at which the car pulled back onto the road. Seeing this may have enabled the jurors to understand, in a way that the testimony alone might not have, that the claimed misperception was plausible.

While the animation thus served a legitimate function, consider several other, arguably less justifiable ways in which it may have enhanced the credibility of Murtha's account. *First*, some of the reasons why jurors may misconstrue purely illustrative evidence as independent proof, explained above in connection with the photo simulations in *Devadas*, apply here as well. Although the animation was not photographic, the jurors might still have construed it as bolstering Murtha's testimony; the animation was easy to process and thus more likely to be believed; and it gave the jurors a visual experience, albeit a schematic one, of the critical events, on which they could draw when they deliberated.

Second, the medium of computer animation may have appealed to jurors who, immersed in simulation culture, understand how reliably informative educational animations can be (Spiesel, Battye, and Feigenson, forthcoming). To be sure, the animated reconstruction of what Officer Murtha claimed to have seen was not *directly* grounded in any expert authority, unlike, say, the typical computer-animated accident or event reconstruction introduced as substantive evidence. It was, however, indirectly supported by expertise. Two defense expert witnesses testified how, in stressful situations like Murtha's, officers can develop "tunnel vision," becoming so focused on one aspect of a situation that they misperceive or remain oblivious to others. This testimony helped the jurors understand how Murtha might have sincerely thought (as he initially reported) not only that the suspect's car had been heading straight toward him but that it had struck him, even though it had not.

Third, the jurors may well have believed they were seeing a reliable depiction of Murtha's subjective misperception of reality because the exhibit was not just an animation, but rather a hybrid or *montage* of dashcam video and animation. Dashcam video is presumptively reliable. Unless we have reason to believe the video has been altered, we accept it as an accurate enough recording of legally relevant reality. This presumption is even stronger for the dashboard camera than for the digital camera in *Devadas*, since Devadas and his wife could choose when to turn the camera on and where to point it, whereas for most police dashcams, automated systems take those choices away from individual officers: the cameras record when the overhead lights are activated,[39] and the camera's position is fixed. Linking the animation to the video clip bolstered the animation's credibility by grounding it in the presumptive truthfulness of the video. The transition from video to animation folded the two into the same level of representation. By starting with the dashboard camera's point of view and swinging around to the defendant's, moreover, the animation implicitly claimed that both the defendant and the camera were "looking at the same reality." Connecting the animation to the video in this way also normalized the more novel medium of animation by associating it with the very familiar medium of surveillance video—a kind of implicit *remediation* (Bolter and Grusin 1999).

Fourth, perhaps the most distinctive rhetorical feature of the visual reconstruction of Officer Murtha's subjective perception is that the video animation presented a *cinematic narrative* of his confrontation with the suspect, designed to support the jurors' belief that Murtha really thought he saw the suspect's car headed toward him *and* that his misperception and his response to it were reasonable. Begin with the display's visual vocabulary. Viewers of photos and videos intuitively align themselves with the position of the camera lens; its perspective on the world becomes theirs. And while the camera gives viewers presumptively reliable knowledge of what's in front of the lens, the point of view, properly speaking, is third-person *limited*. Viewers can know visually what the camera "sees," but their knowledge is bounded. This is especially true of a fixed surveillance camera. In contrast, audiences of traditional Hollywood movies have been trained to identify their experience with that of a third-person *omniscient* point of view (e.g., Baudry 1986). Across cuts and transitions, the camera ranges freely from one exterior view to another and to shots the audience is meant to understand as signifying a particular character's interior perspective. So in the first part of the animated portion of the *Murtha* display, jurors would have grasped that when the computer's virtual camera moved from the dashcam's point of view up, to the left, and clockwise around Murtha's cruiser until it stopped, not just behind his head but "inside" it (the animation quickly moves past his head to a shot in which we see only his hand in the foreground, pointing his gun at the car whose headlights blink brightly only a few feet away), they were being transported from an "objective" point of view to Murtha's subjective one.

Movie audiences also understand how film editing reconfigures the *fabula* of the story being told into the *syuzhet*, or manner of its telling. In particular, they understand (unless the director deliberately tries to upset their expectations) how to reconstruct coherent, continuous narratives from various shifts in time—flashbacks, cross-cuts, ellipses—just as they do when listening to verbal narratives. Thus, when the animation's virtual camera froze three times during the crucial confrontation between Officer Murtha and the car (first, for a moment, after the transition from video to animation; then for two full seconds as viewers occupied his point of view; and finally at the moment when the virtual point of view swung back to that of the dashcam and the animated car drove off), jurors would have understood these pauses not as happening in the "real time" of the depicted events, but as a visual storytelling device that emphasized Murtha's sudden and highly charged engagement with the suspect.

The video animation was designed, ultimately, to present Murtha's subjective perception of the threat and his violent response to it as *reasonable*. On the dashcam video, we see Officer Murtha moving quickly sideways alongside the fleeing car, keeping both feet perpendicular to the car, knees flexed, both shoulders thrust slightly forward to stabilize his weapon as he pumps bullets into the driver's side window—in short, acting like an aggressor. The video animation brings Murtha back into the fold of reasonableness. The behavior of the officer in the animation, in contrast to the dashcam video, faced with the immediate threat of the suspect's car headed directly at him, is reserved. He stands motionless in front of the car, feet planted, arm with hand holding the gun extended, for a full two seconds. The animated officer then moves only to walk alongside the suspect's car, posture erect, while he discharges his sidearm three times—

hardly an aggressor. The stately pace of the animation further removes viewers from the shock of the violence, conveying instead a calibrated response to the threat the suspect posed.

The narrative structure of the animation implicitly underscored this message. By dissolving from the last frame of the dashcam video clip into the same scene in animated form, the montage associated Murtha with the "good" officers in the other cruiser, embracing him in the group rather than singling him out as the renegade shooter who, to the unprepared viewer of the dashcam video alone, he might well have appeared to be. Even more importantly, by smoothly transitioning from the objective, third-person point of view to Murtha's first-person perspective *and then back again*, the visual story *encompassed* Murtha's misperception, his idiosyncratic and temporary deviation from the norm, within the objective world we all presumably share. This is critical because the rhetorical aim of the defense argument in *Murtha*, unlike the primary aim in recreating the subjectivity of personal injury plaintiffs, was not to emphasize how far Murtha's perceptual experience diverged from the norm, but rather to make the claimed divergence plausible and then promptly to *normalize* the behavior that followed. Psychologist Jerome Bruner (1990) describes the function of narrative as "mak[ing] comprehensible a deviation from a canonical cultural pattern" (49–50). Murtha's shooting the fleeing driver at close range seems like a deviation from the level of force we expect officers to use, at least when we hear the incident described, and even more so when we see it on the dashcam video. The video animation sought to make this deviation explicable as a reasonable response to a reasonable perceptual error. It did so not only by illustrating the threat Murtha claimed to have faced, putting the jurors in his shoes as he confronted the suspect's car, but also by reconciling his subjective misperception with the externally observable facts as recorded in the dashcam video.

As in *Devadas*, it's impossible to know whether or how seeing the simulation of Officer Murtha's subjective misperceptions influenced the jury's verdict. The jury may well have acquitted Murtha or at least hung even without it: he was a highly sympathetic defendant, a respected police officer who had worked his way through law school, while his victim was a drug dealer already in prison at the time of the trial on unrelated drug and weapons charges (Collins 2006). Even so, we should ask whether it was appropriate to allow jurors in a serious criminal case to evaluate the defendant's claim of justified self-defense, which depended entirely on his insistence that he misperceived reality at the critical moment, after exposing them to a video animation montage that *proved* nothing about his alleged subjective experience but which the jurors may well have taken up as if it did. *Murtha* does *not* exemplify what I described in chapter 3 as the courts' often complacent attitude toward simulations of subjectivity. Judge Keller appears to have considered the defense proffer very carefully before admitting the exhibit, and she instructed the jury to regard it as the illustrative aid it was. Nevertheless, it seems the judge did not entirely grasp the rhetorical implications of using digital media to simulate the defendant's claimed visual experience.

FIVE

The Science of Subjectivity

The simulations in the previous chapter rested their claims to provide reliable knowledge of subjective experience entirely on the word of the person having the experience: "That's what I see!" The simulations in this chapter and the next are different. Their epistemological claims are based not merely on the litigants' say-so, but on the authority of science. The video simulation in *Smith* (the idiopathic intracranial hypertension case) and the sound files in *Janson* (the tinnitus case) both discussed in this chapter, are examples of *psychophysical* simulations. The data underlying each exhibit are subjective, to the extent that they depend on the respective litigants' conscious responses to test stimuli, but they are objective as well—obtained by a neuro-ophthalmologist (in *Smith*) and an audiologist (in *Janson*), using precise, well-validated measurement tools and protocols. The image simulation in *Schiffer* (another LASIK case), discussed in chapter 6, exemplifies the *machine readout* simulation. It is also grounded in clinical science but is arguably even more objective, in that it is derived solely from physical measurement and is entirely machine-generated. Their scientific provenance enables these two types of simulations to recreate litigants sensory experiences more reliably than an artist's sketch possibly can.

This chapter begins with a brief overview of psychophysics, the discipline that developed in the mid-nineteenth century for producing rigorously quantitative knowledge about sensation. I outline the origins and basic methods of perimetry—the measurement of visual fields, essential to *Smith*—and connect it to the psychophysical tradition.

I then describe the video simulation in *Smith* and explain why its depiction of the plaintiff's constricted visual field conveyed highly reliable and fairly precise knowledge of what it was like to see as Rosalind Smith did. Finally, I explore how the simulation took advantage of the medium of video to *narrativize* the plaintiff's experience, so as to make her visual impairment both accessible and emotionally compelling.

The sound files in *Janson* offer different lessons. Audiometry, like perimetry, comprises an established body of clinical knowledge and practice that can yield reasonably accurate, trustworthy measurements of a person's sensations—in this case, Dennis Janson's tinnitus, a constant loud buzzing in his head. With some grasp of audiometry, we'll be able to understand why these sound files may not have replicated the plaintiff's subjective experience as faithfully as the video simulation in *Smith* did. Yet we'll also see how trial participants variously talked about and deployed the sound files to bolster the belief that by listening to the exhibit, jurors could hear what the plaintiff heard, and thus confidently know what his subjective experience was really like.

Modern experimental psychology arose as a distinct field of empirical science in the mid-nineteenth century, largely as a branch of physiology. In particular, it took the form of *psychophysics*, "the scientific study of the relation between stimulus and sensation" (Gescheider 1997, ix; see also Boring 1950; Danziger 1990).[1] By its very nature, psychophysics has always been a philosophically synthetic discipline. Its object is to understand consciousness or subjective experience, what is given to the mind; in this respect it shares common ground with phenomenology. But it insists that sensation can be examined and objectively measured through experimentation, based on the person's responses or reactions to stimuli; in this respect it shares the approach and methodologies of behaviorism (Hirsh 1952).

Gustav Fechner and other nineteenth-century experimentalists both before and after him developed several basic principles and methods of psychophysical research (see generally Boring 1942, 1950; Gescheider 1997). These include the concept of the absolute *stimulus threshold* (or *limen*), the smallest amount of stimulus energy needed to produce any sensation in any given modality, and the *difference threshold*, the smallest change in stimulus intensity needed to produce a *just noticeable difference* (JND) in the sensation. To determine these values, Fechner developed the *method of limits*, in which the experimenter adjusts the stimulus intensity successively by discrete steps until the person changes his or her sensory judgment. The change may be from not experiencing to experiencing the sensation (or vice versa), if the aim is to measure the perceptual threshold, or from being able to being unable to distinguish one stimulus from another (or vice versa), if the aim is to measure the JND.[2] Early psychophysicists also inferred from their experimental data general laws describing what they believed to be the systematic relationships between perceptual experience and the external world.

The conscious participation of the person whose perceptual experience is being examined is essential to psychophysics. Simulations of subjectivity based on psychophysical data, therefore, depend on the litigant's awareness of her own perceptions, as do the artist's sketch simulations discussed in chapter 4. But they do so in a very different way. In *Devadas* and *Murtha*, the introspective reports begin discursively—"Here's what it's like," elaborated descriptively. While some have argued that people with adequate training can generate verbal reports of sensation that provide something close to "pure" phenomenological data, free from retrospective evaluation (Price and Barrell 2012), verbal data reports are necessarily permeated with the observer's attempts to make sense of her perceptions, introducing various cognitive and emotional constructs into her descriptions of them. Moreover, artist's sketch re-creations of experience are the product of an interactive, collaborative effort. Only after working with the visual consultant and examining successive versions of the simulation in progress does the litigant say, "That's what I see." In *Devadas*, for instance, the plaintiff had to compare each iteration of each photo simulation while using his best-corrected vision to the unedited reference photo while using his uncorrected vision, and then suggest further adjustments in an entirely nonquantitative way. Some of these judgments, as we've seen, involved comparing a present perception to the (recent) memory of a similar perception, a more cognitively complex operation than the ideal phenomenological "snapshot" (Price and Barrell 2012).

In perimetry, audiometry, and other psychophysical measurements, the litigant's participation in the measurement of his subjective experience takes a different form. The patient's conscious contributions to the testing process—the button pushes, knob adjustments, or other indications of awareness (or not) of the external stimuli—are *disciplined* in multiple ways (see generally Danziger 1990). First, self-report is constrained by test protocols and quantitative analysis. Responses are elicited only to present stimuli (or stimuli given moments before), and more importantly, the responses, although they may depend on introspection, are much less deliberate. Indeed, to most of the stimuli used in perimetry (for example), the patient responds reflexively, nearly automatically, with no discernible time for reflection. As a consequence, the judgments on which psychophysical measurements are based are much less prone to the biases that retrospection and the need to translate experience into words can introduce—including the biasing influence of the exhibit-in-progress itself. Second, the results of psychophysical measurement are also less subjective than those of the unconstrained introspection at the heart of the artist's sketch simulation because the warrant for their accuracy is based on systematic third-person observation, not just first-person report. Third, the repeatability of test results (within the limits of test-retest reliability) and the fact that entire clinical professions rely on psychophysical data in their efforts to alleviate people's perceptual impairments further validate and thus enhance confidence in the data's accuracy and objectivity.

None of this guarantees that the patient's subjective perceptual experience will correspond exactly to what the objective measurements indicate. Quite apart from the limits of measurement accuracy and reliability, a person may, for instance, have habituated (or *accommodated*) to her perceptual impairments so that she is not consciously aware of them in her everyday life even though psychophysical testing indicates that her perception is indeed impaired. The converse is also possible: a person may experience impairments that testing does not capture. Notwithstanding Fechner's faith in a functional dependence between the physical and the psychological, the relationship between mind and body remains at least partly mysterious. But while psychophysical measurement, and hence any simulation that relies on it, may be unavoidably subjective, it's not *merely* subjective. The subjectivity of the litigant's self-report as a warrant for the simulation is constrained, and the reliability of the demonstrative re-creation of the litigant's sensations reinforced, by clinical methodology, careful measurement, and professional practice.

To assess the quality of knowledge that scientifically based simulations can provide, we need to know something about the underlying science. We'll see that the tools and methods used to produce the data on which scientifically based simulations depend and the techniques for representing those data have been refined and improved over time, enhancing their precision and reliability.

Perimetry, the clinical science at issue in *Smith*, is the measurement of the visual field, "all the space that one eye can see at any given instant" (Tate and Lynn 1977, 1). The basic technique of describing a patient's visual field by introducing stimuli of different sizes or intensities at different locations on a uniform background and tracking which ones the patient says he can see, an application of the psychophysical method of limits, dates to the second half of the nineteenth century.[3] To a considerable extent, modern perimetry continues to follow the principles and methods of classical psychophysics. The devices for displaying the stimuli have changed from white hatpins at the end of a dark wand moved around a flat, dark background screen to a hemispherical bowl with an optical projection system and fully automated machines, but many of the underlying techniques have not substantially changed (Johnson, Wall, and Thompson 2011).

The two basic strategies used today are *kinetic* and *static* tests. In kinetic perimetry, "the perimetrist selects a stimulus of a given size and intensity and moves it from the edge of the [visual] field towards the cent[er], noting the position at which it first becomes visible" while the patient fixates his gaze on a central point (Henson 1993, 23). By repeating the process along different radii (from the center of the field), the contour of the visual field (or *isopter*) can be plotted for the given stimulus. Static testing, by contrast, measures sensitivities at preselected locations in the visual field. Unlike kinetic testing, the stimulus doesn't move, but it is varied in size and/or intensity so that the patient's threshold sensitivity at each tested location can be determined. Two of the most commonly used tests today are the Humphrey field analyzer, which employs a static strategy to test the central 20–30° of the visual field, and Goldmann perimetry, which combines kinetic and static techniques (see Johnson, Wall, and Thompson 2011).

Clinicians have also been producing *visual field maps* of patients' visual fields since the mid-nineteenth century. These began as rather abstract drawings (von Graefe [1856] 1935) but soon became precisely plotted contours on a circular grid (e.g., Carter 1872; Carter and Frost 1887) resembling the one used in the star maps then being pioneered in astronomy, another scientific field intimately concerned with the accuracy of vision (e.g., Kanas 2012). The production of ever more informative maps continued into the twentieth century. Neurosurgeon Harvey Cushing encouraged the development of *quantitative perimetry*, "plotting of the visual fields with stimuli of graded intensity to give a map of concentric lines demarcating the limits of perception for each grade of visual stimulus" (Simpson and Crompton 2008b, 231). Modern visual field maps recording the results of manual kinetic perimetry tests thus typically display several isopters (e.g., Anderson 1987; Hughes 1954; Rowe 2006).

Computerized static perimetry yields even more precise and informative images of the patient's sensitivity to stimuli of varying intensity. The

Humphrey visual field analyzer, for instance, creates a data map indicating the precise luminance values representing the patient's perceptual threshold—how faint a light the person can perceive—at each location tested within the central 30 degrees of the visual field.[4]

In short, perimetry has long been established as a quantitative clinical science along psychophysical principles. It has been much improved over the past century and a half, spurred largely by the aim of facilitating increasingly precise neurological diagnoses of visual defects and by the development of ever more sophisticated measuring and recording devices.[5] Clinical visualizations of perimetric testing results, on which a demonstrative simulation of a patient's constricted visual field might be based, have become more information-laden as well as more accurate. With this background in mind, let's turn to the case of Rosalind Smith.

Smith v. Jones

Rosalind Smith was an assistant vice president at a local bank in central Connecticut. She suffered from idiopathic intracranial hypertension (also known as *pseudotumor cerebri*), a disease that causes *papilloedema*, a swelling of the optic nerve head. Symptoms often include headaches, nausea, and vomiting, as well as various visual impairments, including loss of visual field. If the condition is not properly managed by frequent visual field and other ophthalmological testing, the patient may suffer severe and irreversible loss of her visual field (e.g., Rowe 2006).

Smith was admitted to a hospital on June 22, 2009, owing to severe hypertension, with symptoms of vision changes and headaches. Her primary care physician administered blood pressure medications, which quickly brought her blood pressure down to normal, where it remained. She continued, however, to experience "floaters," blurry vision, and headaches. She was referred to an ophthalmologist employed by the University of Connecticut Health Center. A visual field examination administered on July 8, 2009, appeared normal. Smith's other symptoms continued, however; yet a second visual field examination was not performed until October 21, 2009, by which time her visual field had deteriorated beyond the normal range. Still, her ophthalmologist did not refer her to a neurologist or neuro-ophthalmologist.

Eventually Smith sought a second opinion and was then referred to a neuro-ophthalmologist, Dr. Robert Lesser, a clinical professor of ophthalmology and visual science and neurology and the former chief of neuro-ophthalmology at Yale University. Dr. Lesser examined Smith on December 17, 2009, and observed the further extent of her visual field loss. The surgical intervention Dr. Lesser recommended at that time was performed, but it was unsuccessful because of the extent of the visual field loss that had already occurred (*Smith* Plaintiff's Mediation Position Statement, October 26, 2012).

Dr. Lesser, upset about the treatment Smith had received from her first ophthalmologist, referred her to Hartford, Connecticut, attorney Michael Jainchill of the firm RisCassi and Davis. On her behalf, Jainchill filed a lawsuit against that ophthalmologist and his employer, the State of Connecticut. Experts on both sides of the case concurred that Smith's visual loss was "permanent" and "profound"; the constriction of her field of vision to 20 degrees or less qualified her as legally blind. But Jainchill realized he would face a challenge explaining to a jury what that really meant—what it was like for an active, thirty-six-year-old mother of two to lose most of her vision. At her deposition, Smith described her eyesight as follows: "The best way I describe it to people is that I have tunnel vision. . . . It's like I took a pair of sunglasses and gave them to a kid to play with so they're kind of smudged. And put blinders on. I have no peripheral vision up, down, left, or right" (*Smith*, plaintiff's deposition, 84, 86).

And yet just by looking at Smith, said Jainchill, "you couldn't tell that she couldn't see. She functions well enough to find her way around."[6] How could they impress upon a jury what it's like to suffer from such an extensive and irreparable visual loss?

The culture of the firm where Jainchill practiced emphasized using demonstrative evidence in court. Senior partner Bill Davis had long insisted that a trial lawyer is a teacher, an educator, and so the firm always had on hand the sort of traditional demonstrative evidence used in medical malpractice cases—anatomical charts and skeletons—to help lawyers teach better. They would also blow up maps or photos to poster-board size so all jurors could look at the same images at the same time, instead of passing pictures around the jury box (cf. Carney and Feigenson 2004). One morning, as Jainchill was wondering what his initial settlement demand ought to be, he realized, looking at Smith's automated visual field tests, that the data were digital. He called Dr. Lesser and asked: if we were to make a video of what a person with normal vision could see, and then we blacked out what Rosalind Smith's visual field tests indicated she couldn't see, would that be a fair and accurate representation of her subjective visual experience? Dr. Lesser said it would.[7]

Jainchill then called Cathie Reese of Geomatrix Productions, a legal video firm in Woodbridge, Connecticut. RisCassi and Davis, and Jainchill in particular, had been working with Geomatrix since not long after the business was created in 1978. He asked Reese whether Geomatrix could make a video like the one he envisioned, and Reese said yes. Jainchill gave video producer and editor Patrick Volk of Geomatrix the results of Smith's Humphrey automated visual field tests. Volk used Photoshop to generate mattes corresponding to the test results. Since Smith's visual field loss in her left eye differed from that in her right eye, and she used both of her eyes to see, Jainchill asked Volk if the video could show Smith's vision through each eye individually and then both simultaneously. Volk went to work.[8]

Meanwhile, Jainchill consulted with Dr. Lesser to see whether the project was on the right track. Jainchill knew that if the exhibit were ever to be offered in court, he would need either the patient or Lesser to testify that it fairly and accurately represented Smith's vision. Dr. Lesser thought the video so far was good, but imperfect: according to his test results, Smith's ability to see colors was also impaired, and in what remained of her visual field, her acuity was reduced. So Volk adjusted his mattes and filters accordingly, consulting with both Smith and Dr. Lesser. Ultimately Dr. Lesser was in a position to say that, based on his tests of the patient's vision, the video simulation was a fair and accurate representation of what she could see.[9] Rosalind Smith, who had also told Volk that she saw "as if looking through a mail slot in your door," said upon seeing the simulation: "That's what the world looks like to me."[10]

There was one more important step in the creation of the simulation. Michael Jainchill thought the video would be more persuasive if it followed Smith in certain settings and activities. Patrick Volk and Smith chose the particulars. She didn't want anyone filming her at work, so Volk and cameraman Bruce Becker shot roughly a half hour of footage at her home, which Volk eventually edited down to about three and a half minutes.[11]

The video fades in on an interior shot of the plaintiff, sitting at a table in her home in front of a laptop. We see her first from behind; our point of view is over her right shoulder. Cut to a close-up of her face, as we watch her concentrating, eyes focused. Now cut to a close-up of what she's looking at: her laptop, a Word document. We hear her typing and clicking. After a few seconds, three-quarters of the video screen goes black, leaving an irregularly shaped area, mostly in the top left, where we can still see a little of the computer screen. This area is bordered by a fuzzy, blurry, and partly opaque grey of varying width. A label set against the dark lower right of the video screen reads, "left eye." As we watch the document scroll, there is a cross-dissolve; now an even smaller, also irregularly shaped opening in the darkness appears to the right, occupying perhaps half of the upper right quadrant of the video screen and labeled (in the lower left) "right eye." As a cursor blinks and what little we can see of the document continues to scroll, the first area of sight reappears with the second, and a label in the center beneath the combined shape reads "binocular vision." The camera holds this shot for about five seconds before fading to black.

The same sequence of shots—establishing shot defining the activity; close-up of Smith's face; first-person point of view, in close-up, of a normal view of what she is looking at; then the succession of simulations of what Smith sees through her left eye, her right eye, and both eyes; then fade to black—follows for scenes from each of several presumably typical daily activities. A quiet ambient soundtrack accompanies each scene. In each sequence, the close-up of the plaintiff's face invites viewers to focus on her eyes as she concentrates on the activity at hand. It's a calm sort of concentration, but seemingly more effortful during the reading scenes, and in the last scene, watching her sons play outside, she blinks and seems to strain with the effort of following their movements through the "mail slot" of her vision. As the video progresses, the audience experiences how much more difficult it is for her to track movement. And because her field of vision is especially constricted vertically, she cannot see either child's entire body at any given time, nor, if she looks at one child's head, can she see the other's, because of their difference in height. After this segment fades to black, the plaintiff reappears briefly, watching the children, and the video concludes with a full-screen shot of the kids smiling for the camera.

Mediation on the case was scheduled for November 2012. Jainchill brought the video simulation in on his iPad and showed it to the judge and to the defendant's lawyer, Robert Silva of O'Brien, Tanski, and Young in Hartford. The case settled that day. Although it's not possible to know for sure what role the simulation played in obtaining what Jainchill characterized as a favorable settlement, he said that the evidence was "extremely effective."[12] Attorney Silva also thought that the simulation was "impressive" and "very well done."[13]

Are we more justified in believing that what we see in the video simulation is just like what the plaintiff, Rosalind Smith, sees than we are in thinking, say, that when we look at the photo simulations in *Devadas*, we can know what it's like to see as Johnson Devadas does? The grounding of the video simulation of Smith's visual perception in neuro-ophthalmological testing would enhance the reliability of that simulation, all things being equal, only insofar as those clinical test results were themselves reliable.

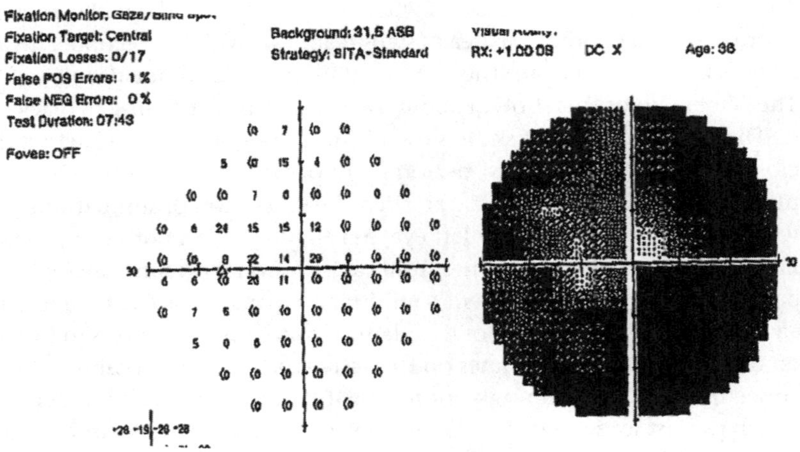

Figure 5.1. *Smith*: portion of plaintiff's visual field test (left eye). Courtesy of Michael Jainchill.

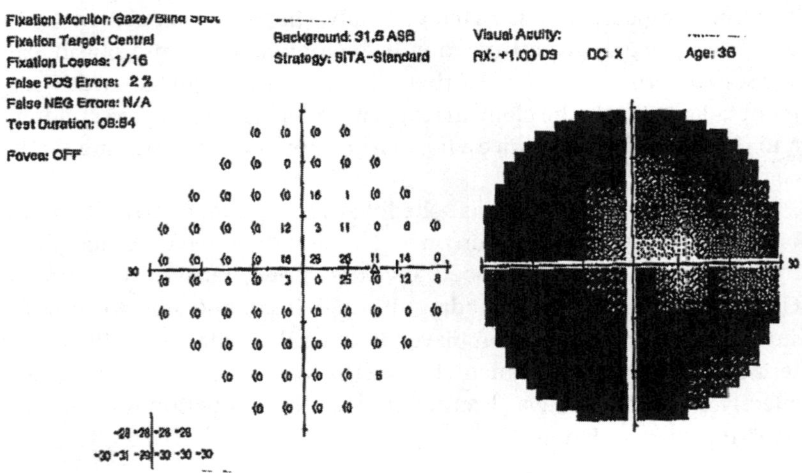

Figure 5.2. Portion of plaintiff's visual field test (right eye). Courtesy of Michael Jainchill.

Were they? How precise and reliable are the measurements resulting from visual field tests? And how faithfully were those test results translated into the mattes superimposed on the underlying video?

Perimetry can yield both highly reliable and relatively accurate depictions of the contours of a patient's visual field, but to evaluate the trustworthiness of the data on which simulations like the one in this case are based,

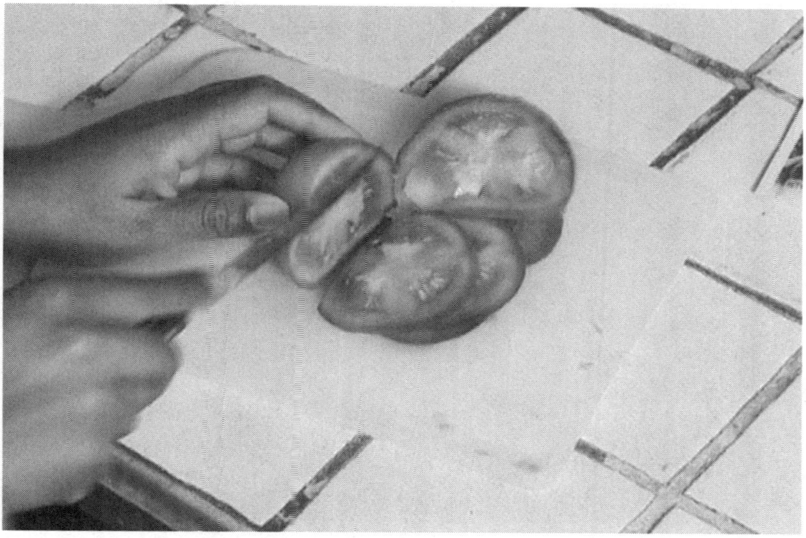

Figure 5.3. Still from video simulation: scene in plaintiff's kitchen. Courtesy of Michael Jainchill and Cathie Reese.

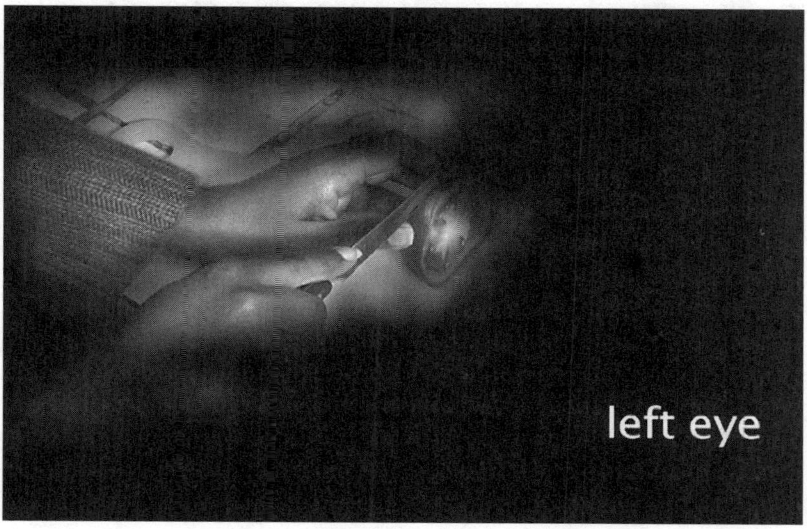

Figure 5.4. Still from video simulation: kitchen scene as plaintiff sees it through her left eye. Courtesy of Michael Jainchill and Cathie Reese.

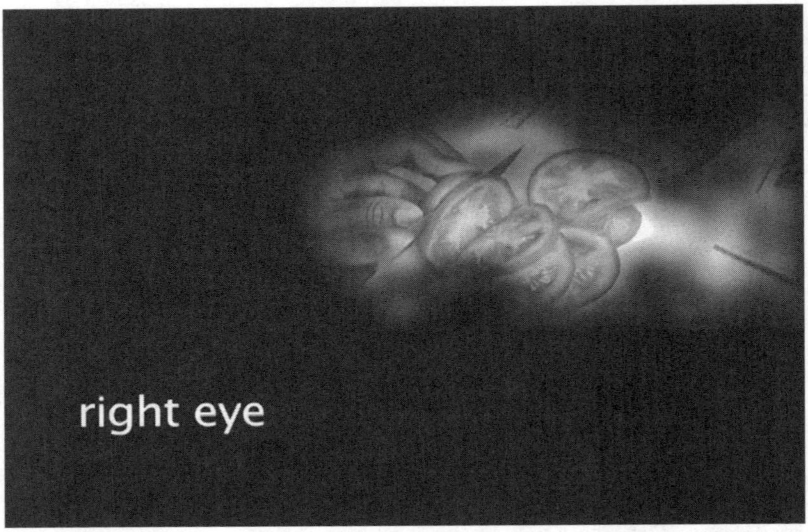

Figure 5.5. Still from video simulation: kitchen scene as plaintiff sees it through her right eye. Courtesy of Michael Jainchill and Cathie Reese.

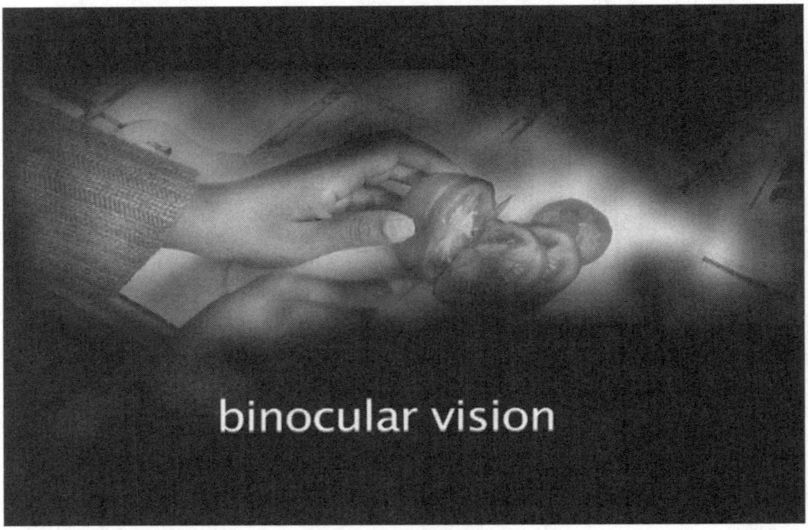

Figure 5.6. Still from video simulation: kitchen scene as plaintiff sees it through both eyes. Courtesy of Michael Jainchill and Cathie Reese.

several concerns must be addressed. First, not every possible location in the visual field can be tested with a stimulus of every size and intensity, so the contours of defective areas and the extent of the defects in those areas are partly approximations based on the responses actually tested (e.g., Anderson 1987). Second, "even for patients who are perfectly alert and attentive, who maintain perfect fixation, and who never blink at the moment of stimulus presentation, there is likely to be a certain minimum variability of responsiveness to stimuli near the boundary between visible and invisible stimuli" (228). The range of short-term fluctuations varies from one patient and test to another.

This takes us to a third, and important, point: the *patient himself* introduces many factors that may undermine test reliability if the perimetrist does not account for them by adjusting the equipment and the administration of the test. Ophthalmology professor and vision scientist David Henson (1993) lists roughly a dozen such factors.[14] Some patients are "trigger happy"; they respond to mechanical noises or features other than test stimuli, so that the test results in a false positive rate that can threaten overall reliability (Budenz 1997). The patient's emotional state may also affect reliability; for instance, depression and irritability significantly increase the variability of responses (Bittner et al. 2011).[15]

The upshot is that at any given location, the isopter as determined by kinetic testing "is probably no more accurate than ± 5°" (Norden 1989). Although random measurement errors would tend to cancel each other out, most viewers would probably notice differences of 5° in the contour of a field of vision simulated in a courtroom exhibit. That said, clinical measurements of the visual field, when properly conducted and used as appropriate in conjunction with brain imaging and other tests, are reliable enough to support the diagnoses of a wide variety of visual defects (e.g., Rowe 2006; Tate and Lynn 1977) and thus are generally accepted in the profession as yielding sufficiently accurate knowledge about the relevant features of the patient's vision.[16] Measurement error or variability of the magnitude described above is seldom of any clinical importance,[17] especially when the patient's perceptual deficit is severe[18]—as Rosalind Smith's was.

The measurements of Smith's visual field appear to have been as accurate and reliable as standard modern perimetry allows. A certified ophthalmic technician in Dr. Robert Lesser's office first performed an automated Humphrey visual field test. This was followed by manual Goldmann field testing to obtain a more complete mapping of Smith's entire visual field, although given the Humphrey test results, the outer contours of her vision, effectively limited to the central 30 degrees or so of the total field, were already known. On the basis of Smith's visual field data, Dr. Lesser was prepared to testify, as already noted, that the video simulation "fairly and accurately represented" her field of vision, as well as her visual acuity within the remaining field. (Dr. Lesser did not have to testify, because the case settled.) Given the literature summarized above, that opinion would almost certainly have been justified.

What about the translation of the visual field tests into the mattes that were superimposed on the video segments from Smith's daily life to simulate her visual experience? In one respect, the process resembled the one involved in making artist's sketch simulations: the mattes were not directly caused by the isopters or contours they purported to represent; they did not bear the physical traces of the plaintiff's behaviors in response to test stimuli. The mattes were thus not indexical representations of the limits of Smith's visual field. Rather, Patrick Volk adapted the visual field maps to create the mattes from scratch in Photoshop.

Nevertheless, the mattes were crucially unlike the artist's sketch simulations in *Devadas* and *Murtha*, because instead of creating and adjusting his work solely on the basis of the litigant's verbal report, Volk himself could see the data readouts the tests had generated. He needed only to convert them into a different medium, from paper to pixels. In addition, Volk could check and recheck his work against the visual field test readouts. Volk's work, therefore, was more constrained than Roger Davis's in *Devadas*. Davis could consult only with Devadas himself, and thus could not help but import into the Photoshopped pictures whatever variability and biases may have affected Devadas's judgments of how well those pictures corresponded to his visual experience. For Volk, the test data and the visual field maps were already fixed (although there were multiple tests, tracking the worsening of the plaintiff's condition). He therefore enjoyed far fewer degrees of freedom in fashioning the mattes' sizes and shapes.

Given the reliability of visual field testing, attentively administered as part of a more extensive battery of tests of a symptomatic patient's complaints, it seems reasonable to state, as one ophthalmologist has, that a matte or mask corresponding to the test results can "fairly accurately" represent the patient's subjective vision.[19] There is always the caveat that the patient's conscious experience may diverge from what the test results indicate she is experiencing. For instance, a study of glaucoma patients, who suffer from progressive visual field deficits, showed that more than one-quarter of those whose Humphrey field analyzer tests indicated visual field loss were completely unaware of any impairment of their vision (Crabb et al. 2013).[20] This subjective compensation for objective visual deficits may be due in part to the well-known phenomenon of "filling-in," by which our brains actively fill in blind spots (or *scotomas*) with visual sensations drawn from the surrounding area (e.g., Ramachandran and Gregory 1991; Safran and Landis 1999).

This sort of gap between subjective experience and psychophysical measurement would not, however, appear to be a concern in Rosalind Smith's case. The glaucoma study just mentioned identified people whose visual experience was *less* impaired than clinical testing indicated it should have been. Presumably, plaintiffs in cases like Smith's would not be pursuing their cases unless they felt their vision was seriously impaired. Smith's legal team would not have prepared to go forward with the exhibit, moreover, if she had not been ready to testify that it fairly and accurately represented her vision. It's reasonable to conclude, then, that the psychophysically based simulation of Smith's severely limited visual field more or less accurately evoked her subjective visual experience.

While the video simulation of Rosalind Smith's constricted field of vision was thus backed by scientific authority in ways that the artist's sketch simulations discussed in chapter 4 were not, its persuasive effects go beyond its purely scientific appeal. Because the case did not go to trial, we have no way of knowing whether jurors would have found it convincing, but there are several reasons why legal audiences might have believed it gave them reliable access to the plaintiff's subjective experience. In particular, by using the medium of video and the genre conventions of the day-in-the-life movie, the simulation constructed her perceptual experience as an immediately intelligible, emotionally compelling narrative.

Begin with the medium of video. In comparison to the still photos used in *Devadas*, video situates Smith's visual experience more thoroughly in the story of her everyday life. It does this in two ways. First, most obviously, video is a time-based medium. It can show behavior as it unfolds in real time. It depicts the plaintiff as she performs activities (and enables the audience to mentally simulate the performance of those activities; see the discussion of mirror neurons in chapter 2), whereas still photography can only suggest performance. Instead of having to infer from a photo of bottles on pharmacy shelves what Devadas would be doing with those bottles—looking at them, reaching for them—viewers of the video can watch Smith as she slices a tomato or cooks hamburger, and then occupy her point of view and vicariously engage in those behaviors themselves.

Second, because the video depicts *sequences* of behavior, it can elicit emotional responses based on the unfolding of action over time. For instance, the second scene opens with a medium shot of Smith at her kitchen counter, slicing a tomato. After the cut to the close-up of her face, shot from below, we see in close-up her hands in action at the cutting board: her left hand holds the tomato, her right wields the knife. The black matte quickly fades in to block all but a portion of the upper left quarter of her visual field, simulating the view from her left eye, just as the sharp edge of the knife touches the top of the tomato. Due to the camera angle, the knife seems poised directly above her left thumb. The viewer automatically tenses, fearing that she may cut her thumb—even while knowing this will not happen (see Gerrig and Prentice 1996). She continues to slice, seeming to miss her thumb by a hair. The visible field then shifts to show what can be seen through her right eye, and then both eyes, but all the while the tension remains. Without having to be told in so many words, viewers immediately understand how unnerving the plaintiff's daily life must be, fraught with small anxieties and larger dangers. The video conveys more concretely and vividly than her own testimony at her deposition did what it's like, at a phenomenological level, to live with her condition.

The video simulation is documentary in nature, but it is obviously not simply an observational documentary (Nichols 1991), a record of the plaintiff's day in real time. Rather, the video simulates Smith's constricted vision as part of a *day-in-the-life movie*, a genre of demonstrative evidence frequently used in personal injury cases. The goal of the day-in-the-life movie is to demonstrate to jurors what the injury means to the plaintiff, in terms of both the plaintiff's physical and mental suffering and its effects on the plaintiff's family and other persons, all of which is relevant to the jury's determination of pain and suffering damages (e.g., Graham and Lapp 1992). The day-in-the-life film must of course represent reality faithfully enough to be admitted as evidence; it cannot, for example, be deceptively edited. But it can be composed to show the plaintiff as a heroic character in a daily drama, struggling to overcome her injuries and be the best person she can be under the circumstances. The editing of the footage shot in the field (typically several hours' worth) down to the 15 to 20 minutes ordinarily shown at trial both condenses the presentation to a length that judges and jurors can tolerate and aims to tell a clear and emotionally engaging story (Feigenson and Spiesel 2009).

The *Smith* video differs from the typical day-in-the-life movie in a few ways. It is only about three and a half minutes long, and the order of the scenes is not necessarily the order in which the plaintiff typically engaged in those activities. But in its most essential features, the video aspires to do what a good day-in-the-life movie always does: to construct the plaintiff as someone who deserves the jury's sympathy and understanding, even admiration. Each segment of the video begins with an establishing shot and then a close-up of Smith, her face calm, pleasant, and focused on the task at hand. The narrative arc of the video starts with the plaintiff working alone on the computer; proceeds to cooking, an activity she presumably performs for her sons (whom we've not yet seen) as well as herself; then to activities she does with her younger son; and finally, as a coda, observing both her sons at play. That is, we see Smith first as simply the main character, but she evolves over the course of her daily activities into a concerned and loving mother. She earns our respect not just by dealing quietly and nobly with her impairment, but by being a continuing presence in her sons' lives. (Smith is in fact married, but since we see no other adult in these scenes, the implication is that she is primarily responsible for taking care of the children, enhancing our sense of her virtue.) At the end of the video, her attentive and appreciative gaze toward her sons at play models the attitude viewers are expected to display toward her.

Thus, unlike the photo sequences in *Devadas* (and the sound files in *Janson*, to be discussed next) but like the video-plus-animation in *Murtha*, the video simulation in *Smith* combines first-person with third-person points of view to achieve its overall effect: getting the audience to understand what the litigant's aberrant perceptual experience is (or was) like, while encouraging the audience to align themselves and sympathize with the litigant. In addition, and in contrast to the cartoon figure in the *Murtha* animation, the video simulation gives viewers a rich source of demeanor evidence about Smith. As noted, she appears positive, determined, loving, and hopeful. The medium of video thus permits a more complete demonstration of the litigant as a *deserving character*.[21]

Because viewers are so cognitively involved with the vicarious experience of seeing with Smith's constricted visual field, so emotionally absorbed in her story, and so accustomed from lifetimes of watching movies to accepting what they see as a more or less direct window onto what the movie depicts, they will probably fail to notice *how* the video constructs their experience of her subjectivity—how deliberately it builds their seemingly unmediated knowledge of her visual world. Consider, for instance, the repeated sequence of shots comprising each scene, culminating with the simulations of the plaintiff's severely limited visual field as seen through her left eye, her right eye, and then both eyes. After a while, this rhythmic repetition becomes just a natural way to depict Smith's visual experience; viewers no longer think about the video maker's choice to show these activities in just this way (if they ever did). And by repeating this pattern of shots, the video maker creates for each new scene an expectation that is always fulfilled, satisfying viewers that they are being competently and thoroughly taught what they need to know.

Note another curious feature of the video: it depicts what is outside the plaintiff's visual field as a black area within the screen. The plaintiff, however, sees nothing like this. She doesn't see black beyond the periphery of her visual field; she simply doesn't see anything. The effect of showing the extensive dark areas may well be to emphasize the contrast between normal vision, identified with being able to see to the edges of the screen, and the plaintiff's impaired vision. In addition, by deploying a color culturally coded as signifying absence, even despair, the design of the video suggests a negative emotional register that could affect viewers' judgments of how bad it is for the plaintiff to have to endure her condition (and thus how deserving she is for enduring it with such resolve). It isn't necessarily misleading to use black spaces to depict what a person with normal vision can see but the plaintiff cannot; Smith's neuro-ophthalmologist, Dr. Lesser, described what she can't see as "black."[22] The point is that even ostensibly sober and accurate elements of the simulation have rhetorical effects.

More generally, that the representation of the plaintiff's constricted visual field is *aestheticized* in these ways does not imply that the video should be regarded as any "less scientific" and hence less credible as a simulation of her subjective experience. Visualizations of medical and other scientific information have always owed some of their appearance, and their appeal, to conformity to aesthetic standards, whether those standards are generated inside or outside the particular discipline (e.g., Breidbach 2011; Elkins 1999; Lynch and Edgerton 1988; Mody 2014; Steinman and Steinman 2011). The scientifically based re-creation of Rosalind Smith's constricted visual field is no exception.

Janson v. J.D.O.R.A.P., Inc.

Janson, the tinnitus case, extends our study of evidentiary simulations in several ways. The exhibit engages a new sensory modality, hearing. Unlike *Smith*, a significant question could have been raised about the clinical measurements on which the simulation was based, problematizing its correspondence to the plaintiff's sensory experience. Yet the simulation was talked about and performed in court in ways that encouraged jurors to believe that, just by listening to the sound files, they could really know what it was like for Dennis Janson to hear the sounds that only he could directly experience.

Dennis Janson was an acoustic engineer and recording studio designer and architect (*Janson* 2011; Miller 2011). Janson bought four "extreme" off-road tires from Extreme Vehicle Builders, owned by the defendant, J.D.O.R.A.P., Inc. Extreme Vehicle Builders installed the four tires on Janson's Jeep Wrangler. Janson drove the vehicle without any problems for a few months. One day, while he was checking the bolts on the right front wheel, the wheel's bead-lock rim sheared off at a weld joint, and the wheel exploded. The force of the explosion knocked Janson backward into a wall, injuring both of his hands. More significantly, the accident also caused "acute acoustic trauma," resulting in a permanent loss of hearing in Janson's left ear, the loss of high-frequency hearing in both of his ears, hyperacusis (reduced sound tolerance, so that even ordinary sounds become excruciating), and tinnitus in both ears (*Janson*, trial transcript, March 2, 2011).

Janson engaged Antonio Ponvert III of the firm of Koskoff, Koskoff, and Bieder in Bridgeport, Connecticut, to represent him in his lawsuit against J.D.O.R.A.P., Inc. Proving the tire seller's liability under a theory of strict products liability would not be difficult. The greater challenge, as so often in personal injury cases, would be making a compelling case for damages—especially since the accident did not prevent Janson from continuing in his studio design business, although he testified that his hearing loss and other ailments were "critical" to his work (*Janson* transcript, March 2, 2011, 22). Ponvert recruited Dr. Richard Salvi, an audiologist in the University of Buffalo's Department of Communicative Disorders and Sciences and its Center for Hearing and Deafness, as an expert. Salvi, in turn, contacted Dr. Edward Lobarinas, then assistant research professor and clinical audiologist at the Center,[23] to run the standard batteries of audiological and tinnitus tests on Dennis Janson (*Janson* transcript, March 1, 2011). Both ultimately testified in Janson's behalf at trial.

Ponvert recognized that the expert testimony in itself might not be enough to convey to the jury what it was like to endure the sort of tinnitus from which Janson was suffering and how seriously his tinnitus and other hearing defects interfered with his enjoyment of life. Tinnitus is the perception of sound in the absence of an external source (Møller 2011b). It can be thought of as a phantom injury to the ear, much like a phantom limb injury (Møller 2011a). The patient hears something that is *not there*. Not only does the plaintiff not appear to be impaired in any way, but jurors may be suspicious whether a condition without any identifiable, objective cause could really be as bad as the plaintiff, or his audiologist, claims it is.

Ponvert asked Dr. Lobarinas whether there might be any way to show the jury what Janson was hearing. Lobarinas responded with the idea of creating the sound files.[24] Lobarinas had made sound files "all the time" as stimulus materials for purposes of his preclinical research on drug therapies for tinnitus, but he had never made a sound file to represent, for courtroom use, a particular tinnitus sufferer's experience. And while there was (and is) no professional literature on making sound files for forensic use, there was a "rich" literature on making sound files for research. In addition, Lobarinas, unlike most purely clinical audiologists, had both the expertise and the equipment to make sound files.

Lobarinas's plan was to "start with the basics"—how loud Janson's tinnitus was, where Janson heard it (e.g., in one ear or the other, both ears, in the "middle of his head," or somewhere else), and whether it correlated with Janson's hearing loss. Once these and other physical characteristics were ascertained, it would be a "straightforward" matter to create the sound files, since every sound has physical properties that can be mathematically broken down. The audiological and tinnitus tests Lobarinas had run on Janson, moreover, indicated that his tinnitus was a "relatively simple" and not a complex sound, and thus all the easier to replicate.

Ultimately six separate files were made, three for each ear, each file representing a different tone that Janson claimed to hear. The idea was to put the complete exhibit on an iPod and make the sound files available to jurors through headphones. As part of his trial preparation, attorney Ponvert presented the case to a focus group. Some participants, upon hearing the sound files, said they couldn't believe how loud the tinnitus sound was: "How could anyone live with that?"[25]

During the first day of trial, Judge Michael Maronich held an evidentiary hearing to determine whether to admit Lobarinas's expert testimony and the sound files. Connecticut courts have adopted a version of the *Daubert* test for the admissibility of expert evidence.[26] The judge listened to the sound files through both speakers and headphones. He ruled that the exhibit was "a fair and accurate representation of what the plaintiff hear[d]" and could be played for the jury (*Janson* transcript, March 1, 2011, 52).

When the jury returned, Lobarinas took the stand. Ponvert led him through his qualifications and the process by which he had tested Janson's hearing and ascertained the extent and nature of his tinnitus. He then asked Lobarinas to explain how he "took this information that [he had] learned about his tinnitus and . . . created an exhibit for the jury to hear." Lobarinas briefly explained how the sound files had been made. Ponvert then produced an iPod and a set of headphones, to give the jurors an opportunity "to . . . hear what Dennis Janson hears." Each juror was allowed to listen for as long as desired and then hand the iPod and headphones to the next juror. Ponvert cautioned the jurors, "Just bring [the headphones] to your head sort of slowly and then put them down if you're comfortable doing it. If you don't want to put them all the way on, you don't have to" (*Janson* transcript, March 1, 2011, 69–70, 72). At least some, if not all, of the jurors put on the headphones and listened.[27]

The trial lasted another day and a half and included testimony from Dennis Janson and his wife. Janson described his tinnitus and its effects on his work as a sound studio engineer and on his daily life:

> From the time I wake up in the morning until the time I go to sleep at night I have an extraordinarily loud high-pitch noise in both ears. It never goes away. Sometimes it'll get slightly worse. It's more recognizable in quiet environments, which is one reason why it's troublesome in my profession, and it's . . . debilitating. It's difficult to live with. I'm lucky if I get four hours of sleep a night, sometimes five. It's very difficult to fall asleep. [I]f I wake up in the middle of the night—and as I mentioned before, in quiet environments it becomes more prevalent—then you begin to dwell on it more, the fact that it's there and it's not going to go away. So it's a problem with sleep. (*Janson* transcript, March 2, 2011, 31, 34)

After the jury retired to deliberate, the foreman and at least one other juror listened to the exhibit again.[28] The jury returned a verdict for $1.2 million, which, according to Ponvert, was one of the largest personal injury judgments ever awarded in that county (Miller 2011).

Could hearing the sound files actually allow the jurors in *Janson* to know what the plaintiff's tinnitus sounded like to him? In the courtroom, jurors were invited to believe that by listening to the files, they could "hear what Dennis Janson hears." The knowledge claim was that the simulation faithfully recreated the plaintiff's subjective reality. How valid could that claim be?

The reliability of a scientifically based simulation, as we've seen, derives from the reliability of the underlying clinical measurements and the translation of those measurements into (in this case) audible form. We begin, then, with the science of audiometry—the measurement of hearing—and in particular, the measurement of tinnitus. Clinical audiometry depends on the *audiometer*, a device used to generate specific, scalable qualities of tone varying in frequency and intensity.[29] Audiometers are used to ascertain hearing thresholds, using the method of limits and other procedures so fundamental to psychophysics (Hirsh 1952; Reger 1950). They are also used to elicit the patient's judgments comparing one or more tones with the sound of his tinnitus. The reliable reproduction of stimulus tones and accurate, broadly interpretable, quantitative descriptions of patients' psychophysical data required standardized equipment, which became widely available by the 1930s. The logarithmic decibel scale for measuring the intensity of the tones used to test hearing also became widely accepted by that time (Kranz 1963; see also Fowler and Wegel 1922). Audiometric equipment and techniques have continued to improve to the present day. Digital audiometers, for instance, are now available in a variety of models for industrial, clinical, and research applications.[30]

The psychoacoustic assessment of tinnitus dates to the early twentieth century (e.g., Henry, Dennis, and Schechter 2005). Today, measuring a patient's tinnitus typically begins with tests of the patient's auditory sensitivity, or hearing thresholds, at different frequencies. Once these are established, the audiologist starts measuring the tinnitus sounds themselves. A standard technique involves what is called a "two-alternative forced-choice" method (e.g., Goodwin 1984; Henry 2004).[31] In this test the patient sits in a soundproof booth, wearing headphones. The audiologist presents the patient with two tones and asks the patient to indicate by hand signal which sound is more like the sound he typically hears.[32] Since most tinnitus patients also have hearing loss and indeed are likely to experience tinnitus at the frequencies at which they have hearing loss (Clark 1984), external tones must be raised in volume, relative to what a person with normal hearing would be able to hear, in order for the patients to hear them. As successive pairs of alternative tones are presented and selected, the audiologist is gradually able to identify the tone that most closely corresponds to what the patient indicates he hears—much as an optometrist figures out a prescription for glasses or contact lenses.[33]

Using this protocol, the audiologist can eventually obtain a match to the pitch (typically measured in increments of 1 kHz) and loudness (typically measured in increments of 1 dB) of the sound the patient claims to be hearing. Repeating the tests yields a high level of test-retest reliability with regard to loudness, although not for pitch (Henry 2004; Tyler 2000).

The measurements of Dennis Janson's tinnitus that Dr. Lobarinas obtained could be trusted in large part because of the objective, disciplined nature of the measurement process. Lobarinas subjected his patient to the rigorous protocol of forced-choice questions described above. The testing environment itself was physically constrained: in the standard procedure, applied here, the patient sits in a soundproof booth, to exclude potentially confounding noises and enhance the value of the signals; he faces 90 degrees away from the audiologist to prevent him from being influenced by any of the audiologist's gestures or other behaviors. The protocol then procedurally constrains the patient's responses. The patient does not engage in open-ended introspection to report what his tinnitus sounds like; he indicates only that one test sound or the other in each pair more closely resembles what he hears. The considerable number of such forced-choice questions, forty for each ear for each of the three parameters used to describe the sound (loudness, pitch, and tone), and the variation in the order in which the choices are presented (e.g., with regard to pitch, sometimes the higher tone is presented first, sometimes the lower), make it very difficult for a patient to fabricate the overall sound profile. This method of testing tinnitus, moreover, has long been used and accepted, not just by individual audiologists and other tinnitus researchers, thus satisfying the "general acceptance" criterion so important to admissibility under Connecticut law,[34] but by the Veterans Administration, bolstering the methodology's credibility with the authority of a routinized, institutional practice.

The measurement of Janson's tinnitus was also, according to Dr. Lobarinas, a *mechanical* process, involving no subjective judgments on the audiologist's part. "I merely keep a tally of what Mr. Janson consistently matches to. So I do not guide Mr. Janson in any way or ask him any questions of whether it's higher or lower. I just present pairs randomly within a range of his hearing until he consistently matches to one of the sounds" (*Janson* transcript, March 1, 2011, 17).

But now we come to a difficulty. Although most audiologists agree that the pitch and loudness of tinnitus can be measured fairly accurately and precisely, they disagree about *what scale* to use when measuring loudness. This is critical, because the choice of loudness scale affects the volume of the sound file, and hence the loudness of the sound jurors will experience when they hear the simulation.

The most common scales of tinnitus measurement are *hearing level* (HL) and *sensation level* (SL), both expressed in decibels (dBs). Hearing level is the dB reading on the audiometer when the patient indicates the tone being played is as loud as (i.e., matches) the tinnitus sound he hears in his head. Sensation level is the dB reading on the audiometer when the patient indicates the tone being played is as loud as the tinnitus he hears, *above that person's threshold* for hearing any tone at all at that frequency (Ward 1965).[35] The loudness of the tinnitus sound measured in dB HL (hearing level) tends to be much higher than when measured in dB SL (sensation level) for the simple reason that the SL measurement controls for the patient's hearing loss at that frequency, whereas HL does not. Most experts report that tinnitus loudness measured in sensation level units usually does not exceed 10–20 dB SL.[36] For comparison, 20 dB roughly corresponds to a whisper at a distance of about five feet (Tonndorf 1965). Loudness measured in hearing level units, by contrast, can be 70–80 dB HL (e.g., Hoffman and Reed 2004), roughly equivalent to a busy office environment or an automobile in motion at a distance of about 20 feet, or even higher.

Neither scale, however, provides a completely accurate measure of loudness (Goodwin 1984). Hearing level tends to *overrate* the subjective loudness of the sound, while sensation level tends to *underrate* it (Baskill and Coles 1999). HL tends to overrate loudness because a tinnitus patient who has hearing loss (as most do) will generally hear external sounds less well than a person with normal hearing, but she will still hear her tinnitus sound at whatever level she hears it because the tinnitus is coming from *inside* her head, not outside, and so its apparent loudness to her is not reduced by her hearing loss. Therefore, the tone being used in the loudness-matching test to correspond to the loudness of the inside (tinnitus) sound has to be played at a higher volume for the person with hearing loss—Dennis Janson, for example—than it would have to be for a person without hearing loss to match an internal sound of the same subjective loudness. Since dB HL measures the level of the tone when, according to the tinnitus patient, it matches the sound inside his head, that measurement exaggerates the loudness of the patient's tinnitus as it would be perceived by a person with normal hearing.

For instance, consider a tinnitus patient who is experiencing a ringing sound in his head. Assume that the patient also has a 50 dB hearing deficit at the relevant frequency. Assume also that the audiologist has to increase the test tone to a volume of 80 dB before the patient says, "That's at the same level as my ringing." But since that tone is only 30 dB above the patient's threshold for hearing any sound at all at that frequency, a person with normal hearing, whose threshold is by definition 0 dB (Ward 1965), would need only a 30 dB tone to experience the same degree of subjective loudness. So, relative to a person with normal hearing, dB HL would, as a first approximation, overestimate by roughly 50 dB (the level of the hearing deficit) the volume of the tone needed to match the subjective loudness of the patient's tinnitus at that frequency.

The dB SL measure, on the other hand, tends to underrate the loudness of the sound the tinnitus sufferer is hearing. Sensation level measures only the difference in dB level between the threshold at which the patient can hear any sound (at that frequency) and the level that matches his tinnitus, but simply subtracting the threshold level from the match level doesn't take account of *loudness growth* (or *recruitment effects*). This phenomenon describes how a person with damage to the ear and/or to auditory processing channels in the brain may be much more sensitive to a given increment in sound intensity than a person with normal hearing is (Hirsh 1952; Ward 1965). That is, a person with hearing loss loses the ability to hear relatively quiet sounds, but once that person's threshold is crossed, loudness grows very quickly. The greater the hearing loss (i.e., the higher the threshold), and the greater the intensity of the external sound, the more quickly the subjective loudness of that sound for the person with hearing loss "catches up" to what the person with normal hearing experiences (Goodwin and Johnson 1980). As a consequence, measuring a tinnitus sound at, say, 5 dB SL from a high threshold may significantly understate the patient's subjective experience of loudness. This is one reason why loudness matching tests using the sensation level scale usually yield results no higher than the 20 dB range (recall that that is about the level of a whisper at a distance of five feet), even where the patient reports his tinnitus as unbearable (Møller 2011b).[37]

Which scale to use, then? Experts disagree, although probably the majority would use sensation level.[38] Dr. Lobarinas chose hearing level. Using this, he measured the loudness of Dennis Janson's tinnitus as 80 dB HL. Janson's hearing threshold at that frequency was about 60 dB, so using the db SL scale, the same subjective loudness would be measured as 20 dB. Thus, using the hearing level scale instead of the sensation level scale to describe tinnitus loudness resulted in the creation of a sound file that would seem much louder to persons with normal hearing.

Audiometric testing produced quantitative measures of a few key characteristics of Janson's tinnitus—pitch, loudness, and noise bandwidth. How were these characteristics converted into a sound that, it could be claimed, closely corresponded to what Janson heard in his head? Dr. Lobarinas explained: "Well, that is actually relatively straightforward because the sound that he matched to has physical characteristics. It has intensity, it has frequency, and it has bandwidth. So once you have those three characteristics, we just used MATLAB software and just generated the parameters in there and the output was the sound file" (*Janson* transcript, March 1, 2011, 12).

Clinical audiologists "commonly" use sound files generated from audiometric data when they present their findings to other professionals,[39] and MATLAB is standard software for audio processing generally and in tinnitus research specifically, for both the creation of stimulus materials and data analysis.[40] Thus, in relevant professional practices, the knowledge generated when test data are converted into sound files is routinely relied upon. That these particular sound files were created with eventual use as courtroom evidence in mind would not appear to undermine that reliability.

Yet during the evidentiary hearing, it emerged that the creation of the files ultimately played in court was not quite the "straightforward," even automatic process that Lobarinas indicated it was. The defendant's lawyers asked Judge Maronich to exclude the exhibit, not on the basis of any substantive reliability concerns of the sort discussed above (e.g., the choice of db HL scale), but on the ground that the files had been "switched." Apparently, Dr. Salvi had previously created a sound file matched to Janson's tinnitus for pitch but not loudness. Lobarinas then "recalibrated" the file so that its loudness as jurors would experience it would match the loudness of the sound that his measurements indicated Janson heard (*Janson* transcript, March 1, 2011, 26). To defense counsel's chagrin, Judge Maronich construed this change as an argument in favor of admission: "It appears to me that there's been . . . an ongoing attempt to make this recording more accurate to what . . . the plaintiff actually experiences" (51). In the judge's view, changing the file not only enhanced the demonstrative exhibit's reliability but also proved its proponents' virtue. Yet the recalibration of the sound files runs counter to the impression Lobarinas gave earlier that the synthesized sounds were simply automatically produced auditory translations of the test data.

So, *can* a simulation faithfully reproduce the sound of an individual's tinnitus, which only he can actually hear? There are likely to be aspects of the tinnitus sufferer's experience that a sound file cannot replicate. For instance, because "tinnitus does not share the same psychophysical characteristics as external acoustic stimuli" (Henry 2004, 222–23; see also Jastreboff 1990), it may be difficult if not impossible in principle to match any external sound exactly to a person's subjectively experienced tinnitus.[41] Tinnitus sounds, moreover, may change from day to day, may be pulsatile (i.e., experienced in synchrony with the patient's heartbeat or respiration rate), and are often accompanied by other hearing deficits, so it may be difficult if not impossible to copy precisely the ensemble of symptoms the patient experiences. Moreover, the subjective intensity of tinnitus is in part a function of the patient's psychological and behavioral coping mechanisms. That said, one leading audiology scholar has written: "Once tinnitus has been measured, a pure tone can be presented at the pitch-match frequency and at the tinnitus loudness so that [an]other person can get some indication of what the tinnitus patient is going through" (Tyler 2000, 150). Yet this same authority has also remarked, "You never really know what a person's tinnitus sounds like to them."[42] It seems fair to say, then, that the tinnitus simulation in this case was capable of conveying *some* knowledge of what Janson heard—knowledge good enough to satisfy many if not most audiologists—but not *exactly* what he heard.

Once the simulation of Dennis Janson's tinnitus entered the courtroom, however, it was *described* and *performed* so as to lay doubts to rest, first for the judge and then for the jurors. I have already drawn on Dr. Lobarinas's testimony at the evidentiary hearing for the descriptions of the test protocol and the creation of the sound files. Here I want to discuss five other examples of courtroom discourse. By variously evoking scientific and popular norms of reliability, the expert and the lawyers encouraged both the judge and the jurors to believe that the simulation gave them the truth of Dennis Janson's subjective experience.

First, observe how, at the evidentiary hearing to determine whether the sound files would be admitted, Dr. Lobarinas used the term "match":

Q (Attorney Ponvert): Is this exhibit a fair and accurate representation of what Dennis Janson hears in terms of frequency, noise, tone, and decibel?

A (Dr. Lobarinas): This sound file, the one that I provided for each ear and the combination, is the match that he consistently matched to (*Janson* transcript, March 1, 2011, 13).

There is some slippage here. The question asked was about the relationship between the exhibit and Janson's *subjective experience*—"what Dennis Janson hears." Lobarinas answered that the sound file "is the match," that is, represented the volume, frequency, and tone of the external sound to which Janson's *behavioral responses* during testing indicated he "matched." The answer is appropriate; without direct access to Janson's inner experience, the audiologist could confirm only that the sound file accurately represented the stimuli that, according to his psychophysical testing, corresponded to the sensations that Janson reported. Yet the judge may have been left with the impression that the sound file fairly and accurately represented "what Dennis Janson hears"—that it offered good enough knowledge of his subjective experience for the jurors to rely on. The gap between subjective experience and objective knowledge of it would have been subtly elided. And this appears to be what the judge ultimately concluded. As already noted, he ruled that Lobarinas's application of the methods generally accepted in his profession was, in the language of the law of evidence, "valid and accurate" and that the sound files were a "fair and accurate representation of what the plaintiff hears" (*Janson* transcript, March 1, 2011, 52).

Second, immediately following this first question and answer, Lobarinas was asked "to what degree of certainty" he could say that "this sound file, the one that [he] provided for each ear and the combination, [was] the match that [Janson] consistently matched to." His response: "95%, which would be at the .05 level, which is the standard for scientific findings" (*Janson* transcript, March 1, 2011, 13). This is a curious response, because Lobarinas didn't answer the question he was asked. The question asked about the correspondence between the *sound file* and the *test results*. But his answer, "95%, . . . the standard for scientific findings," referred to the statistical significance of his *test results* as a measure of *what the plaintiff was hearing*.[43] What Lobarinas's response actually meant was that there was less than a 5% chance that the volume and frequency of the tone he had matched to Janson's tinnitus (e.g., 80 dB HL at 6–8 kHz in the right ear) through the series of forced-choice alternatives had been arrived at just by chance, as opposed to indicating the sound that Janson was actually hearing inside his head. The reference to "the standard for scientific findings" is to the statistical convention for determining when the likelihood of a false positive error is acceptably low. When it is low enough, scientists are generally entitled to say: "There's really something there (and my measurements capture it accurately)." But neither the judge nor the opposing attorney noticed that Lobarinas had reinterpreted the question he was asked and, in doing so, had leveraged a legitimate claim about the statistical significance of the *test data* into one about the correspondence of the *exhibit* to what the testing had sought to measure: Janson's subjective experience. The slippage is comparable to what we saw in the first example, except here it is Lobarinas's answer, rather than the question, that closes the gap between the clinical basis for the simulation and Janson's subjective experience of his tinnitus.

Third, testifying later before the jury, Lobarinas explained: "Actually one of the challenges that we had generating this file is that at those high frequencies it's very hard to get to the levels that Mr. Janson hears. So even at maximum volume you're still going to be just a hair short of where he actually perceives his tinnitus. The pitch is very, very close. It's—it's a perfect match" (*Janson* transcript, March 1, 2011, 71).

Here the audiologist explicitly addressed the relationship between the sound file jurors were about to hear and what the plaintiff "actually perceive[d]." And after a bit of hedging, he committed to saying that the pitch (of the sound that jurors would hear) was a "perfect match" to what Janson heard. Now, as we have already seen, "match" has a routine, literal use in audiometry: the correspondence between the test subject's indications of the sounds he perceives and the readouts on the audiometer. But by speaking repeatedly of a "match" (and, a fortiori, a "perfect" match), Lobarinas may also have evoked for the judge and the jurors a more familiar kind of match—the one often produced by forensic DNA identification tests. The conversion of subjective tinnitus into sound files could thus borrow credibility from what is generally regarded today as the gold standard of forensic proof. In DNA "fingerprinting," a suspect's physical traces are processed by computer in a lab, yielding precise numbers popularly believed to establish an *identity* between the forensic evidence presented in court and the fact of the matter in reality.[44] Similarly, "perfect match" may have suggested that the evidentiary simulation was identical to Janson's subjective reality, even though, as already observed, the most that could legitimately be claimed for the sound files is that they matched the external sounds that Janson had indicated, during audiometric testing, were closest to the sounds he heard in his head.

The *fourth* example of courtroom discourse evokes another technology of objective, machine-generated matching to address the causal gap between the plaintiff's subjective experience and the exhibit's tangible re-creation of it. During the evidentiary hearing, the trial judge and both lawyers repeatedly referred to the sound files as a "recording" of Janson's tinnitus (e.g., *Janson* transcript, March 1, 2011, 23, 28, 30, 31, 52). It's a verbal slip, but a telling one. People are accustomed to accepting recordings—photographic, videographic, and so on—as veridical read-offs from reality. Apparently the judge and the lawyers couldn't help but treat the sound files in the same way, both reflecting and reinforcing their common sense understanding that the simulation simply reproduced the reality inside Janson's head, just as ordinary recording devices, people tend to believe, reproduce the external reality most everyone can hear and see. This usage suggests that Janson's subjective experience was capable of becoming *for them* as reliable a fact as anything else that can be "recorded."

To his credit, Dr. Lobarinas did not call the simulation a "recording." He explicitly corrected the opposing attorney's use of the term: "It's not a recording. A recording requires that you take from another source. Here we're synthesizing a sound" (*Janson* transcript, March 1, 2011, 24). This little vocabulary lesson, however, does not seem to have sunk in, because the judge and both lawyers continued thereafter to use the word "recording" repeatedly. The jurors did not hear the word used. But they heard other words that just as effectively framed the sound files as offering direct access to Janson's subjective experience.

This takes us to the *fifth* and final example. When attorney Ponvert introduced the exhibit through Dr. Lobarinas's testimony, he asked his expert: "And this exhibit has been set so that if the [i]Pod is played at maximum volume with this file with these headphones that will demonstrate *the volume at which Mr. Janson hears the tinnitus in his head*?" Moments later, as jurors were about to don the headphones to hear the exhibit, Ponvert asked Lobarinas: "But am I right, Doctor, that the way *to most accurately hear what Dennis Janson hears* is you should have the headphones on your ears?" (*Janson* transcript, March 1, 2011, 70–71, 72, emphasis added). The plaintiff's lawyer, with the expert's assent, thus primed the jurors to interpret their upcoming experience as "hear[ing] what Dennis Janson hears." If these words were taken at face value—and why wouldn't jurors do so?—the entire *chain of transformations* (Latour 1999) by which Janson's subjective experience had been translated into a tangible exhibit, from the administration of the audiometric tests to the recording of the results, to the creation of the sound files, to their playback in court—would have disappeared. The words encouraged jurors to believe that hearing the sound files offered them direct access to the plaintiff's inner experience.

Furthermore, the sound files were not simply displayed for jurors, as the photo simulations in *Devadas* were. They were *performed*, orchestrated by attorney Ponvert and expert witness Lobarinas. As he brought the iPod and headphones to the jury, Ponvert, in addition to the remarks just quoted, cued jurors to expect a sound that would be painfully loud: "And what I would suggest, Your Honor, is that—and I'll just demonstrate this. When you put these on, just bring them to your head sort of slowly and then put them down if you're comfortable doing it. If you don't want to put them all the way on, you don't have to put them all the way on." But then, in response to Ponvert's question, Lobarinas confirmed that "the iPod at full volume with the headphones on your ears would be the closest" to what Dennis Janson himself heard (*Janson* transcript, March 1, 2011, 72). The jurors themselves then actively participated in the performance, taking turns putting on the headphones and listening to the sound files. At least two of them listened again in the jury room, during deliberations.

This is significant precisely because it underscored the *experiential* quality of what jurors learned about Janson's tinnitus. To return to a question fundamental to our entire inquiry: what sort of knowledge is knowing what it's like for another person to have the sensory experiences she or he does? We can get at this by asking an ostensibly simpler question: what sort of knowledge is involved in sensing what one has not previously experienced *oneself*? As we saw in chapter 2, philosopher Frank Jackson (1986) posed the case of Mary, who is confined to a black-and-white room and, through black-and-white books and television programs, learns everything there is to know about the physical nature of the world. If Mary is let out of the room or given a color television, will she learn anything new? Yes: she will now know *what it's like* for her to see whatever colors she sees. This knowledge could not be conveyed by the propositional lessons Mary read or heard; she just had to experience it for herself. Moreover, having had the experience, Mary can now *remember* what seeing those colors is like, *imagine* the experience, and *recognize* it if it should occur again (Lewis 1997). Thus, experience provides a distinct type of knowledge, one that is not reducible to description.

And if experiencing a color or a sound, say, is an essential component of knowing what it's like to see that color or hear that sound, then experience is also a necessary (although not sufficient) condition for knowing what it's like for *someone else* to have the sensations that person has. The goal of evidentiary re-creations like the sound files in *Janson* is to produce in the audience an experience as much as possible like the litigant's own sensations. And it follows from this that if we seek to know what the litigant's experience is really like, an experience-producing exhibit would seem to be not merely helpful but necessary, because without the right sort of experience, jurors simply can't know what it's like. We are justified, then, in treating the jurors' experience of the simulation as an essential step in the production of legal knowledge of the litigant's subjectivity.[45]

I would like to conclude by suggesting that the experience of putting on the headphones and listening to the sound files gave jurors a more profound sense of knowing what Dennis Janson's auditory sensations were like because it made his subjectivity *present* for them. From a philosophical perspective there is something especially apt in thinking about demonstrative evidence of phenomenal experience as a *making-present* of the subjectivity of the person having that experience. According to cognitive neuroscientist, psychologist, and philosopher Antti Revonsuo (2006), consciousness itself *is* presence; specifically, "to be conscious . . . is to have patterns of phenomenal experience *present*" (126), here and now.[46] This conscious experience is fundamentally nonpropositional and subjective. What it's like to hear what Dennis Janson hears, as already suggested, would be to have the same auditory sensations that he does, here and now. Dr. Lobarinas and Janson himself could *talk about* those sensations on the witness stand, but only the demonstrative exhibit could recreate what purported to be very much like, if not identical to, the experience itself. By doing so, the simulation made Janson's subjective phenomenal consciousness present for others.

I mean this in a different sense from the one in which any visual or audio recording is often said to make present for the viewer or listener what is not there because what is represented occurred in the past or is occurring elsewhere (e.g., Barthes 1981; Belting 2011; Noë 2012).[47] Consider instead an analogy to the function of sacred images in pre-Renaissance Europe. These were understood not so much to represent as to *re-present* an unseen, higher order of reality (Belting 1994; cf. Latour 1988, 1998). The artists' goal was not primarily to offer accurate information about the appearances of biblical persons and events, but rather to *instantiate the presence* of what was to be venerated—the Crucifixion, say—"right here, as if for the first time," allowing the devout to experience the event anew, for themselves (Latour 1988, 23). Importantly, the experience that holy images enabled believers to have was felt to be *unmediated* (Belting 1994), which was possible because it was believed that the images had something of the divine *in them* (Freedberg 1989).[48]

Art historian Hans Belting's (2011) discussion of an even earlier period in the history of images, the origins of image-making in figures of the dead in the Neolithic period, offers especially provocative parallels. First, in those cultures, the image of the recently deceased gave tangible form to what was otherwise forever inaccessible, the person as a body infused with life. By making the image, the survivors replaced the absence of the deceased with the presence of his effigy. Second, by being embodied in a new image, the deceased could rejoin the social realm from which death had removed him.[49] Third, masks made from or based on the deceased person's actual skull would be worn by dancers in communal rituals, "animating the mask [and] thus bringing the dead back to life" (Belting 2011, 93).

Analogously, the sound files in *Janson* made the plaintiff's subjective consciousness *present*, for at least a few moments, in the jurors' own minds. True, that consciousness was not absent in the way a once-living person is after his or her death, nor even in the way events depicted in photos or videos or on television are absent. The plaintiffs in our cases are in the courtroom, and their conscious experience is ongoing. But like the absent referent of other representations, what the simulation depicts is *inaccessible* (in a stronger or weaker sense, depending on one's position regarding the philosophical debates surveyed in chapter 2). By reinstating what would otherwise be always beyond reach, the plaintiff's phenomenal experience, the sound files catered to the same sort of desire that motivated those who made the first effigies of the dead: to make present *again*, as a tangible body, the now forever inaccessible living person. The simulation also had the capacity to overcome the *distance* between Dennis Janson's conscious experience and the experience of the world that the rest of us, lacking his tinnitus, presumably share. It thus allowed jurors an opportunity to acknowledge his suffering as they might not otherwise have done and, by recognizing his sensory experience as a fact on which compensation could be based, to reintegrate him (insofar as the law can) into the community from which his impairments had alienated him.

These same points could be asserted with regard to the other simulations of plaintiffs' perceptual experiences we've examined in earlier chapters. But the sound files in *Janson*, more than those other simulations, made the plaintiff's conscious experience present in the jurors' minds. Consider that, unlike the video simulation in *Smith* or the photo simulations in *Devadas*, which featured explicit comparisons of the plaintiff's perceptual experience with norms of good perception, the sound files in *Janson* consisted *only* of the sounds of tinnitus as the plaintiff supposedly heard them. No third-person point of view was made salient as a context for the re-creation of the first-person experience; nothing in the exhibit gave the jurors any sense of a perceptual world outside the plaintiff's own auditory consciousness. When the jurors donned the headphones, the rest of the audible world disappeared; their awareness was now fully occupied with the sound they heard. That sound, moreover, was not at a remove from them, as pictures on a screen would be, but rather *inside their heads*.[50] And it might well have seemed to them that the sound now inside *their* heads was *the same sound* that was inside Janson's. If "hearing is a way of touching at a distance" (Schafer 1977, 11) and touch is the most personal and intimate of the senses, we can understand how jurors hearing the sound files, which had been presented to them as accurate reconstructions of the plaintiff's tinnitus, might have believed they were not just witnesses to but *in touch with* his conscious experience.

When listening to the sound files, then, the jurors did not merely learn about Janson's subjective experience. They *reenacted* it themselves. By taking hold of the headphones, bringing them to their ears, and listening, the jurors participated bodily in the reconstruction of the sound of Janson's tinnitus. Their knowledge had a performative aspect that made their acquaintance with what purported to be Janson's experience both intimate and profound.[51]

In sum, diverse aspects of the simulation and the way it was presented in court reinforced one another in helping to constitute the sound Dennis Janson heard in his head as a fact the jurors could believe. Dr. Lobarinas imbued Janson's entirely subjective experience with objectivity through professionally disciplined testing and measurement, yielding a computer-generated object, the sound files. Hearing the sound files allowed the jurors to encounter what might otherwise have seemed to be Janson's inaccessible subjectivity and place it inside themselves, where it became *their own* qualia, providing them with what their common sense told them is the surest sort of knowledge. At the same time, the exhibit's tangibility took what was only in the plaintiff's head and put it out into the world as a public object, giving it an independent, enduring existence. And when the jurors listened to the exhibit, its truthfulness was augmented by a kind of social proof: "We all heard the same thing." Thus, the simulation tightly connected subjective to objective knowledge, eyewitness to expert testimony, and mental experience to tangible representation, strengthening the jurors' confidence that by hearing it they could really know what it was like to hear what Dennis Janson heard.

SIX

Ex Machina

The third type of simulation of subjective perception is the *machine readout*. The plaintiff in *Schiffer v. Speaker*, like Johnson Devadas in chapter 4, complained of visual impairments following LASIK surgery. But the exhibit offered to show what his impaired vision was like differed from both the artist's sketch in *Devadas* and the psychophysical simulations studied in chapter 5. The clinical measurements of Mark Schiffer's refractive error caused by the progressive aberration of his cornea, as well as the resulting *image simulation*, were produced entirely by an automated device. This process completely bypassed introspection of his visual experience—which, we recall, was the entire basis for authenticating the artist's sketch simulation as accurate and (albeit in a different form), is an inherent part of psychophysical testing as well. To the extent that our knowledge of what it's like for another person to have the sensations she or he does is more reliable the more objective the methods by which those sensations are measured and then converted into a simulation, the evidentiary exhibit in *Schiffer* promised to provide the most trustworthy knowledge of other minds we can have.

The chapter begins with a brief overview of keratometry, the clinical science of corneal measurement. I summarize the epistemological strengths and limitations of simulations of visual perception based on fully automated *wavefront* measurements of the eye's optics. I describe the *Schiffer* case, the image simulation of the plaintiff's impaired vision, and its admission at trial. I then explore the visual rhetorics of this image simulation, arguing that it was in some respects a more authoritative re-creation of the litigant's subjective experience than were the exhibits discussed earlier, but that in other respects it may have been less persuasive. The chapter concludes with some general reflections on how far the trial process can illuminate or obscure the epistemological status of all kinds of simulations.

How well we see depends on, among other things, how well the eye focuses incoming light. Measuring the curvature and thickness of the cornea is a matter of great importance to optometrists, ophthalmologists, and others who seek to gauge patients' vision and improve it through corrective lenses or surgery, because "the interface of air with the tear layer of the human cornea accounts for approximately two-thirds of the eye's refractive power" (Swartz, Mattioli, et al. 2006, 3). Even extremely small aberrations in the cornea can affect refractive power and hence the quality of vision (Smith 1977).

Most attempts to measure corneal curvature before the twentieth century, whether relying on the physician's unaided vision or on any of a succession of devices (starting with the keratoscope, invented in 1847, and the ophthalmometer, invented in 1851), were based on the same basic technique: observing the reflections of a candle or other illuminated object on the anterior surface of the patient's cornea and then calculating aberrations in the cornea's curvature from distortions in the reflected image (e.g., Gutmark and Guyton 2010; Levene 1965). Once those aberrations were measured, their functional effects on the cornea's refractive power could be computed using standard formulas (Gutmark and Guyton 2010; Swartz, Mattioli, et al. 2006).

In the last third of the twentieth century, computerization made possible the modern era of *corneal topography*. A variety of digital technologies allow both surfaces of the cornea (posterior as well as anterior) and the cornea's thickness to be measured directly and with ever greater precision. Vast increases in computing power then allow those data, along with the crucial functional data specifying the patient's corresponding patterns of refractive error, to be displayed in clear graphics. Thus, a typical computerized topographical display includes a map of the local curvature of the cornea; one or two elevation maps, depicting the height at each point on the corneal surface relative to the surface of a sphere with that cornea's diameter; and a *pachymetry* map of corneal thickness (the distance between the anterior and posterior surfaces) (e.g., Cohen et al. 2006). This information facilitates accurate diagnoses of visual impairments, especially those caused by complex corneal aberrations, and improves ophthalmic surgeons' ability to prepare for corrective surgery. Many kinds of corneal topography devices are in use today, of which the Orbscan system is probably the most widely known (Cohen et al. 2006; Swartz, Liu, et al. 2006).

As topographic systems have become the standard for measuring corneal shape and thickness, so *wavefront technology* has become the standard for measuring the eye's corresponding optics (Tamayo and Serrano 2006).[1] Any light source emits waves of light that can be imagined as a plane, with each ray traveling perpendicular to the direction of the wavefront. If the surfaces of the media through which the light passes are not perfectly smooth or the indices of refraction of those media are not constant, the rays and hence the shape of the wavefront will change; the wavefront will deviate from the ideal and the light will not converge to a point or diverge as though it is coming from a point. This is referred to as an *aberrated* wavefront (Roorda 2004). To measure the precise shape and extent of the aberrations in the light reaching the eye, wavefront devices focus beams of light onto the retina and capture spots of reflected light on sensors, making it possible to determine the displacement of each of the reflected spots from its unaberrated position (Howland 2004). Then a set of mathematical functions known as the Zernike polynomials is fitted to the wavefront data.[2]

The measurement of the wavefront of light striking the retina, and hence the extent to which that wavefront is aberrant, primarily owing to deformations of the cornea, is the first of three steps in the creation of wavefront *image simulations*. To simplify greatly, the second step is the computation from the wavefront data of the point spread function (PSF), a measure of the distortion of a single point of light as it makes its way to the retina. The PSF can be represented as the image the eye forms of that point of light: a more or less perfect disk (the larger the patient's pupil, the smaller the disk),[3] or one that is blurred, bent, or otherwise distorted in accordance with the divergence of the wavefront from its optimal shape. In the third step, the wavefront machine applies the PSF to every point of light making up the entire image of any object—conventionally, the "E" on the standard Snellen eye chart is used, but any image whatsoever will do[4]—through a process known as *convolution*. The result is a simulation of the retinal image of that object for a person with those particular wavefront aberrations (see Howland 2004; Mattioli and Tripoli 2006).

Eliminating the patient's self-report from the construction of the image simulation, not to mention automating the measurement process, does not ensure a perfect re-creation of the patient's subjective visual experience. Wavefront analysis is a highly complex intervention in the reality of the eye's optics. Even without the contribution of the patient's conscious responses to test prompts, variability and uncertainty arising from many sources may affect the visible features of the simulation, and hence our knowledge of the patient's visual perceptions. For instance, wavefront measurements involve *sampling* the wavefront of light entering the eye at different points, so "if the wavefront varies wildly between grid points, then misinformation about the shape of the wavefront is obtained" (Schwiegerling 2004, 85). Wavefront measurements may vary depending on which type of device is used, since each employs a different way of capturing and measuring the light as it enters or exits the eye (Durrie and Stahl 2004). Measurements may also vary depending on whether the clinician or technician performing the test uses the device properly. Finally, the patient himself introduces the largest sources of variability, albeit considerably less than when measurements depend on the patient's conscious responses to test prompts. On the whole, though, wavefront technology, being exceptionally sensitive and fully automated, based in fundamental optical physics, improved over decades, and employing algorithms validated in many other scientific and practical applications, is capable of providing extremely accurate and precise data about the eye's optics.

The wavefront image simulation, moreover, unlike the psychophysical and artist's sketch simulations, arguably stands in something like an indexical relationship to those underlying data. Needless to say, the relationship is here far removed from that of the prototypical footprint in the sand to the animal that left it, and even from that of the analog photograph to what it depicts. The wavefront machine doesn't "take a picture" of a person's impaired visual experience in the way that a camera can be used to take a picture of the external world. The image simulation is computed from the point spread function, which is itself computed from the aberrated wavefront, which is itself computed from the physical data collected by the wavefront sensor. But if we are willing to treat a standard digital photo as an indexical sign of what it depicts, and thus as independent evidence that what it depicts was in front of the lens when the picture was taken (see discussion in chapter 4), it doesn't seem to be too much of a stretch to regard the wavefront image simulation as indexical too.

We seem, then, to have good reason to believe that the wavefront image simulation can yield a very good approximation of a person's subjective visual experience. One vision scientist writes: "The retinal point spread function . . . contains all the information needed to construct what the patient sees" (Karpecki 2006, 203). To be more exact, wavefront technology can claim to provide the information needed to reconstruct the person's *retinal image* (Applegate, Hilmantel, and Thibos 2004), since it does not incorporate any data from the visual pathway leading from the optic nerve into the brain. This is worth emphasizing: wavefront image reconstruction, although superior to psychophysical performance tests as a measure of the optical quality of the retinal image,[5] still takes us only as far as the retina. "Final visual perception is influenced by many factors and compensation mechanisms and therefore the images constructed from wavefront data may not represent the patient's actual perception" (Kohnen et al. 2005, 310).

Yet if we assume that for persons without neural pathologies, the retinal image corresponds to the subjectively perceived image, the wavefront image simulation offers an objective representation of something arguably very close to first-person visual experience. Ophthalmological research scientists Renzo Mattioli and Nancy Tripoli report that a PSF image obtained through corneal wavefront analysis corresponded closely to the patient's own drawing of how a small spot of light in dark conditions appeared to him. "This example shows that the [corneal wavefront] simulations, which directly derive from the corneal PSF, can be especially realistic" (Mattioli and Tripoli 2006, 240)—that is to say, faithful to subjective perceptual experience.[6]

Schiffer v. Speaker was, like *Devadas*, a LASIK malpractice case.[7] Mark Schiffer was an investment banker. On September 29, 2000, Schiffer, then age thirty-two, visited the Manhattan office of Drs. Farkas, Kassalow, Resnick & Associates, an optometric care provider. After a consultation and follow-up tests, one of the practice's optometrists, Dr. Regina Zyszkowski, determined that Schiffer was suffering a retinal irregularity that could be corrected by LASIK surgery. She issued a referral to TLC Laser Eye Center's Manhattan office. TLC Laser Eye Center operates LASIK surgery centers across the country and was at the time the nation's largest provider of LASIK surgery. Schiffer was examined by the office's medical director, Dr. Mark Speaker, a well-known LASIK surgeon. After further tests, Schiffer agreed to undergo LASIK surgery on both of his eyes. On October 6, 2001, Speaker performed the surgery (*Schiffer v. Speaker* 2005).

The following spring, Schiffer began to experience blurred and distorted vision. Additional testing revealed that he was suffering from ectasia, a thinning of the cornea. Schiffer was later diagnosed as having keratoconus, one of the higher-order aberrations (HOAs) of the cornea and a progressively degenerating condition. Eventually Schiffer's deteriorating vision forced him to leave his highly paid Wall Street career and take a less lucrative financial job with his father's company on Long Island (Lin 2005).

In 2003 Schiffer, represented by Todd Krouner, the same lawyer who later represented Johnson Devadas, sued Dr. Speaker and TLC. Schiffer argued that the defendants, because of their high volume of patients, had failed to diagnose Schiffer's preexisting keratoconus, which would have contraindicated LASIK surgery. The case went to trial on July 12, 2005. After a two-week trial, on July 27, 2005, the jury found Dr. Speaker liable and awarded Schiffer $7.25 million in damages, the largest verdict ever for LASIK malpractice, including $2.75 million for pain and suffering (Lin 2005).[8]

During the direct examination of one of the plaintiff's expert witnesses, ophthalmologist Dr. Selig Percy Amoils, attorney Krouner offered a wavefront study done by another ophthalmologist, a Dr. Braunstein, who had treated Schiffer some years after his LASIK surgery. That study included an image simulation of how an "E" on a standard eye chart looked to the plaintiff, using his left eye, at that time, given the further degeneration of his cornea (*Schiffer*, trial transcript, July 14, 2005, 277). Judge Alice Schlesinger, overruling defense counsel's objection but reserving other arguments for later, allowed the wavefront study to be marked for identification and shown.

The wavefront study was produced using iTrace technology, a product of Tracey Technologies (see Wakil, Padrick, and Molebny 2006). The exhibit included various measurements of Schiffer's cornea and its refractive power, and hence the extent of his physical and functional deficits. In the upper center of the exhibit, labeled "Snellen Letter HOA 20/40," was the image simulation of a blurred and smudged "E." In the lower center, labeled "Point Spread Function HOA," appeared a rather faint, sparse, seemingly abstract design of the pattern of light to which the image simulation corresponded.

Dr. Amoils, the plaintiff's expert, sought to explain to the judge and the jurors the scientific basis for the wavefront study and the image simulation in particular. He testified that wavefront analysis yields "a computer-generated simulation of what the patient will see" (*Schiffer* transcript, July 14, 2005, 278). Directing his (and the court's) attention to the upper central portion of the exhibit, Dr. Amoils said: "What is being depicted is how, by means of ray tracing, the patient would see an E . . . at a 20/40 level" (280–81). He then testified that to "a reasonable degree of medical probability . . . this is how Mark Schiffer visualized an E on the Snellen chart at 20/40," and he characterized the "E" in "clinical terms" as "distorted, smudged, or blurred, certainly not clear" (281).

Then Judge Schlesinger spoke: "How is that done? I mean in other words, I'm curious, it almost seems as if this machine is getting inside

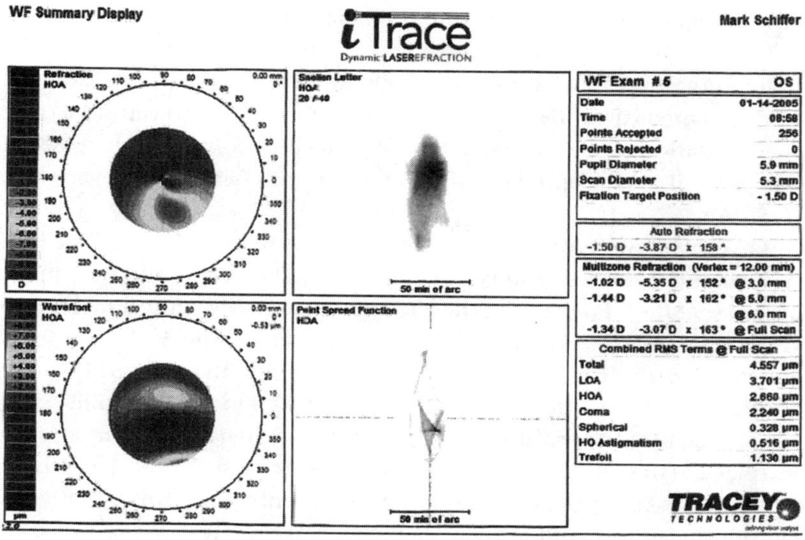

Figure 6.1. *Schiffer*: wavefront display (image simulation at top center). Courtesy of Todd Krouner.

the patient's head. Of course, it isn't. So how is this done?" Dr. Amoils responded: "They shine 29 separate bundles of light into the eye and then it comes out again and the computer simulates the optics of the eye. It's very complicated, your Honor. It is even difficult to explain to ophthalmologists. It's based on astronomic polynomials. But the fact is it does work, your Honor" (*Schiffer* transcript, July 14, 2005, 281–82).

The following day, the trial judge convened an evidentiary hearing on the admissibility of the image simulation. In New York state courts, a preliminary hearing on the admissibility of scientific or other expert evidence is known as a *Frye* hearing. Under *Frye v. United States* (1923), the proponent of the evidence need only show that the principles and methods on which it is based are "generally accepted" in the relevant scientific community. At the hearing, Judge Schlesinger took up a specific objection that defense counsel had raised earlier: even if wavefront analysis as a whole is generally accepted in the relevant scientific community, the "reproduction or simulation of the plaintiff's vision that is shown [in the exhibit] is not generally accepted within the medical or scientific community for an objective interpretation of the patient's actual vision" (*Schiffer* transcript, July 15, 2005, 497). On direct examination by attorney Krouner, Dr. Amoils testified that "wavefront studies [were] generally accepted as reliable in the scientific community" (501); that wavefront technology was in "broad use throughout the world" (511); and that it had been shown to be reliable in two peer-reviewed articles and a professional presentation (511–15). Finally, and most to the point, Dr. Amoils affirmed that "with a reasonable degree of medical probability, . . . the utilization of this wavefront to give the simulation of the Snellen letter was generally accepted in the medical and particularly the ophthalmological community" as of the relevant date (515–16).

On cross-examination by defense counsel Ralph Catalano, of the firm of Catalano, Gallardo, and Petropoulos in Jericho, New York, Dr. Amoils agreed that he "underst[oo]d the Snellen letter 'E' to be an accurate objective reproduction of . . . how the patient [per]ceives the 20/40 line 'E' at the time" (516). Catalano then walked Dr. Amoils and the court through the basics of ray tracing, in order to draw out two potential reliability concerns: first, that the wavefront measurement would be affected by any abnormalities in structures of the eye *other* than the cornea through which the light rays being measured pass, or by tears or other fluid in the patient's eye during the test; and second, that there was no standard procedure or method for preparing the patient before the test is begun. Neither of these concerns, however, kept the judge, applying the relatively permissive *Frye* standard, from admitting the wavefront study and the image simulation as a trial exhibit. Later on the same day of trial, the plaintiff, Mark Schiffer, was asked on direct examination whether the image simulation was "a fair and accurate representation of how [he] visualized an E on a Snellen letter chart at line 20/40." He answered that it was (*Schiffer* transcript, July 15, 2005, 706).

Since the wavefront image simulation is, at least in principle, the most objective and thoroughly scientific of re-creations of subjective perception, an evidentiary hearing offers an opportunity for the legal system not just to exclude an exhibit properly found to be deficient, but also to explain to trial participants and interested observers why a well-made image simulation can offer highly trustworthy knowledge about the litigant's inner experience. *Schiffer* shows that when the defense counsel and the trial judge are sufficiently alert, at least some grounds for gauging the reliability of this type of simulation can be brought to light.

But only some. New York's use of *Frye* rather than *Daubert* tended to stunt the inquiry into the scientific basis for the image simulation, focusing as it did on the general acceptance (according to the expert witness) of the simulation rather than requiring a more thoroughgoing examination. The plaintiff's counsel did direct the trial judge's attention to the existence of two peer-reviewed articles on the reliability of wavefront technology in general. And defense counsel brought out, in a general fashion, some of the factors that might affect the wavefront measurement, although only one (the presence or absence of fluid in the patient's eye) went to the accuracy of the resulting simulation.[9] Yet on the whole the trial judge learned less than she might have about how wavefront technology is used to generate image simulations.

Almost none of the information she learned, moreover, was made available to the jurors, who would ultimately have to decide how bad it was for Schiffer to go through life with his LASIK-induced visual impairments. In the presence of the jury, the trial judge, not the attorneys, was the one who asked about the wavefront process, and the judge and the jurors were left with Dr. Amoils's ipse dixit rather than any specific substantive reasons for believing that the wavefront analysis could in fact yield a highly reliable re-creation of the plaintiff's retinal image.

Significantly, the judge remarked that "of course" the wavefront device can't "get inside the patient's head," signaling to the jurors who were listening that the image simulation was not a *recording* of the plaintiff's subjective experience. But we can only wonder whether Dr. Amoils's brief response, in place of an actual substantive explanation—"It's very complicated, your Honor. It is even difficult to explain to ophthalmologists. It's based on astronomic polynomials. But the fact is it does work, your Honor"—may have left the jurors rather mystified. In short, the proceedings did not enlighten the judge or the jurors as much as they might have about the epistemological value of the wavefront image simulation as evidence of Mark Schiffer's visual experience.

The wavefront display in *Schiffer*, unlike the other re-creations of subjective perception we've encountered in this book, was made in the course of routine clinical scientific practice. It was not created at a lawyer's behest for purposes of litigation. Not coincidentally, unlike the other simulations, it bore on its face indicia of its scientific provenance. This manner of representing the plaintiff's visual impairment had obvious persuasive benefits. The exhibit was likely to appear "more scientific," and therefore more objective and less partisan, than the displays crafted by visual consultants, even those made with the collaboration and support of clinical experts. Yet the wavefront display also lacked some of the immediacy, most of the vividness, and all of the narrativity of the exhibits discussed earlier. For these reasons, even as it may have allayed many of the doubts raised by, say, the artist's sketch demonstratives examined in chapter 4, the wavefront image simulation may have been somewhat less effective in convincing jurors that they could vicariously participate in the plaintiff's sensory experience.

Let's look more closely at the wavefront summary display. The wavefront operator can choose to display "any possible data" the test generates (Molebny et al. 2004, 147); the data display in the *Schiffer* exhibit appears to have been one of many standard variations. On the left are two diagrams, data maps of, respectively, irregularities in the refractive power of the plaintiff's eye and the corresponding wavefront errors at each location on the cornea (in this case, his left eye). The colors—blue, green, yellow-green, yellow, orange—are keyed to scales that run vertically to the left of each map. The colored patterns allow ophthalmologists to see at a glance the gist of the patient's condition—the form and severity of the deviations of his eye's refractive power from the ideal. In the center of the display are the point spread function (bottom) and the image simulation of the distorted "E" (top), both in shades of black, bluish-gray, and light blue on a blank white background. On the right are summary data identifying the test, test conditions, and basic measurements, including the size (in microns) of the different types of aberration. Each component of the summary display is set off in its own box. At the top center is "iTrace Dynamic Laserefraction," the equipment name and logo; at the bottom right, the manufacturer's name and logo, "Tracey Technologies."

To appreciate the visual rhetorics of this display, consider first the PSF and the image simulation, and then the display as a whole. What do the wispy PSF and smudged "E" evoke in us? It's often been remarked that practices in new visual media are initially guided by, and thus representations in those media are interpreted in terms of, the conventions of older media (e.g., Bolter and Grusin 1999). So, for instance, the traditions of painting governed the composition of many early photographs. Consequently, viewers are inclined to interpret new sorts of pictures in terms of older viewing habits—as we saw in *Devadas*, in which the Photoshopped simulations were presented so as to invite jurors to assimilate them to ordinary photography.

It's less clear what habits might have governed jurors' viewing of the wavefront PSF and image simulation. Neither bears an obvious relationship to culturally familiar pictures. Some viewers might, perhaps, see a resemblance to spectral images of distant astronomical objects (e.g., Elkins 2008).[10]

I would like to suggest two impressions likely to come to mind: the *trace* and the *shadow*. Both are importantly evocative in this context. The trace, needless to say, is verbally primed by the name of the machine at the top of the display and the manufacturer's logo in the lower right, if not also by the expert witness's mention of *ray tracing*, the source of those eponymous commercial names. But the picture of the PSF itself could appear as if it were a trace left by something. We understand that both shadows and traces are produced by actual physical things, and this knowledge restores to the wavefront images the prototypical sense of indexicality which, as discussed earlier, is otherwise quite attenuated. More than that: classical Roman writers posited that the first drawing of a human being was created by tracing the outline of a person's shadow (Belting 2011). And in the late eighteenth and early nineteenth centuries, the *physionotrace* enabled silhouettes or profiles of sitters to be produced by mechanically tracing the outlines of their heads (Tagg 1988). Viewers who perceived the PSF and hence the "E" as traces, closely connected to Mark Schiffer's *person*, would have been all the more inclined to believe that the "E" presented the *true image* of his conscious experience.[11]

The living, biological source of what the PSF and the "E" represented was further emphasized by the contrast between these images and the diagrammatic maps to the left of the display. The boldly colored, wavily shaped areas in the center of each map, depicting patterns of refractive aberration, are triply constrained. The colors are keyed to identical color samples in the vertical scales just to the left. The central area of each map (representing the cornea) sits inside a larger circle circumscribed by the numbers 0–360 in ten-degree increments. And the central area itself, we see on closer inspection, is overlaid by concentric circles of dotted white lines and a grid of solid white lines—the *grid* being a primary signifier of mathematization and measurement (Lynch 1988; cf. Elkins 2008).

Contrast to these maps the PSF and the image simulation, which are free-floating images, unconstrained by grids or numbers (although below each there is a small scale indicating "50 min of arc"). We intuitively read the variations in the density of the images (from black to dark grey to lighter bluish-grey to a faint bluish-white) and their blurs or smears as signifying objects in motion, sketches of ephemera. Classic psychology experiments inform us that people tend to perceive moving shapes as animate (Heider and Simmel 1944). To read the PSF and the "E" this way would be to misconstrue them; they don't depict motion, or even objects in three-dimensional space, and of course, things in motion needn't be alive. Nevertheless, these cognitive viewing habits, of which the jurors themselves were probably unaware, could have bolstered their belief that in seeing the image simulation, they were looking not (only) at a computer *model* derived algorithmically from physical data, but at the sign of a living person.

At the same time, the juxtaposition of visualizations, as well as the format of the display as a whole, anchored the simulation of Mark Schiffer's subjective visual experience in the quantitative data and scientific method from which it was derived. It announced to the viewer that the simulation was grounded not in the plaintiff's say-so alone, but in thoroughly objective measurement: machine- and computer-generated, comprehensive and precise. We don't see the wavefront apparatus itself, much less observe the plaintiff being tested, but the "iTrace" logo at the top of the display and the readout of the test date, time, and other conditions in the upper right gesture at the process behind the information presented. Everything visible in the display bespeaks the reliability of automated medical measurement, routinely performed and using the most advanced technology.

More specifically, by starting with the blurred "E" and looking down to the point spread function and then to the data maps on the left, jurors could symbolically *retrace* some of the steps that connected the subjective phenomenon to their presumptively reliable knowledge of it. The image simulation was derived from the PSF beneath it, plotted onto the eye-chart "E"; the PSF, in turn, is how a point of light would have been displaced, having traveled along a wavefront through a cornea that caused the refractive errors depicted in the maps on the left. The plaintiff's subjective experience, represented in the simulation, was thus linked to its physical, biological substrate: his defective cornea. The "view from inside" was connected to the view from the outside, suggesting that after all, the first-person and third-person accounts of subjective experience can be *aligned*, brought into very close association, even if the one is not completely reducible to the other. We can imagine this as the scientific analog to the embedding of first-person within third-person points of view that we saw in *Murtha* and *Smith*, except the visual logic here is that of scientific method rather than cinema. If jurors could trust the wavefront machine outputs, they could place equal faith in the image simulation.

The rhetorical strengths of the image simulation in situ as a piece of clinical scientific discourse may, however, have weakened it as a means of offering viewers the vicarious experience of the plaintiff's own phenomenal life. The blurred "E" is quite small: the box it occupies is only about a sixth of the entire display, and the distorted "E" itself covers only about one-twelfth of that area. As a re-creation of how the plaintiff saw an "E" on a standard eye chart, the simulation alluded to clinical practice and the measurement of vision, something with which every juror could identify. But it would have required effort to imagine how the distorted vision indicated by the blurry "E" affected the plaintiff's everyday visual experience, which is more closely related to the judgment that the jurors had to make: how bad was it for the plaintiff to have to go through life with his impairment? The photo simulations in *Devadas* and the video simulation in *Smith*, by contrast, did that work for the jurors. Furthermore, the quantitative data and graphics surrounding the image simulation, while providing it with scientific bona fides, also tended to divert viewers' attention from it. So the image simulation, shown as part of the wavefront summary display, was far less vivid than the re-creations of subjectivity in *Devadas* and *Smith*; it did not offer the immediate, at least somewhat immersive experience of subjectivity that the photo and video simulations did.

As the picture of a moment in time, moreover, the wavefront image simulation, unlike the simulations in *Murtha* and *Smith* (and, to a lesser extent, *Devadas*), did not tell a story. The blurred "E," floating in its box in the summary display, did not invite the jurors to imagine themselves participating in the litigant's experience. It did not create any of the drama and emotional engagement that even simple narratives can. The wavefront display may well have strengthened the jurors' belief that their knowledge *about* the plaintiff's impairments was highly reliable. Yet they may not have come away from the image simulation feeling that they knew what it's like to have those impairments as strongly as they might have had they experienced the impairments more fully for themselves. And this would be ironic if, as I have argued, the machine readout simulation really does make the best-warranted claim to provide accurate knowledge of the litigant's sensations.[12]

We've now examined the full range of evidentiary re-creations of subjective perception, looking closely at the knowledge claims that can legitimately be made on behalf of each type of simulation as well as the claims their proponents in fact advanced. We've seen potential epistemological weaknesses go uncriticized and potential strengths left unarticulated. In every instance, we've also seen how the simulation's medium, its style, and sometimes its manner of presentation may have induced audiences to believe they were experiencing what the litigants themselves did. It's worth stepping back at this point and reflecting more generally on how well the trial courtroom can function, in legal scholar Jennifer Mnookin's (2006) felicitous phrase, as an *epistemological public space*: a venue in which the competing knowledge claims that simulations raise can be put to enlightening tests, with the potential to influence the acceptance or rejection of those claims in the culture at large.

As with respect to most other sorts of demonstrative evidence, the courtroom can provide only an imperfect forum for vetting simulations' knowledge claims. The low threshold for admissibility, especially for merely illustrative aids, means that triers of fact will be exposed to re-creations of sensory experience running the gamut from minimally to highly probative, often without much guidance as to their actual epistemological status. Even if judges at evidentiary hearings properly scrutinize these exhibits (especially scientifically based ones) before admitting them, that scrutiny won't educate jurors unless counsel or expert witnesses develop the points again at trial. Proponents will often lack strategic incentives to elaborate on the strengths of scientifically based simulations, relying instead on what they hope will be jurors' intuitive belief in the realism and accuracy of computer-generated exhibits. Opponents may be unprepared or unwilling to challenge them adequately.[13] Because jurors don't have to explain how they arrived at their judgment (indeed, absent a special verdict or jury interrogatories, they do not report even the particular facts they found), we usually can't tell whether they believed they really knew, thanks to the simulation, what the litigant's perceptual experience was like. And the absence of published opinions on the admissibility of these simulations makes it difficult to determine whether the law is actively endorsing or merely tolerating the knowledge claims that advocates make in their behalf. For these and other reasons, the legal treatment of evidentiary simulations can, it seems, only equivocally inform our understanding of the kind of knowledge of other minds these re-creations of subjective experience can offer.

Still, the law can enlighten us more than it has so far. Judges can investigate more closely the epistemological warrants for scientifically based simulations in particular. They can instruct jurors more clearly on the probative value of the different types of simulations,[14] explicitly anticipating the misconceptions to which jurors are most prone. Opposing counsel, finally, should understand more fully the clinical science invoked to support psychophysical and machine readout simulations and the psychology and rhetoric of all simulations. This will enable them to articulate challenges to admissibility that will better educate judges and will help them to cross-examine more effectively the witnesses who vouch for the simulations, thus better educating jurors as well.

SEVEN

Judging the Person

Evidentiary simulations of perceptual experience offer more than knowledge for its own sake. In personal injury cases, plaintiffs present these simulations to support their claims for what the law calls *noneconomic* damages (i.e., items other than calculable medical expenses, lost wages, and so on), including, most importantly, damages for their pain and suffering. Jurors want to know what it's like for the plaintiff to experience what she or he does because they need to determine how severely the plaintiff has been injured and then (assuming that they find the defendant liable) to decide on appropriate compensation for the plaintiff's physical, mental, and emotional distress and loss of life's enjoyments.

The primary evidence of the plaintiff's pain and suffering usually consists of the plaintiff's own words—her testimony describing her impairments and their effects on her life. The plaintiff's physician also typically testifies; so, too, may members of her family. Given this testimony, what difference can a re-creation of the plaintiff's subjective experience make? Possibly quite a lot. Anecdotal evidence in the form of the verdicts reached in *Devadas*, *Janson*, and *Schiffer* suggests that simulations can lead to very substantial damage awards: in *Schiffer*, for instance, the largest verdict ever in a LASIK malpractice case; in *Janson*, one of the largest personal injury judgments awarded in that court.

Our goal in this chapter is to understand *how* simulations of plaintiffs' sensory experience can affect jurors' evaluations of plaintiffs and their suffering. I begin with an overview of the law and psychology of noneconomic damages. I then turn to plaintiffs' testimonial accounts of their pain and suffering. Spoken language, for all its limitations, is especially well suited to translating the subjectivity of suffering into the shared normative judgments that jurors must make. Through testimony on the stand, the plaintiff constructs a character, ideally one whom jurors will be strongly motivated to help by awarding damages.[1]

What, then, can a simulation add to a credible plaintiff's testimony? Jurors' vivid experience of what purport to be the plaintiff's own sensations can anchor the rest of their knowledge of her impairments, as well as their appraisals of how bad it is for her to have to endure them. Simulation and testimony can interact in the other direction as well: the impressions that jurors gather from the plaintiff's testimony can influence how credible they find the simulation to be and what they glean from it.

Throughout the book I have noted but not emphasized another important feature of almost all simulations. "Emotion is at the heart of jurors' experience of the personal injury case," says Antonio Ponvert III,[2] Dennis Janson's attorney. Jurors' vicarious experience of the plaintiff's sensations may encourage them to sympathize with her, which would incline them to award more damages. It can be argued that this outcome is morally justified. Yet by prompting additional sympathy as well as inducing other cognitive biases, simulations can also lead jurors to overestimate the severity of the plaintiff's suffering and hence the amount of damages she deserves.

The chapter concludes by addressing a broader jurisprudential concern. By inviting jurors to identify with the plaintiff, simulations threaten to confuse jurors' judgments about how bad it is for the *plaintiff* to have to endure her impairments with how bad it would be for *them* to do so. This conflation is exactly the kind of thinking that the law's traditional ban on "Golden Rule" arguments is meant to prevent. Some may contend that jurors who personally experience the plaintiff's subjectivity cannot remain detached from the litigant in the way the law considers fundamental to good deliberative judgment. I argue, however, that the more empathic way of assessing pain and suffering damages that simulations prompt can actually enhance justice in personal injury trials.

Insofar as money can do it, the plaintiff is to receive fair, just and reasonable compensation for all injuries and losses, past and future, which are proximately caused by the defendant's [culpable conduct]. . . . In this case, plaintiff claims non-economic damages. Non-economic damages are monies awarded as compensation for non-monetary losses and injuries which the plaintiff has suffered, or is reasonably likely to suffer in the future. They are awarded for things such as physical pain and suffering, mental and emotional pain and suffering, and loss or diminution of the ability to enjoy life's pleasures. As far as money can compensate the plaintiff for such injuries and their consequences, you must award a fair, just, and reasonable sum. You simply have to use your own good judgment in awarding damages in this category. (*Janson* transcript, March 3, 2011, 19–20)

Nowhere in tort law is the impossibility of perfect justice more obvious and more widely acknowledged than in the use of money damages to compensate tort plaintiffs for their general or noneconomic losses, their pain and suffering in particular.[3] Liability determinations can be thoroughly just in the sense of completely fulfilling their normative goal: a recognition that the defendant has violated the plaintiff's legal right or entitlement. Other types of remedies can more or less completely achieve corrective justice. Specific performance can restore the status quo or fulfill the parties' agreed-upon expectations; special or economic damages can fully compensate the injured party for quantifiable past or expected future loss. But everyone knows that money damages cannot make a physically or psychologically injured person "whole" in the sense of restoring the person to the same condition he or she would have been in had the injury never occurred,[4] even if those damages may mitigate some of the suffering that the injury has caused.

Pain and suffering awards are also imperfect because they're imprecise and even, it has been argued, unprincipled. The imprecision is easy to explain: there's no approved metric in the law for measuring suffering, and even if there were—for instance, empirically validated units of "hedonic value" or the like (e.g., Bronsteen, Buccafusco, and Masur 2014; Posner and Sunstein 2010)—there's no reliable way to translate those units into dollars. As the instructions quoted above indicate, jurors are given no standard for gauging what the plaintiff's pain and suffering are worth (Chase 1995; Olender 1962; Plant 1958). Not surprisingly, jurors struggle to come up with an appropriate figure (e.g., Mott, Hans, and Simpson 2000). Telling them to reach a dollar amount that's "fair" produces considerable variability in awards (e.g., Greene 1989; Greene and Bornstein 2003), frustrating horizontal equity (Wissler, Kuehn, and Saks 2000) and creating at least the appearance of injustice in that sense.[5] Some commentators believe the process by which these awards are reached is so flawed that they have advocated capping pain and suffering damages, implementing specific guidelines for allowable awards, or doing away with these damages altogether (see, e.g., Chase 1995; Geistfeld 2006; Sunstein 2008).

And yet awarding injured tort plaintiffs *something* for their pain and suffering is surely just, even if the amounts can't be pegged to measures of actual loss as economic damages can. Noneconomic damages serve multiple purposes. They advance tort law's goal of corrective justice by putting the plaintiff closer to the position she would have been in had the defendant's culpable conduct not harmed her. In doing so, they also further a goal that the law has recognized at least since the time of the *wergild*: peaceful dispute resolution, making it likelier that the victim will accept and adjust to her new condition. The pain and suffering award also has *expressive value* (see Adler 2000). It is a public recognition that plaintiffs have been harmed, their lives diminished, over and above the costs of medical and related care and the wages they must now forgo. It acknowledges their physical and mental suffering as real and thereby expresses the community's affirmation of the value of a life free from tortious personal injury.

This last observation points to an essential feature of pain and suffering awards: they are inherently normative. Legal scholar Linda Meyer writes that "suffering in law is normative all the way down, resistant to any simplistic reductionism or unmediated 'experience' of the other" (2014, 16). This is not to say that these damages aren't about the facts of the plaintiff's experience, but that jurors perceive and evaluate those facts through intersubjective and community norms to arrive at a judgment of what the plaintiff's suffering is worth.[6]

Thus, in deciding what's "fair, just, and reasonable" compensation for the pain and suffering the defendant has culpably caused the plaintiff, jurors must "consider [both] the individual circumstances and local community norms" (Vidmar and Hans 2007, 284). Jurors indeed appear to do this. Legal scholars Valerie Hans and Valerie Reyna (2011) have proposed a model to explain how jurors translate their responses to personal injuries into damage awards (not limited to pain and suffering awards specifically). Jurors first form "gist" judgments about whether any damages at all are warranted and, if so, whether the plaintiff's specific injury is severe or not severe, and thus whether the damage award should be high or low. (If the injury can't be coded as severe or not, it is coded as medium.) Jurors then map the ordinal gist judgment onto a corresponding number. The particular plaintiff's injury is the judgment target, but social norms and community values enter into the process at every stage (see also Hans 2014).

For pain and suffering damages, jurors also consider how much the plaintiff, as a person, *deserves* to be compensated. This, too, is based on jurors' perceptions about the plaintiff himself, filtered through their sense of social norms and values. As we'll see, deservingness can reflect judgments regarding the plaintiff's responsibility, if any, for the accident or malpractice that caused his injuries (see, e.g., Wissler, Kuehn, and Saks 2000). Here I want to emphasize that deservingness also includes an evaluation of whether the plaintiff is the *sort of person* whose physical, mental, and emotional distress resulting from his impairments is to be highly valued. Although money damages cannot make an injured person "whole," they reflect jurors' evaluation of what the life of the *whole person*, free from the tortiously inflicted pain and suffering, is worth (Levine 2009, 43–46).[7]

To appreciate how evidentiary re-creations of plaintiffs' sensory experiences may affect pain and suffering awards, we'll start with the baseline: how jurors ordinarily reach those awards in the absence of simulations—largely on the basis of the plaintiff's testimony about her injuries and her suffering.

We cannot help but rely on what others say (or have said or written) for most of our knowledge of the world (Coady 1992). Jurors, similarly, must rely on testimony. Even when there is nonverbal documentation of the events in question (e.g., forensic evidence, surveillance videos, and so on), that evidence doesn't "speak for itself" (see Mnookin 2012). Testimony remains at the heart of any trial.

In personal injury trials in which the plaintiff is able to speak, the plaintiff's account is ordinarily a principal source of evidence about the events he claims caused his injuries. As evidence of pain and suffering, his testimony becomes even more important. Jurors may infer the extent of the plaintiff's physical pain from the objective evidence of his bodily injuries, the testimony of other eyewitnesses (such as nurses or other health care professionals), and expert testimony about the extent of the pain itself (Olender 1962; Plant 1958). But they certainly depend on the plaintiff's own words to learn what it is like for him to live with that pain. And regarding the plaintiff's "mental and emotional pain and suffering, and loss or diminution of [his] ability to enjoy life's pleasures," to quote again the typical jury instruction from *Janson*, the plaintiff's testimony is far and away the most critical proof.

Through his testimony, the plaintiff seeks to convince the triers of fact of two things. He must persuade them that the physical and psychological injuries he now endures are *severe*, warranting substantial compensation, and that he *deserves* that compensation. Four overlapping features of the plaintiff's testimony advance these rhetorical goals.

First, to persuade jurors that his physical, mental, and emotional distress, his loss of life's pleasures, is severe, the plaintiff has to describe his pain and suffering so as to make it intelligible to others. At the outset we face a potential difficulty. Pain, literary theorist Elaine Scarry has written, is essentially incommunicable and untranslatable. "Whatever pain achieves, it achieves in part through its unsharability, and it ensures the unsharability through its resistance to language" (1985, 4). Scarry's claim is that there is something distinctive about the experience of physical pain, as opposed to other subjective phenomenal experiences, that makes it especially resistant to being known by others.

Even if we accept that bodily pain is ultimately unsharable,[8] though, it doesn't follow that personal injury plaintiffs are thereby rendered effectively speechless. A sufferer can communicate something about her pain by grimaces, tears, and gestures. Her posture, demeanor, and behavior can convey that she is in distress, as well as some sense of how intense that distress is. All these nonlinguistic signs can communicate immediately and powerfully.[9] But the plaintiff's words vastly extend her ability to make her subjective condition known to others. Because language is necessarily public, not private, it consists of shared concepts, and it is through these common concepts that the plaintiff's pain can be better understood. For all their vagueness, words can disambiguate the messages sent by facial expression and bodily movement, giving others more precise information about what's wrong. And for plaintiffs like Dennis Janson, who are not in the sort of pain or discomfort that triggers tears, grimaces, or other observable, involuntary bodily movements, words would seem to be the *only* way to make their feelings known.

More importantly, "pain and suffering," though often said together, aren't the same thing. Trial lawyer Ted Koskoff has been credited with popularizing the distinction between physical pain, on the one hand, and the attendant fear, despair, anguish—in a word, suffering—on the other (Werth 1998). In Koskoff's view, "You just can't make someone feel another person's pain," whereas misery and suffering are things with which jurors can empathize, and from there, be moved to award significant damages (106). "Pain and suffering" as an element of damages, at least in the cases with which we're concerned, is more about the suffering than the pain. The typical jury instructions from the *Janson* case, quoted above, reflect this. Noneconomic damages encompass "physical pain and suffering, mental and emotional pain and suffering, and loss or diminution of the ability to enjoy life's pleasures"—much more than bodily sensations alone.

Language is also crucial in making plaintiffs' predicaments intelligible to others because of the temporal dimensions of consciousness. At every moment, our conscious life—sensation, perception, thought, and emotion—is the product not just of the specious present (James [1890] 1950) but also of our past, whether we remember it or not, and our anticipated future.[10] Suffering, moreover, extends over time. Simulations in time-based media—the video simulation in *Smith* or the sound files in *Janson*—provide, for a few minutes or even seconds, samples of plaintiffs' ongoing present experiences of impaired sight or hearing.[11] But only through words can plaintiffs describe their past and expected future suffering; only through words can they convey something of the mental and emotional distress caused by knowing their suffering is likely to endure indefinitely.

Second, plaintiffs' words on the stand also explain the *significance* of their injuries—how those injuries have affected and continue to affect their lives. The plaintiff's testimony necessarily relates these matters from the first-person point of view, which helps jurors understand what it's like and how bad it is *for him* to have to live with his impairments. His words must also, however, appeal to *jurors'* sense of what's important to the kind of life a person in the plaintiff's position might reasonably expect to live. The plaintiff conveys the meaning of his pain and suffering through the incidents he chooses to recount and the words he uses to explain what his life is now like.

These testimonial choices are especially critical in the cases we're studying. Because these plaintiffs' impairments are not obvious—the plaintiffs are not, for instance, multiple amputees or paraplegics—jurors cannot readily infer just from observing them (or from hearing expert testimony, for that matter) how seriously their impairments are affecting their psychological well-being.[12] The plaintiffs' testimony has to carry much more of the burden of persuasion.

The next two features of the plaintiff's testimony advance the goal of persuading jurors that the plaintiff deserves substantial compensation for her severe injuries. The *third* is that the plaintiff, on direct examination, presents a *narrative* of her predicament, or rather, interlocking narratives of how her suffering came about and how it has changed her life. As legal and literary scholars have repeatedly observed, storytelling is central to many aspects of law and legal decision making (e.g., Brooks and Gewirtz 1996; P. Meyer 2014; White 1973). One basic idea from the academic literature is that many stories, including personal injury plaintiffs' narratives, follow a fundamental plot structure: an initial "steady state" that is disrupted by some sort of "Trouble," which prompts efforts to redress or transform (which may succeed or fail), leading to a struggle in which the initial state is restored or a new, transformed steady state is created (Amsterdam and Bruner 2000). The Trouble that launches the story, as folklore scholar Vladimir Propp explained, comes in two versions: tales of *villainy* and tales of *lack* (Propp 1968; see also Amsterdam, Hertz, and Walker-Sterling 2005). In a tale of villainy, a "bad guy" is responsible for the harm that befalls the protagonist. In a tale of lack, the protagonist must confront some sort of want or absence.[13]

The personal injury plaintiff relates both kinds of stories. His account of the accident or malpractice leading to his injuries aims primarily to persuade jurors that he is *not to blame*. If he fails in this, his recovery for his losses, economic as well as noneconomic, may be reduced or even eliminated (depending on the law of the jurisdiction and how much fault jurors attribute to him). So the plaintiff, drawing on all the elements of narrative construction from character and plot down to the microlinguistic level of verb tense, sentence structure, and metaphor, will try to appeal to the cognitive habits jurors use to determine causation and responsibility, encouraging them to conclude that the defendant is blameworthy and the plaintiff is not (see, e.g., Feigenson 2000; see also Amsterdam, Hertz, and Walker-Sterling 2005).

Following and partly overlapping with his account of how the harm occurred, the plaintiff also tells another kind of story. He portrays himself as the hero in a "lack" story: someone who is struggling to overcome the adversity the defendant's negligence has caused, but who needs the jury's help to be set aright. The *character* the plaintiff presents himself as being is essential to bringing off this kind of story and gaining the audience's allegiance. Recall that whether jurors will be inclined to award the plaintiff substantial damages depends significantly on what they think of him as a person.[14] "Jurors give money not for a prize but for a purpose. . . . If the jury regards the plaintiff as the kind of person they do not want to help, they will minimize the size of the verdict even if they are fully convinced of the defendant's liability" (Ball 1997, 163). The plaintiff's narratives of how he grapples with his suffering—and there may well be several, just as well-told folktales, novels, or movies often involve several "mini-stories" that heighten the drama by depicting the protagonist's increasingly dire predicament—prove him to be the kind of person whom jurors will want to help.

Fourth, the plaintiff constructs her deserving character through *performance* as well as narrative. To some extent, every witness, through his or her testimony, provides jurors with character evidence. Evidence scholar Robert Burns (1999) argues:

> How [the witness] puts [the events he describes] tells the jury *who he is* to such an important extent that the formal evidentiary rules prohibiting "evidence of character" are almost trivial. . . . Telling the story of a past event is a moral enterprise that reveals a great deal about the storyteller. To do it perfectly, to tell a story as it happened, . . . certainly requires [the witness] to make one choice after another among the infinite possibilities for characterizing any event, choices that cannot but reveal a great deal

of who the witness is and to which our tacit abilities of assessment and recognition are highly attuned. (54, 133)

The entire trial, as Burns (1999) explains, is structured as a series of dramatic performances, in which time is condensed and the audience's attention is concentrated, heightening the perceived importance of what is being told. For the personal injury plaintiff in particular, however, testifying under oath in a highly formalized, public setting while knowing she will be subject to cross-examination serves as a kind of test or *proof* (in the original evidentiary sense; see Haack 2014) of her claims—less painful than trial by ordeal, but still a singular performance on which everything depends. As jurors listen to and observe the plaintiff on the stand, they simultaneously appraise her credibility, the severity of the harms she claims to be suffering, and her deservingness as a person. These evaluations are tightly bound up with one another, because the plaintiff is both jurors' source of information about her pain and suffering *and* the target of their judgment. The more compelling the plaintiff's testimonial performance, the more jurors will believe her account of her distress and the more seriously they will take her suffering, and hence the more they will want to do something about it.

To recap: The plaintiff's testimony is central to jurors' determination of how much his pain and suffering are worth. His words make his suffering intelligible to jurors in a way that no one else's words can. And through his narrative performance, the plaintiff offers jurors essential insight into his character, who he is as a person, and thus how deserving he is of compensation. His testimony is the *moral focus* of his claim for pain and suffering damages.

There is, in addition, a distinct moral value in having jurors decide their damage award on the basis of the plaintiff's testimony. The presentation of evidence in the form of words spoken live at trial engages the jurors as auditors, connecting them to the speaker. In particular, the speaking plaintiff is present to the jurors, "mak[ing] the trial an intersubjective experience in a way that reading written transcripts c[an]not" (Burns 1999, 135) and triggering in them a moral obligation to *listen* to his story. As jurors struggle to decide what his suffering is worth, they necessarily decide how far they are willing to trust his words—not simply how much they believe those words, but also, in the course of weighing his account of his suffering, how much they trust and value *him*.

This is ultimately a moral decision. When we build our normative worlds together, we are constantly (although not always consciously) relying on others' words, and so we are constantly deciding whose stories to believe and which ones matter enough to stake our actions on them.

And we always risk misplacing our faith. Jurors, as representatives of their community, must decide how far to include the plaintiff's words, spoken in court, in the shared construction of that part of their *nomos* that their verdict will constitute. By putting the plaintiff's testimonial performance at the center of the trial, we proclaim that compensating injured plaintiffs for their pain and suffering is not only about deterrence or corrective justice or even responding to need. It's about deciding how much a fellow member of the community is to be valued, based largely on her own terms—the words she uses to convey her experience to the rest of us.

To illustrate these general observations, let's examine the testimony of one of the plaintiffs we've encountered, Dennis Janson. Janson, we recall from chapter 5, was an audio engineer in his early sixties. On direct examination, he described his educational background, his wife and college-aged daughter, his love of his work as an audio studio designer, and then the accident that befell him and its aftermath. At this point, his lawyer, Antonio Ponvert III, asked him to describe what it was now like for him to live with his hearing loss, hyperacusis (increased sensitivity to sound), and tinnitus:

> The hearing loss is, you know, it's critical in my work. . . .
>
> All studios are quiet by nature because of what's happening in there, . . . and we deal a lot with the nature of how sound reacts and responds to the four walls and the ceiling and the floor. And while there are instruments to test things, in almost all instances with studios it also comes down to what the human ear hears in that particular space, whether it's a warm feeling or it's a bright feeling. . . . Even if you close your eyes and you were to be led into the room, you can feel the room. You can feel the fact that it's quieter, that it has less sound echoing around. There are certain rooms and certain studios where it has a sort of a warm, rich feeling, tonality, and there are certain studios that might have a more bright feeling. . . . [People] rely on [me] to make sure that these rooms perform up to their expectations; and, if they don't, that's a very bad thing.
>
> [Now] if I go into a studio, the first thing I do is I hear a tremendous noise, which is very loud, from the tinnitus. And anything above seven or 8,000 hertz I can't hear that for the most part at all. [Since the accident] I can no longer rely on the accuracy of what I'm hearing . . . and the tonality of what I hear now is completely different. What I used to think would be warm and rich and is not that anymore. I just can't trust them

anymore. It's embarrassing and it's sort of debilitating. I've done this for many, many years now and it's taken away some of my ability and enjoyment of what I do for a living, which I thoroughly do enjoy. (*Janson* transcript, March 2, 2011, 22–23, 27–29)

Janson proceeded to describe the effects of his tinnitus on his life outside of work (we have already encountered some of these words in chapter 5):

Well, from the time I wake up in the morning until the time I go to sleep at night I have an extraordinarily loud high-pitch noise in both ears. It never goes away. Sometimes it'll get slightly worse. It never gets any better than what it currently is actually. It's more recognizable in quiet environments, which is one reason why it's troublesome in my profession, and it's something that—it's debilitating. It can be—it can make you irritable. It's a—it's difficult—it's difficult to live with. . . .

Now I'm lucky if I get four hours of sleep a night, sometimes five. It's very difficult to fall asleep. Once I'm asleep, obviously, I don't pay attention to that. But if I wake up in the middle of the night—and as I mentioned before, in quiet environments it becomes more prevalent—and then you begin to dwell on it more, the fact that it's there and it's not going to go away. So it's a problem with sleep. [To fall asleep,] I turn the TV on, because that's become sort of a masking device for me. [That helps] a little bit, [but my wife is] not too happy about having a television on in the bedroom. . . . [Since the explosion, I get] just four or five [hours of sleep each night.] It's sort of a constant drain, tired, and it's difficult. . . . I've developed bad habits, like being cranky. Being cranky and being less tolerant of little things that never used to bother me before. (*Janson* transcript, March 2, 2011, 31–35)

Janson's description of his tinnitus, his explanation of its significance, and his self-presentation as a deserving person are all intertwined. (We are not considering the portion of his testimony relating to his lack of responsibility for his injuries.) We can start by asking whether this testimony makes his tinnitus intelligible to jurors. How far they credit his account of the tinnitus's impact on his work and life would depend, one might think, at least partly on what they imagine the tinnitus actually sounds like. But it's hard to derive from Janson's description a very definite idea of that sound. "An extraordinarily loud high-pitch noise in both ears" could encompass a wide variety of sounds. Each juror might understand this brief description quite differently.

And yet, for two reasons, Janson's words may still have described his auditory experience fairly effectively. First, even if each juror imagined a different sound, each one may have imagined a sound that was loud and annoying enough to cause real distress. This is especially so since the sound "never goes away." That fact may have impressed them as much as the sound's reputed loudness or pitch. Second, rather than basing their understanding of the impact of Janson's tinnitus on his life on what they imagined the tinnitus sounded like, jurors may have drawn the converse inference: if they were persuaded by his account of how pervasively the tinnitus interfered with his work, they would be more inclined to believe that the sound must really have been as loud, intrusive, and continuous as he claimed.

So let's turn to Janson's explanation of the significance of his impairments. He needed to make the jurors understand how his tinnitus undermined his ability to do his job and intruded on his daily life and, in doing so, convince them that these effects on his life mattered deeply. The effect of his tinnitus on his work is obvious enough from his account. Janson told the court that doing his job depended on "what the human ear hears" and, more than that, on his professionally experienced sensitivity to the significance of what the ear hears—how a room "feels warm" or "bright" or "rich." Since the accident, however, he said, "I can no longer rely on the accuracy of what I'm hearing . . . and the tonality of what I hear now is completely different. What I used to think would be warm and rich and is not that anymore. I just can't trust them anymore."

Through this testimony, Janson made it clear that he couldn't do his job the way, or as well as, he used to, but he also explained why his tinnitus was causing a profound blow to his personhood. Jurors learned from Janson's testimony that he *heard for a living*. His ability to make fine discriminations in sound environments had been essential to his self-identity. His choice of words—the "feel" of sound and of the room in which the sounds occur, the evocative adjectives "warm," "bright," and "rich"—*displayed* his auditory sensibility to the jurors, making his self-description as an auditory expert all the more credible. These words also drew the jurors into his phenomenal world, enabling them to understand how sensory experience can be a way of perceiving and knowing something, beyond the sensations themselves. Hearing is not just an isolated modality; as much as if not more than sight, it is a way of being in the world (e.g., Levitin 2006; Sacks 2007). When the explosion of the defendant's defective product impaired Janson's hearing, the defendant did more than force Janson to endure annoyance and pain. Through no fault of his own, Dennis Janson was now alienated from the world he had known and enjoyed. Tinnitus had damaged his sense of self.

On top of that, Janson knew he was letting down those who had trusted in him. "[People] rely on [me] to make sure that these rooms perform up to their expectations; and, if they don't, that's a very bad thing." The words explicitly refer to his clients' needs for their studios, but it's plain that

Janson wanted the jurors to understand he was concerned about clients' expectations for *him*—and, consequently, his expectations for himself. He was no longer able to do what was expected of him, no longer able to live up to his self-image. And he knew it. This sense of falling short, resulting not from lack of effort but from his uncontrollable impairment, the constant awareness of not being able to repay the trust that others placed in him, was surely a psychologically significant injury.

Janson's testimony also inclined jurors to value his suffering highly because it presented a character whom they would find deserving of their recognition, their sympathy, and their help. Although we could construe his testimony as a kind of "lack story," these excerpts are more portrait than narrative. Janson explained that he was an accomplished acoustic engineer who loved his work and who continued to work despite his tinnitus because he took pride in his job and (as he said in a portion not excerpted above) had to pay his daughter's college tuition. He was a true professional and a responsible parent. And far from giving in to his ailments, he was trying to make the best of a barely endurable situation.

Janson's description of the tinnitus's impact on him reinforced this portrait of a man stoically dealing with his impairments. He wasn't superhuman; he admitted to being "cranky" from the loss of sleep the constant tinnitus caused. But neither was he a complainer. The closest the transcript comes to indicating an emotional display is Janson's hesitation in characterizing the effect of the ever-present ringing—"It's a—it's difficult—it's difficult to live with"—as if he were reluctant to complain even this much. The snapshot of his domestic life rounded out the picture. By recounting how he needed to turn on the TV at night to mask the tinnitus so he could get to sleep, while acknowledging that his wife was "not too happy" about that, he simultaneously let the jurors know that his tinnitus intruded even into the bedroom and displayed his solicitude toward his spouse.

In sum, through his testimony, Dennis Janson revealed himself to be a decent, responsible husband and parent as well as a hardworking professional who took great pride in his abilities and who now had no break, no relief, from the psychological distress his tinnitus caused him. His words on the stand enabled the jurors to comprehend why his sensory, mental, and emotional suffering was so severe, and those words may well have motivated them to compensate him generously.

Compared to this baseline, what difference can a simulation of the plaintiff's sensory experience make? I will explain that simulations can affect jurors' impressions of the plaintiff and her suffering, and hence their judgments about how much compensation is "fair, just, and reasonable," in several, complexly related ways. First, jurors' experience of the simulation can anchor their understanding of the plaintiff's impairment and thus their assessment of its severity. Second, the simulation itself can be normatively loaded: simulations can (although not all do) invite jurors to evaluate the plaintiff as a particular sort of deserving sufferer whom they should want to help. Third, the simulation can interact with the plaintiff's testimony to shape jurors' judgment of the character the plaintiff presents on the stand: the testimony may frame jurors' experience of the simulation, and/or the simulation may lead them to reevaluate the testimony. Fourth, by giving jurors such a powerful experience of the plaintiff's own consciousness, the simulation may even shift the trial's center of gravity, partly displacing the plaintiff's testimonial performance as the moral focus of judgment.

First, an evidentiary simulation of the plaintiff's sensory experience can anchor jurors' knowledge of that experience. One person's subjective experience, if knowable to others only through his first-person report, can seem to be a pretty malleable kind of fact. In theory, litigants can fashion their words in a variety of ways to mesh with the other available evidence. One might think of Officer Murtha, who (as we recall from chapter 4) stated in his initial incident report that he fired his weapon because the suspect's car had struck him; when he later saw the dashcam video from the following cruiser, clearly showing that the car did not hit him, he changed his story to the one he presented at trial. Even if jurors believed Murtha's trial testimony, they would, upon learning he had previously given a different account, be confirmed in what they presumably believed from their everyday lives: people's reports of their private mental states are, to put it mildly, adaptable. In addition, as we've seen, plaintiffs' testimonial descriptions of their sensory experiences are more or less vague. Their words do convey something about what those experiences are like, but they can't give any very precise idea of, for instance, the intensity of the impairments—How blurry is "blurred"? How loud is "extremely loud"?

A credible evidentiary simulation makes the plaintiff's subjective experience seem much more substantial. Jurors aren't left to their imaginations in the same way. They can see or hear for themselves what the plaintiff's sensations are like. The demonstrative gives them tangible proof, or at least a vivid illustration that the plaintiff has sworn is accurate. This solidifies the plaintiff's subjective experience as more of a *fact*, not to be gainsaid or pushed around.

By recreating the plaintiff's subjective experience in its own sensory modality, moreover, the simulation preserves the particularity of that experience, its strangeness, as verbal description alone cannot. Language relies on concepts, and thus on generalities that jurors will then try, with greater or lesser effort to visualize for themselves. When Johnson Devadas describes his vision as "blurry" or says he sees "halos" when he looks at streetlights at night, jurors must imagine what that visual experience might be like. Context guides our interpretation of ambiguous visual stimuli (e.g., Balcetis and Lassiter 2010), and ordinarily the context most available to people is their own imaginations, as guided by their personal experience. Thus jurors' mental imagery will err, if it does, in the direction of their own ideas of blurred vision or haloed lights.

Evidentiary simulations resist this egotistical bias. If jurors believe a simulation is accurate, they must believe it shows them what the plaintiff's vision or hearing is really like. That can be surprisingly different from what jurors without access to the simulation may have imagined the plaintiff's experience to be. Recall that before the *Janson* trial, some focus group members reacted to hearing the sound files by exclaiming, "How could anyone live with that?" The impassioned response reflects the difference between merely knowing *about* the plaintiff's sensory experience and *knowing* it in the way the simulation made possible.

Jurors' shared experience of the simulation in court can also anchor their deliberations. Without the exhibit, jurors may find it more difficult to reach consensus on what the plaintiff's pain and suffering is worth because each knows that she or he is working from her or his own imagined version of the plaintiff's sensory experience. The simulation can resolve at least that doubt because all jurors know they've seen or heard the *same re-creation* of that experience. They may still disagree about what the plaintiff's suffering is worth, of course, but they are more likely to feel they are on solid ground as to one crucial component of what they are evaluating.

Second, at least some simulations—the photo sequences in *Devadas* and the video in *Smith*, for instance—offer normatively charged versions of plaintiffs' subjective experiences. These simulations connect the plaintiffs' sensations with their personhood by presenting their perceptual acts as attributes of their identities and by casting the plaintiffs as the protagonists in their own life stories.

A simulation of phenomenal experience can construct the plaintiff as a particular kind of *perceiving subject* who is situated in his world through what he sees or hears and how he sees or hears it. For instance, the photo simulations in *Devadas* present Johnson Devadas as someone engaged in particular acts of seeing. The first set of pictures offers close-up scrutiny of the bottles on Devadas's pharmacy shelves. Viewers understand at a glance (and thus more immediately and viscerally than they would from the plaintiff's testimony alone) that a pharmacist is someone whose professional livelihood depends on routinely, carefully, and repeatedly *looking* at arrays of sometimes very similar-looking bottles. With one set of pictures made to stand in for ten or more hours of work, day after day, the simulation conveys at least some idea of the level of visual attention and concentration Devadas must exercise without fail, for every patient and every prescription.

The discrepancy between the original image and the blurred and doubled images then strikingly illustrates the constant threat to the plaintiff's ability to do his job well. The distorted images invite viewers to imagine an act of stressful seeing repeated hundreds of times each day. It's a source of physical stress because seeing well enough requires Devadas to wear irritating contact lenses and to strain his eyes (and even so, the contacts do not correct for some of the higher-order aberrations of the cornea with which the surgery has left him). And it's psychologically stressful because of the ever-present danger of making a mistake. For Devadas, seeing well every time is both a matter of pride and a professional obligation. The acts of seeing that the photo simulations recreate convey how his impaired vision has undermined his confidence in his work and hence his very sense of self.

The video simulation in *Smith* reveals even more about who Rosalind Smith is. It accomplishes this by alternating first-person and third-person points of view of each scene from Smith's daily routine. When the scenes are shot from the first-person point of view, the camera identifies viewers' access to Smith's reality with the plaintiff's own, just as in *Devadas*. Viewers' imaginative identification with Smith's acts of seeing—working on her computer, preparing meals for her son, reading to him, and so on—is, however, heightened by the medium of video as opposed to still photography. As observed in chapter 5, video enables viewers to participate vicariously in action over time, triggering their innate tendency to mentally simulate those actions for themselves.

When the scenes are shot from the third-person point of view, viewers can also occupy their more accustomed role as observers of a documentary film that provides presumptively objective, credible information about the world. The choice and sequence of scenes construct a story—a typical day in Rosalind Smith's life—and a character: Smith as the heroine of her daily drama. She is a wife and working mother, conscientiously and intimately caring for her sons. Watching Smith engaged in each of her everyday activities, viewers *see* and thus appreciate how much patience and quiet determination are needed for her to sustain her peaceful and happy home life despite the extreme limitations (and even danger; recall the tomato-slicing scene) that her constricted visual field imposes on her. It's this perseverance that elevates her character, letting viewers know who she really is.

Third, simulations and testimony are likely to *interact* in different ways to shape jurors' conceptions of what kind of person the plaintiff is, how severe her perceptual impairments are, and how much she deserves in compensation for her suffering. To begin with, jurors' impressions of the plaintiff from her testimony, appearance, and demeanor on the stand may influence their uptake of the simulation. Most obviously, if jurors think the plaintiff is a trustworthy witness, they will be more inclined to believe her when she says that the demonstrative fairly and accurately represents her experience. All things being equal, this would enhance the exhibit's persuasive force. That's no small matter when the perceptual impairments the exhibit recreates are quite different from what jurors would otherwise imagine. It would seem to be especially important in the case of artist's sketch simulations, which lack independent probative value. On the other hand, if jurors do *not* find the plaintiff to be a very credible witness, they might not believe the simulation either. For instance, if jurors, on the basis of other evidence, think the plaintiff is overreaching in his description of his impairments, an artist's sketch simulation illustrating that exaggerated account might not be believed and could even be "counterproductive."[15]

Simulation and testimony may also interact in the opposite direction: the exhibit may influence how jurors interpret the plaintiff's testimony. The presumptive accuracy of the simulation—the judge has, after all, allowed it to be shown, so it must be reliable enough to be considered—would tend to allay any concerns that the plaintiff is exaggerating her impairments. And having assured themselves of the plaintiff's credibility regarding her sensory experience, jurors may also be more inclined to trust the plaintiff's testimony in other respects—in particular, her account of the psychological effects of her impairments.

Jurors' encounter with the simulation may also improve their opinion of other aspects of the plaintiff's character. Consider Dennis Janson. His own story of his suffering, supported by expert testimony about the audiological test results, may not have required any further corroboration. Jurors would have had no trouble appreciating, at least on some level, his verbal account of his inner experience. As we've seen, though, they would still have had only a vague notion (or rather, different vague notions) about how loud the "extraordinarily loud" noise he said he heard was, and they might have wondered how "debilitating" the noise could have been if Janson could still work and get around. Hearing the sound files, though, the jurors would have had no such doubts. They experienced the simulation before they heard Janson's detailed narrative of how his impairments affected his life. Assuming that listening to the sound files convinced jurors that Janson's injury was truly severe, they may well have concluded later, when they heard and saw him testify the next day, that he was *understating* the extent of his suffering. That stoicism may have made Janson seem all the more credible as a witness ("he's not exaggerating") and more deserving as a plaintiff ("he's not a complainer").[15]

The narrative theory presented above helps us to appreciate the deeper significance of this point. Recall that a personal injury plaintiff's stories of suffering are "lack" stories (Propp 1968), which depict how the protagonist, through strength of character, confronts and transcends his injuries. The audience of the folktale responds by admiring the protagonist's character; jurors, the plaintiff hopes, will respond by compensating him in accordance with the *value* they assign to his character. When a simulation is integrated into the plaintiff's case, jurors are presented with a new, holistic narrative that compels jurors to shift their point of view of the story of suffering, at least in part, from third-person to first-person. Without saying a word, the simulation invites jurors to inhabit the plaintiff's world as he himself does, and thus to experience his story in the sensate and uncritical way that effective narratives make possible. The simulation helps jurors to appreciate the plaintiff's character by allowing them to *become* that character, for a brief but sufficient moment, which in turn may well incline them to value that character more highly.

A highly credible simulation, especially one backed by scientific authority, might also compensate for perceived deficits in the plaintiff's testimony. The shift of the focus of proof from testimony to credible demonstrative evidence could at least partly divert jurors' attention from any unfavorable estimate of the plaintiff's reliability, attenuating if not reversing the effects of any negative evaluations of her character.[17] The simulation may also "smooth out" the gaps and glitches in the testimony of a credible but relatively inarticulate plaintiff, elevating jurors' opinion of her.[18]

Fourth, simulations of subjectivity may change personal injury trials in yet another way. Earlier I explained that the plaintiff's testimonial performance is typically the moral focus of the trial. It's ordinarily the most probative source of evidence for the normative judgments that jurors must make regarding the severity of the plaintiff's suffering and his deservingness. In addition, judging the plaintiff on the basis of his live testimony in court is itself a moral act. Yet introducing demonstrative evidence of the plaintiff's subjective experience could partly shift the focus of the trial from the testimony to the demonstrative proof, tending to *displace* the testimony as the basis for jurors' moral judgments.

Consider an analogy from the history of medicine. As late as the eighteenth century, doctors, in diagnosing disease, relied mainly on the patient's description of her symptoms. Physical examination was secondary, if done at all. Over the course of the nineteenth century, doctors began increasingly to rely on new, or newly improved, mechanical devices—ophthalmoscopes, laryngoscopes, thermometers—which objectively registered the patient's internal functions (Reiser 1978). The patient's narrative was gradually displaced from the center of diagnosis, a trend that has continued to the present (see also Pasveer 2006).[19]

What are the consequences? Remarking on a seventeenth-century patient's account of her symptoms to her doctor, medical historian Stanley Joel Reiser (1978, 2) writes: "The narrative technique permits a subjective portrait of the illness, greatly influenced and perhaps distorted by the patient's intellect and personality. . . . [The patient herself] is the chief witness to and interpreter of the events of her illness. She manipulates the memories of the sensations she experienced while ill, diminishing or magnifying their severity as she chooses. Her account is not an objective description of the events but a personal statement of their meaning. The listener is being drawn into the human drama of this illness." The patient's words communicate the personal significance of her ailments—their meaning and their human drama. They can sometimes be less reliable as a guide to what the patient's physical symptoms actually are. To the extent that successfully treating the illness depends on ascertaining the fact of the matter, some physicians would prefer to rely on diagnostic techniques and tools that appear to yield more objective information. As medical practice increasingly becomes a business of measurement, what can't readily be measured tends to be diminished. The patient's story of her suffering, the primary locus of its meaning to her as a person, becomes less important to the course of her medical care.

In the very different context of the personal injury trial, something similar could occur. When a scientifically based simulation is introduced, the main epistemological warrant for believing the plaintiff's sensory impairments are what the plaintiff claims they are may shift from her credibility as a witness to whatever jurors take to be the indicia of reliable science. This moves judgment into an entirely different episteme. Instead of trust in the first-person discursive account, jurors are invited to rely on the clinician's protocols, devices, measurements, and methods of translating the clinical data into demonstrative form. To the extent that jurors put more faith in scientific expertise than in eyewitness testimony, even where the eyewitness is uniquely positioned to report on the subjective fact of the matter, there will be a shift of epistemological emphasis.

This, in turn, implies a shift of moral focus. The simulation, it could be argued, makes jurors' opinion of the plaintiff's character and credibility less important, and their belief in the credibility of the science behind the simulation more important, to their judgments of what it's like for the plaintiff to experience her impairments. Screening a simulation like the video in *Smith*, which offers a nearly self-contained documentary portrait of the plaintiff as a deserving sufferer, would tend to diminish further the importance of the plaintiff's live testimony.

In addition, when an expert witness introduces a scientifically based simulation, jurors' attention may be diverted away from the plaintiff and toward the expert. Plaintiffs often share the spotlight with experts. But the shift may be greater when the matter to be proved concerns the plaintiff's subjective experience, something to which the plaintiff, through his testimony, would otherwise be expected to provide privileged if not exclusive access. In deciding how much weight to give the simulation as proof of the plaintiff's subjective state, jurors should be very interested in the testimony of the expert witness, whose application of scientific principles and methods provides the support for the simulation's reliability.[20] The salience of jurors' impressions of the expert, as opposed to those of the plaintiff herself, in their evaluation of the plaintiff's suffering may loom even larger because jurors' encounter with the scientific simulation is separated in time from the plaintiff's testimonial performance. In *Janson*, for instance, the expert introduced the sound files and jurors listened to them on the first day of the trial; Janson didn't testify until the next day.

Any such redirection of jurors' focus away from plaintiffs' narratives of suffering and toward scientific demonstrative evidence (both the exhibit itself and the expert testimony offered in its behalf) would seem to be of a piece with not only the progression of modern medical diagnosis described above, but also other positivist, antinarrative trends in science and culture. Perhaps most pertinent is the supposed "*CSI* effect," in which the suspect's physical traces, revealed through computerized forensics, purport to prove guilt conclusively, obviating the need for a trial at which the defendant's behavior will be variously explained or excused by being placed in the context of competing stories (Spiesel 2014). Antinarrativism is especially notable in the contemporary study of the mind. Neuroscience proposes to explain more and more of mental life in terms of mappable brain functions,[21] while psychiatry, largely for economic reasons, has increasingly abandoned talk therapy for pharmacology (e.g., Angell 2011).

Scientific simulations, by representing subjective experience as measurable fact and inviting jurors to leverage that factual knowledge into moral judgment, seem to suggest a similarly positivist approach to consciousness.

Ultimately, however, even the most probative and convincing simulations won't supplant the plaintiff's testimonial performance. Television dramas of forensics notwithstanding, proof at trial is always verbally framed—by witness examination and cross-examination, opening statements and closing arguments, and jury instructions. The trial remains a "consciously structured hybrid of languages" (Burns 1999, 183), and any demonstrative exhibit of subjective experience at trial will always be presented and taken up in the context of the plaintiff's and others' narratives. Simulations of subjective experience may change how jurors judge personal injury plaintiffs and arrive at their awards for the plaintiffs' pain and suffering, but they won't entirely displace plaintiffs' testimony from its central role in the trial.

If "emotion is at the heart of jurors' experience of the personal injury case," as Antonio Ponvert III, Dennis Janson's attorney, has said,[22] then plainly it's important to think carefully about how simulations, in conjunction with plaintiffs' testimony, can elicit or intensify jurors' emotions and how those emotions may affect jurors' evaluation of plaintiffs' suffering. The most important emotion in this context is surely sympathy, which may be defined as a heightened awareness of another person's suffering, accompanied by the urge to alleviate that suffering (Wispé 1991). Any additional sympathy that simulations prompt jurors to feel for the plaintiff may inform their judgments; it may also bias those judgments.[23]

Increased sympathy can inform jurors' judgment because, *first*, emotions embody cognitive content. As many philosophers and psychologists have argued, each emotion reflects a specific appraisal of changes in the environment that are relevant to the person experiencing that emotion (e.g., Lazarus 1991; Ortony, Clore, and Collins 1988; Smith and Ellsworth 1985). Emotions send bodily signals (Damasio 1994), telling the person that a particular situation deserves attention and inclining the person toward a given behavioral response. A person without emotions is not a superior decision maker; to the contrary, without the "somatic markers" (Damasio 1994) that emotions provide, the emotionless person becomes incapable of making decisions at all. Emotions also reflect judgments of value (Nussbaum 1992). Our passions offer us physical and psychological evidence of what we truly care about and how favorably or unfavorably we judge it. To experience the right emotion in the right situation, moreover, reveals one's good character—one's proper attunement with the world (Nussbaum 1986).

Experiencing an emotion, then, is at least potentially a *source of knowledge* about whatever has provoked that emotion. The knowledge the emotion conveys depends on that emotion's cognitive structure (Ortony, Clore, and Collins 1988). To feel sympathetic toward the injured plaintiff is to recognize that he is suffering significantly and undeservedly. By prompting jurors to feel more sympathy for the plaintiff, a simulation informs them that her suffering is that much more significant.

Second, and relatedly, certain emotions also reflect *intuitive moral judgments* (e.g., Haidt 2001, 2007). A growing body of psychological research associates specific emotions (e.g., disgust) with particular sociomoral concerns (e.g., preserving purity) (Rozin et al. 1999; but cf. Cameron, Lindquist, and Gray 2015). Most relevant to our purposes, compassion or sympathy is associated with "caring for and reducing harm to others, particularly those in need" (Horberg, Oveis, and Keltner 2011). When people respond to a situation with sympathy, their feeling represents an intuitive moral judgment that the target of their sympathy is in need and deserves their help. Thus, to the extent that a simulation of the plaintiff's perceptual impairments intensifies jurors' sympathy toward the plaintiff, that sympathy sends jurors a signal that reducing the plaintiff's harm, insofar as money damages can, is morally the right thing to do.

Simulations may also increase the risk that jurors will *misjudge* personal injury plaintiffs, in particular by overestimating the severity of their pain and suffering. The law of evidence provides the basic framework for thinking about the threats simulations may pose to good judgment. Rule 403 authorizes the trial judge to "exclude relevant evidence if its probative value is substantially outweighed by a danger of . . . unfair prejudice, confusing the issues, [or] misleading the jury" (Federal Rules of Evidence 2014, 403). Where these risks are not great enough to justify excluding an item of evidence entirely, they may distort jurors' decision making, perhaps especially if the risks are not called to jurors' attention by opposing counsel or counteracted by other evidence.

Simulations may confuse or mislead jurors or cause unfair prejudice to the defendant in several ways. *First*, whatever the arguments supporting the judicious use of emotions in legal decision making, sympathy and other emotions can also pull jurors away from deciding in accordance with legal norms. There are good reasons for the standard jury instruction that jurors not let their emotions sway their decisions. Indeed, the risk that an item of evidence may lead jurors to rely too much on their emotions is often considered to be the core of Rule 403's concern about unfair prejudice (for a critical discussion, see Gold 1982).

Sympathy can bias judgment because of the factors affecting the intensity of emotional arousal. For instance, the arousal of sympathy is subject to a *salience bias*. All things being equal, the stronger the stimulus, the greater the sympathy, even if stimulus strength doesn't accurately reflect the sufferer's degree of need or deservingness. A more compelling performance on the stand, a more dramatic account of the effects of perceptual impairment on the plaintiff's life, provokes more sympathy; another plaintiff suffering the same degree of psychological distress but less able to articulate that distress convincingly would elicit less. An evidentiary re-creation of the plaintiff's perceptual impairments, by making those impairments so vividly present, may prompt more sympathy than another plaintiff's merely verbal description of the same condition. Feelings of sympathy are also prone to a *similarity bias*: we tend to be more sympathetic to those who are like us. Simulations depicting the plaintiff as "one of us," or even showing familiar scenes from a first-person point of view, may induce sympathy based on these or other perceived similarities rather than on the plaintiff's actual levels of pain and distress.

This might not matter, except that the resulting sympathy can also bias legal outcomes. I suggested above that it may be morally appropriate, even if contrary to legal norms, for jurors' sympathy toward the plaintiff to lead them to increase their damage awards. But if the degree of sympathy is itself the product of bias, any resulting effects on damage awards would also reflect that bias. Moreover, the urge to compensate injured accident victims, which sympathy heightens, has been shown to make mock jurors more likely to find the defendant liable in the first place, since jurors know that the law allows them to compensate only if they hold the defendant responsible (Bornstein 1998). By inducing jurors to feel more sympathy for the plaintiff, therefore, a simulation could bias jurors' underlying liability decision.[24]

Second, jurors may be confused or misled as to the simulation's actual evidentiary status. In chapter 4 I explained several reasons why jurors may be prone to mistake merely illustrative simulations for independent, substantive evidence of the plaintiff's perceptual state. Other, related confusions could also occur. For instance, as suggested by the evidentiary hearing in *Janson* in chapter 5, jurors may mistakenly believe that the simulation is a recording of the plaintiff's experience rather than merely a model of it. In either case, jurors may attribute too much weight to the simulation as proof of what the plaintiff's subjective experience is really like.

Third, the vividness and immediacy of the demonstrative exhibit may overwhelm jurors' critical faculties, especially when the exhibit is presented with the imprimatur of scientific expertise. Having experienced for themselves what the plaintiff purportedly experiences, jurors may be so intuitively convinced of the reality of that experience, and thus of the accuracy and reliability of the simulation, that they will not pay sufficient attention to any shortcomings in or doubts about the scientific principles or methodologies used to create it. Consequently, they may, once again, give the simulation too much weight.

Fourth, the simulation may induce a *focusing illusion* (Schkade and Kahneman 1998), leading jurors to exaggerate the significance of the plaintiff's perceptual impairments for his overall well-being. Management scholar David Schkade and psychologist Daniel Kahneman have found that "when a judgment about an entire object or category is made with attention focused on a subset of that category, a focusing illusion is likely to occur, whereby the attended subset is overweighted relative to the unattended subset" (340).[25] Simulations spotlight the plaintiff's sensory impairments. Their very purpose, as we know, is to recreate the phenomenal feel of those impairments. But to the extent that jurors rely on the simulation to evaluate the impact of the plaintiff's diminished vision or distorted hearing on her well-being, focusing on it and not on the plaintiff's other sensory abilities and on all of life's events and enjoyments that her condition leaves relatively unaffected, they may overestimate how bad it is for the plaintiff to have to endure her condition.

Specific features of the simulation may exacerbate the focusing illusion. Consider the sound files in *Janson*. Janson, like other subjective tinnitus sufferers, hears the ringing or buzzing sound "inside his head," but he also hears other sounds emanating from the external environment (to the extent that his hearing loss allows). When he is not in an otherwise silent sound studio or in the dead of night, he does not hear *only* the ringing or buzzing. The simulation, however, depending on the type of headphones the jurors used, may have entirely blocked sounds other than the sound files, or at least reduced their volume to below the level at which the plaintiff would be able to hear them. If so, then the simulation could well have misrepresented Janson's subjective experience by making his tinnitus seem to be an even larger part of his aural world than it really is. This, in turn, might have prompted jurors to overestimate the severity of his suffering.

Fifth, and closely related, the simulation could also mislead or confuse jurors by leading them to overestimate, on the basis of their temporary but vivid personal experience of the plaintiff's impaired eyesight (for instance), how bad it will be for the plaintiff to have to endure that perceptual impairment over the long term. Generally speaking, people are poor affective forecasters (Blumenthal 2005; Gilbert 2006). If asked to imagine how good or bad they would feel some years after experiencing a given very good event (say, winning the lottery) or a very bad event (say, suffering a serious and lasting injury), people consistently tend to overestimate the intensity of their hypothesized future good or bad feelings. A primary reason is the focusing illusion: when thinking about this sort of question, people tend to pay attention to the condition posited in the question and fail to take into account that in the future, as at present, being a lottery winner or injury victim will occupy only a part of their experience and will therefore not have as great an effect on their overall happiness as they tend to believe it will.[26] Another reason is that "human beings are unexpectedly resilient" (Sunstein 2008, S164). People who suffer severe physical and emotional injuries often *habituate* to their new condition, a process known as *hedonic adaptation* (Frederick and Loewenstein 1999). They get used to it, if they can. They can also take affirmative steps to minimize the adverse impact of their injuries. In sum, the hedonic value of their postaccident life is not as much reduced as they or others might have expected beforehand.[27] For these reasons, jurors who are exposed to the possibly unpleasant short-term experience of a perceptual impairment and invited to determine on the basis of that experience (as well as the testimonial evidence) a dollar value sufficient to compensate the plaintiff for having to endure that impairment indefinitely may overestimate its long-term disvalue to the plaintiff (Sunstein 2008).

An important qualification is that people do not appear to adapt as well to constant noise (e.g., from a nearby highway) or chronic pain or depression (see Frederick and Loewenstein 1999). Specifically, "[the sound of] tinnitus does not habituate even when its perceived loudness is weak" (Jastreboff 1990, 237). Thus, the focusing illusion and affective forecasting errors may not lead jurors to overestimate, on the basis of their unpleasant temporary exposure to the simulated sound of a plaintiff's tinnitus, the long-term distress that experiencing that sound indefinitely would cause. Indeed, by making the experience so salient, the simulation of tinnitus may well help to correct for what would otherwise be jurors' tendency to *undervalue* that long-term distress (Sunstein 2008).

Sixth, particular sorts of simulations may give rise to specific cognitive biases. For instance, recall that in *Janson*, the volume of the sound files was perhaps their most salient feature. Focus group participants said that they "couldn't believe how loud it was." It would be entirely natural for jurors to infer their "gist" judgment of Janson's injury severity (Hans and Reyna 2011) from the loudness of the sound files: louder equals worse. Yet many clinical audiologists believe that loudness is not strongly correlated with a tinnitus patient's actual suffering.[28] The convincing experience of hearing the sound files might dominate the other factors jurors should also take into account in gauging just how bad it is for the plaintiff to experience his tinnitus, distorting their overall evaluation of injury severity and hence their pain and suffering award.

I have saved for last the most striking effect simulations may have on jurors' judgments about personal injury plaintiffs and their suffering. By putting jurors in the plaintiff's place, enabling them to hear or see what the plaintiff does, simulations invite jurors to confuse how bad it is for the *plaintiff* to have to live with his impairments with how bad they think it would be for *them* to endure that condition. Because this raises a deeper jurisprudential issue as well as evidentiary concerns, I address it separately.

When a plaintiff's lawyer, in closing argument, proposes that jurors determine her client's pain and suffering damages by putting themselves in the plaintiff's place and asking themselves how much money would be needed to compensate *them* if they were suffering as the plaintiff is, she is said to make a "Golden Rule" argument. She's encouraging the jurors to "do unto others [that is, the plaintiff] as they would have others do unto them" (Brown 1984; Tellier 1960). Golden Rule arguments are generally disallowed,[29] even though in practice, trial advocates can easily skirt the prohibition by not *explicitly* inviting jurors to step into the plaintiff's shoes (see, e.g., Mauet 2013).

The rule against Golden Rule arguments can be understood in terms of evidentiary Rule 403. They're prohibited because they encourage jurors to become partial rather than disinterested decision makers, potentially biasing their judgments in favor of the plaintiff with whom they are asked to identify and thus unfairly prejudicing the defendant.[30] They also threaten to confuse judgment by inviting jurors to inject irrelevant considerations into their decision making—specifically, to use their own experience and sensibilities rather than the plaintiff's in evaluating how bad it is for the plaintiff to have to live with his impairments.

Simulations of plaintiffs' subjective perceptions are offered during the evidentiary phase of trial, not during summation, and the simulations themselves do not appeal in so many words (or any, for that matter) to Golden Rule reasoning, so the ban technically may not apply to them. By purporting to allow jurors to experience what the plaintiff does, however, they arguably raise the same risks of bias and confusion.

The rule against Golden Rule appeals is anchored in an ideal of good legal judgment that is firmly entrenched in our jurisprudence, one that requires impartiality and cognitive and emotional distance between jurors and those whom they judge. Simulations of subjectivity challenge this ideal. They encourage jurors to evaluate the plaintiff's pain and suffering by sharing her sensory experience. Regardless of whether simulations avoid the letter of the ban, they could be seen as such a direct threat to fair and just decision making that they should be excluded for that reason.

I will argue that the jurisprudential benefits of simulations are worth the costs. First, any costs are not as great as might appear at first glance. Even without simulations, jurors naturally draw on self-relevant thoughts and feelings when passing judgment on litigants, although simulations increase this tendency. Other features of the task and process of legal judgment, however, limit the pull of egotistical thinking, with or without simulations. Second, on the benefit side, simulations can improve legal decision making. Good judgment involves a balance of detachment and sympathy; simulations can help the law strike this balance more properly. The intersubjective thinking about the plaintiff's pain and suffering that simulations, unlike traditional Golden Rule arguments, encourage is anchored in reliable information about the *plaintiff*, and thus it facilitates plaintiff-oriented and not merely egotistical thinking. And by inspiring a deeper attentiveness to the plaintiff's felt experience, simulations can help jurors to appreciate better the moral significance of the plaintiff's otherness, in itself an ethical, and hence jurisprudential, good.

First, we should put the judgmental risks of simulations in perspective. Even in the absence of a simulation, jurors are likely to gauge the severity of the plaintiff's suffering by asking, "How bad would it be for me?" People always draw on their own experiences and world knowledge in reaching their judgments. And when people reason about others—what others think, feel, or know—they are especially likely to use their self-perspectives as their default mode of thinking (Decety and Jackson 2004). People tend to overimpute their thoughts and knowledge to others (Nickerson 1999) and to take for granted that others will share their judgments and preferences (Pronin 2008; Ross, Greene, and House 1977).[31] In the typical case, jurors might use their thoughts about themselves and their own preferences as reference points for evaluating the plaintiff's suffering by imagining how upsetting, frustrating, or painful it would be for them to suffer from the sensory impairments the plaintiff describes, extrapolating from that to estimate what the plaintiff feels.

Simulations of subjective states might increase the risk of basing judgments of the severity of the plaintiff's suffering on self-assessment. When the plaintiff's perceptual impairments are recreated for jurors in the form of a demonstrative exhibit, it may be harder for jurors to disentangle "how bad would that be for me?" from "how bad is it for him?" because the thoughts on which the jurors are basing their judgments are derived in part from their own vivid experience, happening to *them* during the trial. For these jurors, "*my* (extremely recent) experience of the plaintiff's tinnitus" (or blurred, doubled, or constricted vision) would be predicted to play a larger role in their reasoning than would mere recollections of relevant (but still dissimilar) personal or secondhand experience.

Nevertheless, any self-oriented thoughts that simulations engender are unlikely to overwhelm jurors' decision making. Understanding what the plaintiff's sensory experience is like is only part of the pain and suffering judgment. As we've seen, in order to gauge the extent of the plaintiff's mental distress, jurors must also evaluate his story of how his impairments affect his work and personal life, and some of their thinking about that will be no more self-oriented than it would be in the absence of a simulation. In addition, the impact of any additional self-relevant thinking on jurors' pain and suffering damages is tempered by the fact that the damage award always reflects more than a dyadic adjustment between the plaintiff's subjectivity ("how bad is it for her?") and the jurors' ("how bad would it be for me?"). There is always a third term: the *social norms* that jurors, as representatives of the community, bring to bear on the target of judgment. "Damage awards and community values are deeply intertwined" (Hans 2014, 937). Any egotistical bias that simulations add to what jurors may already be inclined to express is filtered, in the course of deliberations, through a shared sense of what the plaintiff's suffering is worth.

Perhaps most importantly, even to the extent that simulations reduce the psychological distance between jurors and plaintiffs, many aspects of trial doctrine and practice continue to maintain it. For instance, jurors are not supposed to know the parties or others closely related to or affiliated with them, nor should they have prior knowledge of the litigated facts. Jurors are also instructed not to let their decisions be swayed by sympathy or anger toward any party. Although completely avoiding emotional influences may be psychologically impossible and even (as argued above) undesirable (e.g., Bandes and Blumenthal 2012; Maroney 2006), these instructions at least encourage jurors not to become too personally invested in the litigants.

The nature of the trial as a dramatic performance reinforces the psychological distance between jurors and the parties they judge. The trial is theater. The deliberate dialogues of direct and cross-examination are conducted as if on a stage in the front of the courtroom, in a space from which jurors, as audience, are physically separated by some distance and by a railing or low wall. The judge, the lawyers, the witnesses, the court reporter, the bailiff, and the jurors themselves all play their parts (Ball 1981; Burns 1999). And jurors are fully aware of this. They recognize that they are watching and hearing both a complex representation of truth *and* a ritualized performance. Their awareness that legal truth is being performed by speaking actors creates an *alienation effect*, helping to maintain "the distancing necessary to good judgment" between the jurors and the people and events they are judging (Ball 1981, 60).

Second, simulations can improve decision making in personal injury cases. Detachment, to be sure, is a judgmental virtue. It promotes impartiality. It enables the decision maker to adopt in turn the perspectives of all parties, and perhaps of others who may be significantly affected by the case. Distance from the parties and the case tempers excessive emotional influence, which can distort judgment in the ways discussed earlier, among others. The decision maker who maintains psychological distance from the object of his decision can, in theory, be more objective, more deliberative, and thus reach more considered, justifiable outcomes.

Philosopher and novelist Iris Murdoch has expressed the moral virtue of the exercise of detachment, the abnegation of the self from judgment (Murdoch 1970), in terms relevant to legal decision making. As quoted by legal scholar Robert Burns (1999, 180), Murdoch explained:

> Morality itself involves "an exercise of justice and realism that is really *looking*. The difficulty is to keep this attention fixed upon the real situation to prevent it from returning surreptitiously to the self. . . . Realism, whether that of the artist or of the agent, is a moral achievement. This explains the central insight of Kantian ethics: "The more the separateness and differences of other people [are] recognized, and the fact seen that another man has needs and wishes as demanding as one's own, the harder it becomes to treat a person as a thing."

Getting the facts right matters in law. It matters most, we see now, because legal judgment involves moral judgment. By keeping their attention fixed on the plaintiff's separateness and distance from themselves, on the real facts of her situation rather than on a partially self-oriented imagining, jurors are more likely to regard the plaintiff as the unique person who she is, and to judge accordingly.

But detachment is not all we ask of legal decision makers. Many philosophers and legal scholars, and even some Supreme Court Justices, have emphasized the importance of compassion and empathy in good judging (e.g., Henderson 1988 [discussing former Associate Justice Brennan]; Sotomayor 2013). As law professor Anthony Kronman has explained, excellence in deliberation, whether on the part of judges and jurors or in everyday life, demands both detachment and sympathy, imaginative involvement and the ability to suspend it. It requires "the compassionate survey of alternatives viewed simultaneously from a distance" (1987, 853).

Simulations of subjectivity, I argue, promote a more empathic form of judgment, which can help jurors achieve the balance Kronman posits. Consider the epistemological rationale for admitting simulations of litigants' sensory experiences in the first place. As we saw in earlier chapters, simulations can provide jurors with more complete and accurate knowledge of what it's like for the plaintiff to see or hear as he does, and they do this by enabling them to experience a bit of what the plaintiff experiences. Simulations incline jurors to generate and use more self-relevant thoughts in assessing the plaintiff's suffering, but only by making available more concrete, specific, dependable knowledge about the *plaintiff's* perceptual experience. Simulations, as mentioned earlier, preserve the uniqueness and even strangeness of the plaintiff's subjectivity and thus counter jurors' tendency to assimilate or normalize his actual experience to what, on the basis of his words and their own imaginations, they might have assumed or expected it would be. By presenting more definite and complete information about the plaintiff's sensory experience, simulations can help correct for egotistical bias instead of exacerbating it.[32]

More profoundly, simulations point to a *phenomenological* conception of justice in which a more intimate connection between the perspectives of the jurors and the plaintiff is not bias or confusion, but instead a judgmental virtue. From a phenomenological stance, jurors' task is not to measure the plaintiff's experience somehow, as a subject might size up the features of an object. Judging the plaintiff's pain and suffering is instead a question of *articulating a relationship* between themselves and the plaintiff, a relationship that arises from the "primordial communication" (Merleau-Ponty 1964, 17) between persons who already have in common the perceptual experience of being-in-the-world. The simulation makes this quality of jurors' judgment salient by reconstituting that common experience; it enables jurors, by looking at or listening to the exhibit, to share the plaintiff's experience of the world. For jurors then to refer to this recent sensory experience when evaluating the plaintiff's condition is, from the phenomenological stance, not a flaw in judgment. It's an essential recognition of the fact that each juror, as a human being capable of knowing anything, is already a being-in-the-world together with the plaintiff, as with all others (see Meyer 2010). To put a value on the other's suffering is therefore to put a value on one's own existence as well. It need not, of course, be the same value. Jurors can and do make allowances for perceived differences between themselves and the plaintiff, and through these modulations, jurors articulate how highly they value the different ways they and others can be in the world.

Developing these last two points, we can see how, by immersing jurors in the plaintiff's perceptual experience in as much sensory fullness and specificity as the evidentiary medium allows, simulations can help jurors to recognize and accord proper moral significance to the *otherness* of the plaintiff. The philosopher Emmanuel Levinas, also working in the phenomenological tradition but diverging significantly from Heidegger and Merleau-Ponty, emphasized the fundamental fact of our being in the world with other people who are different from us. That difference means (in the words of legal scholar Linda Meyer), "I cannot know others completely, and the very incompleteness of my knowledge generates, at the same time, a profound call of responsibility and compassion (as I am drawn to others) and a humble respect (as I perceive their uniqueness and difference from me)" (2010, 357). Simulations promote this moral stance toward the plaintiff precisely by offering a slice of her distinct subjectivity as a rich perceptual experience that not only invites but commands jurors' attention. Thus, the moral objective—to recognize the "separateness and differences" of the other person—is the same as Murdoch advocated, but simulations advance that objective through empathy rather than detachment.

This more empathic mode of justice is not without its hazards. As Murdoch (1970) understood and psychological research (e.g., Decety and Jackson 2004) has confirmed, lapsing into selfish concerns is natural and easy. The phenomenological conception of justice risks the return to the self as the price of the fuller knowledge of the plaintiff that simulations can offer. We cannot know for sure whether the more intimate appreciation of the plaintiff's experience that simulations enable will in fact lead jurors to accord more respect to the plaintiff's personhood and to assess his pain and suffering more justly. The arguments above, if persuasive, merely indicate why this could happen. As more simulations of subjectivity are introduced in cases to come, we can hope to learn more.

EIGHT

The Future of Simulations

Demonstrative exhibits of sensory experience have been used in only a handful of cases so far. The number and variety of uses is likely to grow, however, and as it does, it will become all the more important to understand both the kind of knowledge of other minds this evidence offers and the effects it may have on legal decisions. In this brief concluding chapter, I explain why we're likely to see more simulations of subjectivity. I then survey some of the evidentiary and other issues that will arise as more aspects of more litigants' inner experiences are recreated in court.

There are several reasons to expect that the demand for simulations will increase. As I've argued throughout, jurors may well believe that simulations provide especially persuasive evidence of litigants' subjective experiences (although empirical research testing this claim has yet to be conducted). Lawyers will want to appeal to that belief if they think that doing so will improve their clients' prospects. Some lawyers may also be inclined to use these simulations because being known for doing so is a way to avoid being "out-technologized" by other lawyers who use them, and thus to stay ahead of the competition for potential clients. And the better known and better regarded this sort of demonstrative evidence becomes, the more often savvy clients will ask their lawyers to use it.

As lawyers offer more simulations, courts will have more opportunities to rule on their admissibility. It seems reasonable to suppose, given judges' record on this question to date, that many more simulations will be admitted. Even if judges adopt a more critical attitude toward them, the sheer number admitted will rise, owing to the low threshold for allowing those characterized as merely illustrative aids, as well as the ostensible reliability of many scientifically based simulations.

As more lawyers use evidentiary exhibits to recreate their clients' subjective states, word will spread, albeit unevenly. Opinions in cases in which simulations are introduced may not mention them; and the exhibits themselves, like most demonstratives, may not be available online through links in the opinions or on courts' websites (see Feigenson 2011b). But simulations may be reported on blogs, in professional publications, or in the general media, and trial lawyers who use them may eventually share their knowledge with others at continuing legal education seminars, in other professional development venues, and informally.

As the demand for simulations grows, moreover, more resources will be invested in developing the technologies for producing them, so that those technologies will likely become better, cheaper, and more widely available. One consequence is that more of the experts whom litigators consult and engage as potential trial witnesses will be using these simulation technologies in their own professional and forensic practices and/or will have ready access to them when the lawyers decide to create exhibits of this sort for trial. Those experts will become more practiced at laying the necessary foundation for the admission of this evidence, making judges even more inclined to admit it.

In addition, in at least some personal injury cases in which the plaintiff's lawyer seeks to introduce a clinically based re-creation of the plaintiff's subjective state, the defendant's lawyer may respond not only by challenging the plaintiff's exhibit but also by fashioning a simulation of his own, which the defendant will argue more accurately recreates the perceptual state in question. The defendant should have access through civil discovery to the results of the plaintiff's clinical examination. Imagine, for instance, competing auditory simulations in a case like *Janson*: first the plaintiff's, then the defendant's, the latter using a different loudness scale and resulting in a quieter sound file. Indeed, where the plaintiff has put his mental or physical condition in issue, the court may order an independent mental or physical examination, which the defendant could use as the basis for its own simulation (Federal Rules of Civil Procedure 2014, 35).

All this is necessarily speculative. But the indications point in the same direction: in the years to come, we can expect to see (and hear) more simulations of subjective perception offered and admitted as evidence in legal proceedings.

Another reason why simulations of subjectivity are likely to become more common is that enterprising lawyers will seek to use this powerful form of demonstrative evidence to illustrate or prove an expanding range of subjective states. More or less discrete sensations (like tinnitus or blurred or constricted vision) are the most probable new candidates. Consider, for instance, giving legal decision makers the vicarious experience of chronic visual impairments such as flashes or floaters, of the kind that may be symptomatic of a detached retina or the consequence of unsuccessful surgery to correct it. Lawyers may also contemplate recreating various sorts of physical pain. For instance, the US Army has experimented with a device that can deliver, at a distance, pulses of uncomfortable heat, leaving no lasting physical trace or pain (Turner 2012).[1] Developed as a crowd-control device, this sort of technology could be adapted to provide demonstrative evidence of a litigant's relevant pain.

Almost a quarter of a century ago, a California trial court admitted the visual component of the defendant motorcycle manufacturer's virtual reality display recreating a motorcycle ride over bumpy terrain, offered to prove that the terrain was too treacherous for the motorcycle to be operated safely.[2] Attorney Jeffrey Dunn, discussing that case, speculated that virtual reality might also be used to recreate, for instance, the shock and mental suffering experienced by a bungie-jumper whose rope had snapped and was hurtling to his death (Dunn, n.d.). Dunn suggested further that virtual reality could enable jurors to relive vicariously not only what a litigant saw (or sees), but also the temperature, pressure, and other sensations the litigant experienced during the events in question. Fully immersive virtual reality has not yet been offered in court to recreate litigants' subjective perceptions, but as the technology becomes more widely available and more user-friendly (including overcoming problems such as motion sickness; see Wingfield 2015), it may soon be offered.

Re-creations of more complex subjective states, involving more cognitively nuanced sensations, may follow. For instance, mental health professionals, pharmaceutical companies, and law enforcement officials have made use of audiovisual simulations that purport to evoke the disorienting, confusing internal experience of schizophrenia (e.g., Ando et al. 2011). Some of these utilize virtual reality technology (e.g., Banks et al. 2004; Tabar 2007).[3] With proper expert authentication, such simulations might someday be offered into evidence, for example, in support of a criminal defendant's claim of incompetence to stand trial or plea of not guilty by reason of insanity. These exhibits would, at least at first, have to be generic in nature, illustrating an expert's testimony about what the sights and sounds of schizophrenia are like in general. Offering them to prove a specific person's experience of schizophrenia would require a considerably more detailed evidentiary foundation.

Subjective experiences characterized by more subtle phenomenal features will be less amenable to demonstrative re-creation. What does it feel like to *intend* something? Does intention have any phenomenal characteristics at all (cf. Güzeldere 1997)? And if it does, how would one reliably recreate them for others to experience? The increased psychological complexity of certain conscious states and the technological challenge of accurately simulating them impose further obstacles.[4]

Within the realm of phenomenal experience, however, scientific and technological advances will further expand the capacity of demonstrative evidence to simulate others' mental lives. Leading neuroscientists have claimed that the "reconstruction of the subjective contents of human perception may soon be a reality" (Kay and Gallant 2009, 246). For instance, someday soon it may be possible to retrieve from another person's conscious brain the data needed to simulate that person's visual experience, without needing to rely, as in artist's sketch or psychophysical simulations, on the person's own report of her perceptions. Researchers have already taken steps toward what they call *visual image reconstruction*: by scanning a person's brain while she looks at a picture, neuroscientists can reconstruct the picture.

In one of the early studies, neuroscientist Yoichi Miyawaki and colleagues (Miyawaki et al. 2008) showed participants a series of images (abstract shapes or letters), each consisting of a grid of 10 x 10 elements of low or high contrast, while researchers recorded fMRI signals from the participants' visual cortexes. Using a complex statistical decoder, the researchers were able to reconstruct from the fMRI data the shape or letter at which each participant was looking when scanned. "The reconstructed images reveal[ed] essential features of the original shapes" (916), so that the computer was able to identify correctly, at levels far above chance, which image the participant was perceiving.[5]

More recent work has extended the digital reconstruction of subjective visual perception via fMRI to moving images. Neuroscientist Shinji Nishimoto and colleagues (Nishimoto et al. 2011) showed participants two hours' worth of brief segments of color movies of various subjects, measuring fMRI data from each participant's occipito-temporal visual cortex to train the decoding algorithm. Participants then watched nine minutes' worth of different brief movies (not included in the training set) ten times each, while the researchers recorded their brain activity. The decoder reconstructed from participants' fMRI data moving images that, while noisy, could be identified at levels far above chance as corresponding to the particular movies the participants had been watching when scanned.[6]

Yet another team of researchers has successfully reconstructed images of individual faces at which participants were looking when scanned (Cowen, Chun, and Kuhl 2014). Distinguishing faces is an especially challenging task for our brains, and hence for computer reconstruction, because all normal faces are grossly similar—everyone has two eyes on either side of a nose and so on. To differentiate particular faces requires greater computational resources and sophistication than the visual identification tasks previously simulated.[7] Psychologist and neurobiologist Marvin Chun, his then-student Alan Cowen, and psychologist Brice Kuhl first performed principal component analysis (PCA) to extract the quantitative features of a large set of photographed faces. Using a machine learning algorithm, they then mapped the component scores onto the fMRI data they had collected from participants while participants were looking at those photos. The researchers now had a formula for translating brain activity into PCA data, from which images of faces could in turn be generated. Participants were then scanned while looking at photos of faces they hadn't seen before. From their brain activity, the algorithm predicted component scores, and from these a corresponding facial image was reconstructed. By both objective (pixel comparison) and subjective (independent observer judgment) tests, the reconstructed faces were found to be closer than a randomly chosen "lure" face to the original target image—a statistically significant measure of accuracy (Cowen, Chun, and Kuhl 2014).[8]

Visual image reconstruction arguably takes us even closer than do other scientifically based simulations to the objectively reliable re-creation of phenomenal experience. Recall from chapter 2 that because other people's conscious experiences are not directly observable, we must make do with various second-best forms of knowledge. The scientifically based ones depend on measuring an observable proxy for that experience and translating those measurements, more or less indexically, into tangible form. Psychophysical simulations record behavioral responses to test stimuli. In the machine readout, the proxy is the retinal image (inferred from the measured wavefront of light reaching the retina). Visual image reconstruction measures activity in what is presumed to be the neural substrates of visual experience, further narrowing the inferential gap between others' conscious experience and its objective representation.

Astonishing enough in its own right, visual image reconstruction by no means exhausts the subjective experiences that neuroscientists, with the help of digital technology, may someday be able to recreate. Other researchers have extended the neuroscientific reconstruction of mental life from present perceptions to memories. Taking the first steps toward episodic memory identification, a team of researchers led by neuroscientist Martin Chadwick had participants watch three short video clips and then asked them to concentrate on remembering one of them. Scans of each participant's hippocampus allowed researchers to identify at above-chance levels which of the three scenes the subject was remembering (Chadwick et al. 2010). More recently, neuroscientist Jesse Rissman and colleagues have shown that fMRI pattern analysis can discriminate with near-perfect accuracy between participants' recognition of past events in their own lives (photographed with a wearable device one to three weeks earlier) and other events photographed by others (Rissman et al., 2016). If the reconstruction of visual perception via brain scans is ever to be used to support or even in lieu of eyewitness accounts, memories, not present perceptions, would have to be recreated. Combining visual image reconstruction and episodic memory identification could then yield visual memory reconstruction—scans that yield videolike simulations of what the person is remembering (Feigenson 2011a). Still more ambitious simulations of subjective experiences based on brain imaging may also be possible (e.g., Cerf et al. 2011).[9]

Litigants and lawyers would surely want to take advantage of these advances in neuroscientific technology, if and when their reliability for recreating subjective perception is established. We turn next to some of the impediments they'll face.

Practical, evidentiary, rhetorical, and ethical considerations will constrain the range of courtroom simulations of subjective experience. For instance, for the foreseeable future it will be difficult or impossible to capture transitory subjective states as they existed in the past, at the time of the litigated events.[10] Whether the defendant in a case like *Murtha* actually misperceived the threat to his safety at the crucial moment cannot be scientifically ascertained after the fact; the only epistemological function that a simulation can perform is to illustrate what he says he recalls. Re-creations of subjective experience will be limited to enduring states, like those of which personal injury plaintiffs complain, and (as discussed above) to litigants' memories of previous states that can practicably be measured at a later time.[11]

Reliability, of course, will remain a prerequisite for the admission of all evidence, and as with any new form of evidence, especially expert evidence, establishing that new sorts of simulations are sufficiently reliable will take some time. In particular, we can expect that machine readout simulations such as visual image reconstruction via fMRI will be contested, and at first sometimes excluded, on reliability grounds. Broad use in relevant practice communities always lags behind experimental innovation, so in jurisdictions following the *Frye* general acceptance test for the admissibility of expert evidence, it may be that much more difficult to establish that novel simulation technologies are reliable enough. Even in jurisdictions following some version of *Daubert*, it will take time before new scientifically based technologies and methods for simulating subjective experience are experimentally validated and their reliability sufficiently confirmed in peer-reviewed publications. Relatedly, because the potential probative value of each new psychophysical or machine readout simulation will remain less certain until the principles and methods on which it is based are better established, the Rule 403 balance of probative value against prejudicial risks will, all things being equal, be less favorable to admissibility.

Rhetorical and strategic considerations will also limit the use of new forms of simulations, as they do now. For instance, if a plaintiff's lawyer anticipates that experiencing the simulation of the plaintiff's subjective state would make jurors more likely to think "That's not so bad" than they would if they had to rely solely on the plaintiff's testimony and medical records, the lawyer won't use the simulation. Counsel and client also have to weigh the expense of developing and presenting proof against the expected benefits. Assuming that novel forms of evidence are less likely to be admitted and, if they involve outside expertise and novel technology, generally more costly, some lawyers may be disinclined to innovate.

Ethical considerations will also set bounds on lawyers' and litigants' ability to simulate some subjective conditions in court. Recreating extreme physical discomfort or pain, for instance, would (let us hope) be prohibited even if highly probative.[12] Even less extreme sensations may be more disturbing than jurors can reasonably be expected to endure as part of their obligation to serve (see Dunn, n.d.). Simulations may also raise a different sort of ethical issue, having to do with the fairness of the proceedings: a trial judge may decide to exclude a simulation if the parties' resources are so unequal that only the proponent can afford to create one (*Commonwealth v. Serge* 2006).[13]

Despite these constraints on the creation and use of simulations, there will likely be many more of them in trials and other legal proceedings to come. Plaintiffs in many thousands of malpractice and products liability cases claim to suffer from impaired eyesight or hearing; compare that number to the perhaps dozens of cases in which simulations have been introduced to date, and one can see the potential for much greater use. Add the advances in neuroscientific research and digital imaging technologies that will enable more kinds of sensations to be recreated for judges and jurors. Finally, if "everything of value depends on subjective experience" (Kolber 2011, 588), then subjectivity will always be central to the law, whether in personal injury cases, harassment claims, or elsewhere. As simulations of subjective experience become increasingly available and reliable, it's only reasonable to expect that litigants and their lawyers will offer, and judges and jurors will see and hear more of them.

My aim in this book has been to describe what makes simulations of subjectivity so fascinating and puzzling and, by thinking through the puzzles systematically, to explain how the law has grappled with this peculiar form of demonstrative evidence. I hope to have provided some guidance to the judges, jurors, lawyers, and experts who must confront the problems this evidence poses. And I hope that readers in general can now better appreciate the scientific, technological, cultural, and other factors shaping the knowledge of other minds that simulations can offer.

Acknowledgments

One afternoon in the spring of 2011, a student of mine told me about a conversation she had recently had with a local trial lawyer. The lawyer said that he had just represented a man who suffered from severe tinnitus as a result of an accident. To enable the jurors to get some sense of the plaintiff's lived experience, the lawyer had played in court a set of sound files that purported to recreate the loud buzzing sound the plaintiff now constantly heard.

I had been teaching, researching, and writing about demonstrative evidence for more than a decade. But I had never heard of an exhibit purporting to recreate a litigant's internal sensations. How could I not have known about this? And how could this sort of exhibit possibly be admissible? Another lawyer to whom I later described the exhibit exclaimed, "You can't do that!"

I decided to look into the matter further. I contacted Antonio Ponvert III, the lawyer in *Janson*, the tinnitus case. Ponvert generously shared his time and expertise, as well as the sound files and other case materials, enabling me to understand how the simulation was created, why the trial judge admitted it, and how it functioned in the context of the trial. I sought out other trial lawyers who had used or said they knew about other demonstratives of subjective experience. Todd Krouner was equally generous in making available to me the simulations he used in *Devadas* and *Schiffer*, two of his LASIK malpractice cases, and disclosing the thinking behind the exhibits. Michael Jainchill did the same for *Smith*, the case involving the woman suffering from idiopathic intracranial hypertension. These lawyers' willingness to give me access to the simulations they used and to talk frankly and extensively about their cases made this book possible.

Other lawyers, experts, and consultants involved in these and the other cases I discuss or reference in the book were also extremely helpful, and I am grateful for their assistance: Robert Beal, Mark Budzinski, Ralph Catalano, Paul Hoffman, Hugh Keefe, Robert Lesser, Edward Lobarinas, Richard Plattner, Ted Schmidt, Daniel Schultz, Robert Silva, Jeffrey Taylor, Royce Vehslage, and Robert Volk.

The nonspecialist who ventures into others' areas of expertise risks superficiality and error. I want to thank the audiologists, ophthalmologists, and other vision scientists who did their best to help me avoid these pitfalls, graciously answering my questions about audiometry, perimetry, and keratometry, the clinical disciplines behind the scientifically based simulations I discuss in chapters 5 and 6: Natan Bauman, James Henry, William Martin, Aron Rose, Janet Serle, Richard Tyler, and Michael Wall. Melissa Grafe, Librarian for Medical History at the Yale University Medical Historical Library, helped me find some of the nineteenth-century sources for the histories of perimetry and keratometry on which I draw in those chapters. Marvin Chun, Richard M. Colgate Professor of Psychology and Professor of Neurobiology at Yale, kindly walked me through his neuroscientific research, discussed in chapter 8.

Many people assisted this project as it progressed from preliminary questions to completed book. Wesleyan University's Center for the Humanities invited me to present a very early version of my thoughts as part of its "Fact and Artifact" series in fall 2011. I want to thank Jennifer Tucker, Associate Professor of History and Science in Society, for prompting the invitation; Jill Morawski, Wilbur Fisk Osborne Professor of Psychology, for extending it, and Cecilia Miller, Associate Professor of History, for bringing me back to speak to her class later that fall. Adam Kolber, Professor of Law at Brooklyn Law School, later read the notes for my Wesleyan talk and offered comments. The Canadian Initiative in Law, Culture and Humanities gave me the opportunity to share a more developed version of the project at its "Sensing the Law" workshop in spring 2013. Workshop organizers Sheryl Hamilton, Diana Majury, Dawn Moore, Neil Sargent, and Christiane Wilke, all members of the faculty of the Department of Law and Legal Studies at Carleton University, created a wonderfully welcoming and productive interdisciplinary event. My talk there appears as a chapter in Hamilton et al. 2016. I later presented various aspects of my work at the University of Tulsa College of Law, the biennial International Academy of Law and Mental Health, and, more than once, to my colleagues at Quinnipiac University School of Law. Deans Brad Saxton and Jennifer Brown of the School of Law provided research support throughout.

Several friends and colleagues were kind enough to read and comment on drafts of the manuscript. My Quinnipiac School of Law colleague Linda Meyer offered her characteristically thoughtful and incisive responses to an early, sprawling draft; without her encouragement, and that of Nancy Marder, Professor of Law at Chicago-Kent College of Law, Illinois Institute of Technology, the book would not have proceeded further. School of Law colleagues Steve Gilles, Leonard Long, Sandy Meiklejohn, and Brad Saxton read chapters and offered invaluable, highly practical criticism. My long-time co-teacher and coauthor Christina Spiesel, Adjunct Professor of Law at Quinnipiac and Senior Research Scholar at Yale Law School, sharpened my understanding of photography and semiotics, now addressed mainly in chapter 4 but touched upon elsewhere as well. The discussion of the *Murtha* case in chapter 4 is adapted from Christina's and my book *Law on Display* (2009). Greg Battye, Professor in the Faculty of Arts and Design, University of Canberra, read parts of chapter 5 and shared his wisdom regarding photography and presence. Joshua Knobe, Professor of Philosophy, Psychology, and Linguistics at Yale, read and commented on the discussion of the philosophy and psychology of mind in chapter 2; Philip Meyer, Professor of Law at Vermont Law School, critiqued my analysis of courtroom narrative in chapter 7. My former research assistant Wade Luckett, whose investigative skills and healthy skepticism helped me to probe the entire subject more deeply, reviewed the manuscript, as did another research assistant, Allison Pfeiffer.

Finally, I am grateful to my editors at the University of Chicago Press, Christie Henry and the late Chris Rhodes, copyeditor Lois Crum, editorial assistants Jillian Tsui and Gina Wadas, and three anonymous reviewers. Their careful attention, constructive suggestions, and unflagging support have helped make the book, which spans multiple disciplines and delves into sometimes technical material, as accessible as it could be.

Notes

CHAPTER ONE

1. I use the terms *perceptual experience, subjective perception,* and the like where some others might insist on other words to distinguish sensory experience from the apprehension of external objects (Boring 1942). See chapter 2 for further clarification.
2. It's impossible to determine exactly how many such cases there have been to date. There are no reported judicial decisions on the topic, trial or appellate, and only occasional passing references in the secondary literature (Dunn, n.d.; Watts 2000), with the exception of my own book chapter summarizing the topic and discussing the tinnitus case (Feigenson 2016). Some of the difficulties in acquiring information about evidentiary simulations of subjectivity may be inherent in the topic of demonstratives generally: published opinions rarely discuss them and even more rarely provide audiovisual links to the exhibits in question (see Feigenson 2011b, 13); in most cases neither the court nor the attorneys keep the exhibits for very long after the cases have ended. (Several attorneys to whom I spoke claim to have used simulations of one sort or another but did not keep the simulations or could not provide identifying case information.)

   There is some reason to believe that these cases represent the tip of a smallish iceberg. For instance, Roger Davis, the visual consultant who created the image simulations in *Devacas,* has done so in perhaps dozens of other LASIK malpractice cases as well (Todd Krouner [plaintiff's lawyer in *Devadas*], telephone interview by author, August 7, 2013); presumably, other consultants have created similar demonstrative exhibits for other clients. Jeffrey Taylor, the consultant who created the animation in *Murtha,* has created similar animations in behalf of police defendants in several other excessive force cases (Taylor, telephone interview by author, August 5, 2013); again, there may well be other consultants who have done this. Similarly, Dr. William Martin, the director of the Oregon Health and Science University Tinnitus Clinic, has created auditory simulations of tinnitus that have been used as illustrative exhibits in "several" trials and arbitrations (Martin, e-mail message to author, July 22, 2011). Shelley Watts, president of Med-Art & Legal Graphics, a medical illustrator, reported in *Trial* magazine in 2000 that she had created visual simulations of clients' impaired vision after suffering eye injuries (Watts 2000), and she now estimates that she has created simulations of impaired vision in "at least 25" cases over the years (Watts, telephone interview by author, March 27, 2015).

Nevertheless, the total number of simulations used in litigation is still likely to be relatively small. The very fact that most attorneys to whom I've mentioned the idea of simulating sensory impairments have never heard of the practice says something, as does the absence of any discussion of this sort of display from treatises and law review discussions of demonstrative evidence more generally. Inquiries to the trial consultant community through *The Jury Expert,* the online journal of the American Society of Trial Consultants, produced no responses beyond those documented in this book. In sum, my best guess is that there may be several dozen cases in which simulations have been used in one capacity or another—a minuscule proportion of the cases tried in the United States during this period, much less of the cases filed and settled—but I would not be surprised to learn that there have been more.

3. *Wilke v. Dudley* 2011, decided February 12, 2014 (discussed briefly in chapters 4 and 6).
4. Anyone who doubts the profound difference between hearing or reading a credible story of events and seeing (or hearing) a recording of those events might consider, among innumerable other examples, the saga of professional football player Ray Rice. In February 2014 Rice knocked his then-fiancée Janay Palmer unconscious while the two rode in a hotel elevator. Surveillance video shot from outside the elevator, showing the aftermath—Rice dragging the unconscious Palmer out of the elevator and standing over her—plus Rice's own verbal admission of his acts, resulted in his suspension by the league commissioner for two games of the coming football season. (Rice was also indicted for aggravated assault; charges were dropped when he agreed to undergo court-supervised counseling.) When, however, further video from the camera inside the elevator was released, showing the actual punch, outrage ensued, and the commissioner, largely responding to public opinion, revised Rice's punishment to an indefinite suspension. (Rice was reinstated in November 2014 after an arbitrator threw out the second, longer suspension as an abuse of the commissioner's discretion.) All the relevant

facts were already known or easily inferable from the first surveillance video and Rice's statements, but actually seeing the punch aroused immensely stronger and sustained reactions. Sports blogger Brian Phillips explained: "The video didn't tell us anything new. We'd already known that Rice had hit Palmer. But somehow the fact that we could now see the punch, rather than only picture it, took the reaction from intense but still normal-spec cable-channel sports shouting to full-scale cultural meltdown" (Phillips 2014).

CHAPTER TWO

1. I will also ignore (for the most part) the panoply of a person's beliefs, memories, desires, intentions, and emotions that may shape those perceptions and feels.
2. We are already entering definitional and hence conceptual minefields, and I'd like to avoid them. I use the term *perception* throughout the book to refer to sensory experience, whereas others might distinguish perception, as the apprehension of external objects, from sensation (e.g., Boring 1942). (Cf. Peacocke 1997, 341: "Corresponding to the historical distinction between sensation and perception, we can draw a distinction between sensational and representational properties of experience. Representational properties will be properties an experience has in virtue of features of its representational content; while sensational properties will be properties an experience has in virtue of some other aspect—other than its representational content—of what it is like to have that experience.") It's true that perception is usually thought to be perception *of* something, and the evidentiary simulations we'll study usually purport to recreate the litigant's perception of something. But our topic is not limited to perception in this sense, since it includes experiences (such as subjective tinnitus) that have no external, objective cause, as well as impaired perceptions or misperceptions of the external world. So, unless otherwise specified, our focus will be on what is given to or appears to the litigant rather than on what may actually be the case in the world, because our concern is with whether others can know what it's like to have the litigant's (perceptual) experience. I will also assume, contrary to some philosophers (e.g., Lewis 1956; cf. Varela and Shear 1999), that it is possible to have *knowledge* of qualia apart from the conceptualization of those experiences in language.
3. To be clear, to ask whether we can know what another person's phenomenal experience is "like" is not to ask what that experience may be *similar to.* Rather, limiting ourselves to perceptual experience, the question is whether, to what extent, and in what sense we can know *just how* things look or sound or feel to another person.

   Behind the question of how anyone can know another person's phenomenal experience stands an equally troublesome question: Do *we ourselves* actually have the phenomenal experiences we think we have? Some scientists and philosophers think the answer is no—that "perceptual consciousness . . . is a kind of false consciousness. Perceptual experience is a 'grand illusion'" (Noë and Thompson 2002, 8). That is, "it may seem to you as if your [visual] perceptual experience is detailed, continuous, and gap-free. In fact, it is fragmentary, discontinuous, and sparsely detailed" (9). Although the psychophysiology of visual perception indicates that what we *think* we see diverges from what we *really* see, these issues are not directly relevant to our inquiry, for two reasons. First, the phenomenal level of experience with which we're concerned just *is* what we *think* we see (or hear), that is, the sights or sounds that we *seem* to experience, the qualia that are available to consciousness, and not what we "actually perceive," to the extent that that is different. Second, what is most frequently at issue when simulations of subjective perceptions are offered in legal proceedings is not the top-down neural processing that enables most normally functioning persons to experience as detailed and continuous (i.e., the "unity of perception") bottom-up inputs that, owing to the nature of our optic systems (e.g.), are necessarily received as sparse and discontinuous, but rather *atypical impairments* of perceptual experience (e.g., constricted visual field, hypersensitivity to ordinary sounds, etc.) that can be differentiated from normal experience *regardless* of what the relationship may be between any given person's subjective experience and that person's bottom-up sensory inputs.

4. Practically every assertion in this part of the chapter could be and has been challenged; philosophers of mind, cognitive scientists, and others have disagreed, at great length, on pretty much every point raised, including the definitional ones. Many of these debates engage issues (e.g., whether there is anything to phenomenal experience over and above its representational content, where qualia [if they exist] are, or how phenomenal experience arises from the physical or material world) that my framing of the basic question—how can we know what it's like for another person to have the phenomenal experiences he or she does?—deliberately sidesteps. Many of the remainder are too fine-grained and technical to be helpful for my very limited introductory purposes. In the following notes, therefore, I only occasionally mention perspectives at odds with those stated in the text.
5. An extensive philosophical literature takes issue with the common sense claim that phenomenal beliefs, that is, beliefs about one's own phenomenal experiences, are incorrigible or infallible (e.g., Dennett 1991). For a nuanced response, see Shoemaker 1996.
6. Another way of putting it: philosophers and psychologists have famously had difficulty defining "consciousness" and, in particular, "phenomenal consciousness." Ned Block (1995, 230), has written: "I cannot define P-consciousness [phenomenal consciousness] in any remotely noncircular way. . . . The best one can do for P-consciousness is . . . point to the phenomenon." That is, the phenomenal consciousness with which we're concerned can best, and perhaps only, be defined *ostensively*—"there it is"—not descrip-

tively. And yet the only phenomenal consciousness to which any of us can definitively point is our own.

7. Nagel (1974), seems to go even further, not just arguing that the first-person, subjective point of view is an essential feature of experience but questioning "whether any sense can be made of experiences' having an objective character at all. Does it make sense, in other words, to ask what my experiences are *really* like, as opposed to how they appear to me?" (448). (This is not to be confused with our main question in this book, which could be rephrased as "Can we possibly know what someone else's phenomenal experiences are like *for that person?*") Another way of putting this is that it seems impossible to separate the *appearance* of conscious experience (to the person experiencing it) from *reality,* a conflation that is unique in all the world of possible objects of knowledge (Güzeldere 1997, 9–10). Similarly, John Searle says about conscious experience: "*Where appearance is concerned we cannot make the appearance-reality distinction because the appearance is the reality*" (1997, 456). Since, according to Nagel (and others), explanation consists of replacing our sense of the appearance of things with an understanding of the reality that (causally) accounts for that appearance, we cannot explain phenomenal consciousness the way we can, at least in theory, explain anything else, because there is no reality distinct from the appearance to serve as its explanation.

8. There are a variety of theories of the supervenience of mental states on physical states. Searle describes the "intuitive" notion that "mental states are totally dependent on corresponding neurophysiological states in the sense that a difference in mental states would necessarily involve a corresponding difference in neurophysiological states" (Searle 1992, 124), although not vice versa.

9. One reason is that color vision is best represented not by a two-dimensional spectrum in which hue is the only variable, but by a three-dimensional color space in which variations in saturation and lightness are also taken into account (as in the Munsell color solid; see Palmer 1999). There are asymmetries in this color space, so that a red-green inversion (say) would have other perceptual ramifications that could be behaviorally detected (Byrne 2014).

10. Philosophers who have wielded the inverted-spectrum scenario or its variants as an argument for the ontological independence of qualia from physicalism or functionalism must suppose that any such inversion would be physically, functionally, and behaviorally undetectable (e.g., Shoemaker 1996, 141: "The existence of complete intersubjective inversion would be behaviorally undetectable"). Despite some fascinating support for the empirical possibility of undetectable color inversion (Nida-Rümelin 1996), the weight of vision science seems to be against it (for a review, see Byrne 2014). Some philosophers argue that the mere *logical* possibility that one person's qualia could vary from the norm without our having any way of knowing that was the case is enough to support their claim that we cannot be sure that we know what another person's phenomenal experiences are like. I do

not address that argument here, since my concern is with reasons for and against believing, as a *practical* matter, that we can know what another's qualia are like.

11. This is known as the "theory theory" of mind perception: Starting in early childhood, we develop intuitive theories of how people's mental states explain their behaviors, and then we use our observations of their behaviors (and the situation) to draw inferences about their mental states (e.g., Epley and Waytz 2010, 1:498). The main alternative theory of mind perception in psychology (and neuroscience) is "simulation theory," to be discussed next.
12. One indication of how good most people are at gauging others' mental states is the extensive research on autistic persons, who lack this ability (e.g., Baron-Cohen, Tager-Flusberg, and Cohen 2000). Indeed, Baron-Cohen and others refer to "mindblindness" as an essential component of autism (Baron-Cohen et al. 2005).
13. "Once eyes and bodies are merged, our minds tend to merge as well. Thoughts and feelings come from what we're looking at and how our bodies are reacting to it, so when two people are watching something and reacting similarly, they are likely to be feeling and thinking similarly as well" (Epley 2014, 44). Philosophers sometimes refer to this as the *argument from analogy.*
14. Our inferences about others' mental states are systematically anchored by the most immediate, accessible information: our own mental states. Projecting our own minds onto others, we tend to overestimate our ability to see or feel what they do (Epley 2014; Epley and Caruso 2009, 300–302), and this problem becomes larger the less we know about those others' minds.
15. Any mental representation arising from merely observing another person perform an action, as opposed to performing it oneself, moreover, would presumably lack the feedback and further subjective awareness that would result from actually having performed the action, and so it would not produce a robust sense of what it's like for the person observed to have the experience of actually performing it.
16. Peter Carruthers (2000, 28) argues for a *recognition* principle to define "knowing what it's like": "You know what it's like to undergo a certain kind of experience when you can (either from memory, or using suitably-rich background knowledge) construct an imagistic representation of the experience, which is then sufficient to enable you to *recognise* that experience, without interference, *if* you were to undergo it. By this criterion, it is probably possible for a woman who has never undergone labour to know what it is like to undergo labour." Although I can't set out a full critique here, this criterion for "knowing what it's like" seems to me to be too weak. The woman who has not undergone labor would surely know on the basis of background knowledge that it usually involves tremendous pain, often prolonged, in certain parts of the body, and on that basis would be able to "recognize" the experience of undergoing labor (as opposed to, say, being knocked on the head). But I imagine that when having the actual experience for the first time, if

able to think about it at all, she would say something to the effect of, "So *this* is what it's like. I had *no idea*" (not to mention not being able to anticipate the other thoughts and emotions, most importantly those associated with impending motherhood, that might well endow her pain with profound meanings).

17. Hume expressed it this way:

> Suppose therefore a person to have enjoyed his sight for thirty years, and to have become perfectly well acquainted with colours of all kinds, excepting one particular shade of blue, for instance, which it never has been his fortune to meet with. Let all the different shades of that colour, except that single one be plac'd before him, descending gradually from the deepest to the lightest; 'tis plain, that he will perceive a blank, where that shade is wanting and will be sensible, that there is a greater distance in that place betwixt the contiguous colours, than in any other. Now I ask, whether 'tis possible for him, from his own imagination, to supply this deficiency, and raise up to himself the idea of that particular shade, tho' it had never been conveyed to him by his senses? I believe there are few but will be of opinion that he can; and this may serve as a proof, that the simple ideas are not always derived from the correspondent impressions. ([1739] 1896, pt. 1, sec. 1)

See also Alter 2008; Carruthers 2000.

18. Nagel argues a similar point within the framework (discussed earlier) about subjective versus objective knowledge: "There is a sense in which phenomenological facts are perfectly objective: one person can know or say of another what the quality of the other's experience is. They are subjective, however, in the sense that even this objective ascription of experience is possible only for someone sufficiently similar to the object of ascription to be able to adopt his point of view—to understand the ascription in the first person as well as in the third, so to speak. The more different from oneself the other experiencer is, the less success one can expect with this enterprise" (1974, 442).
19. In short, for phenomenologists, experience as a potential object of knowledge is always *pre-interpreted* (through the concepts that phenomenology elucidates), and that's equally true of others' experiences and our own. Instead of the seemingly unbridgeable gulf between your qualia and mine, we have common ground on which reliable understanding of perceptual experience can be founded.
20. Husserl "seeks knowledge of how we *represent* or *constitute* the world and its features in our experience, not knowledge of mere sensory qualia. . . . Ultimately, it is not knowledge of my or anyone's *individual* conscious experiences that Husserl hopes to acquire through phenomenology, but rather of the *essences* of *types* of conscious experience and their interrelations" (Smith and Thomasson 2005, 126). Thus, sense data with qualitatively distinct "feels"—the way things look or sound, say, to the perceiver—matter to the

extent that they motivate the perceiver to become aware of intentional objects (McKenna 1997).

21. Some phenomenologists would recommend reframing the question of knowing what others' experiences are like. For instance, philosopher Shaun Gallagher argues that, as against the "theory theory," simulation theory, and the mirror neuron approaches outlined earlier, all of which depend on third-person observation, "our relations with others are better characterized in terms of second-person interaction where most of what we need for a pragmatic understanding of the other person are not hidden mental states, but embodied expressions that we can easily perceive on their faces, in their postures, movements, and gestures. . . . On the phenomenological view, *interaction,* rather than observation, constitutes our primary way of being with others" (2012a, 87–88). Furthermore, drawing on Heidegger, Merleau-Ponty, and others, Gallagher and philosopher Dan Zahavi write:

    > Our typical understanding of others is contextual and . . . empathy, properly understood, is not a question of feelingly projecting oneself into the other, but rather . . . an ability to access the life of the mind of others in their expressive behavior and meaningful action. . . . In contrast to theory-of-mind approaches that define the problem as trying to access the other person's mind, phenomenological approaches suggest that a more productive focus is on the other person's world. . . . In effect, to understand other persons I do not primarily have to get into their minds; rather, I have to pay attention to the world that I already share with them. (2012, 213)

    In chapter 7 I return to the topic of phenomenological knowledge of others in the context of legal judgment.

22. "The Inner Life of a Cell," for instance, created by scientific animator David Bolinsky for cellular biology students at Harvard University and available online, visualizes microbiological knowledge with exceptional vividness ("Inner Life" 2006).

23. I have more to say about indexicality in chapter 4 and elsewhere.

24. Philosopher of science R. I. G. Hughes (1999, 141–42) explains that computer simulations (he is writing about what he calls "computer experiments") can yield "information about the actual world, about possible worlds, or about impossible worlds. . . . The fact that computer experimentation can give us information about many kinds of worlds, however, tells us something that should have been obvious all along: that, lacking other data, we can never evaluate the information that these experiments provide."

25. For instance, writing about a computer simulation of atomic interactions, physicist Fritz Rohrlich remarks, "There is clearly a tendency to forget that these figures are the results of a computer simulation, of a calculation; they are not photographs of a material physical model" (quoted in Hughes 1999,

130). (Cf. the characterization of the auditory simulation in *Janson* as a "recording," discussed in chapter 5.)

26. At the same time, and contributing to this epistemological anxiety, we must recognize "that primal, never-satisfied desire to reproduce [in art] consciousness-altering conditions. Virtual reality is only the latest in a long series of cave-like boxes seeking to recreate the brilliance and immediacy of the brain traces we see during altered states" (Stafford 2007, 122).

27. Any inquiry into the kind of knowledge of other minds that evidentiary simulations of subjectivity can yield is necessarily conducted at a particular point in our cultural and intellectual history, at which notions of the self are contested in particular ways. The sense of human subjectivity that Turkle and others I mention in the text seem anxious to protect appears to be rooted in an idea of the conscious (and self-conscious) unitary self that is consonant with ordinary intuition. The conception of individuals as distributable *data*—regarding their physical persons, their social situations, and their behaviors—generates one of the most important contemporary challenges to that traditional, intuitive understanding. Ian Hacking (1990, 3) writes that the collecting of personal data beginning in the early nineteenth century "has affected . . . the ways in which we describe our neighbor. It has profoundly transformed . . . who we try to be, and what we think of ourselves." The bureaucratic and, following Foucault, essentially disciplinary practices employing and furthering the conception of individuals-as-data have expanded immeasurably in our own time, aided by digital data gathering and analysis. Turkle herself recognized something similar when she wrote in *Life on the Screen* that "windows [on computer screens] have become a powerful metaphor for thinking about the self as a multiple, distributed system" (1995, 14) (see Dormehl, 2014). My concern in this chapter and throughout the book, however, is with the notions of the self that judges and jurors are most likely to bring to court. Turkle's sense of the self as self-conscious, embodied, and shaped by a subconscious, and thus inherently resistant to adequate digital representation, certainly resonates with popular belief.

28. To be more precise, the proponent would think that a simulation would help her or him achieve a more favorable outcome only when it makes the client whose experiences are being digitally simulated a more credible and sympathetic figure than the client would be without that evidence.

CHAPTER THREE

1. Analyzing the probative value of simulations of subjectivity in terms of the *reliability* of the underlying data and of the translation of those data into the visible or audible form of the exhibit omits what is ordinarily another requisite element of probative value: *how far* the item of evidence tends to *support*

the fact it is offered to prove. For instance, an item of circumstantial evidence may fully deserve belief yet not establish the fact it is offered to prove because other, contrary factual conclusions may also be inferred from that evidence. As evidence professor Charles McCormick's famous aphorism has it, "a brick is not a wall" (Broun 2006, 308). Not to overdo the metaphor, but the more bricks (in the right places), or rather, the greater the proportion of bricks to those needed to construct the whole wall, the greater the support.

In the case of a litigant's subjective perceptual experience, however, the "feel" of that perceptual experience just *is* the fact of the matter, so to the extent a demonstrative exhibit faithfully recreates (or, if you prefer, accurately models all relevant aspects of) that experience, it would seem to be not just a brick or even many bricks, but the whole wall. *If* the simulation is sufficiently reliable, then there would seem to be no further question about how far that simulation tends to support the fact it is offered to prove. Philosopher Susan Haack (2014, 14) explains that in general, "how well a body of evidence supports a conclusion [of fact] depends on the degree of explanatory integration of this evidence with that conclusion" and that where the evidence is experiential, there is a need for "propositional proxies" for that evidence because the explanatory account is itself a set of propositions. But where the factual conclusion is *what it's like* for the litigant to experience what he or she does (i.e., is itself experiential), then no propositional integration of experiential evidence and conclusion of fact need be constructed. Instead of substituting a propositional proxy for the experiential evidence (that is, the experience the simulation provides) and then seeing how well that proxy can be integrated with the propositional factual conclusion, the experiential evidence claims simply to *recreate* the experiential factual conclusion itself. Thus, the issue of evidentiary support as a separate element of probative value disappears.

One counterargument might be that the factual conclusion a simulation of subjectivity is offered to prove (in a personal injury case) is what it's like for the litigant to *live with* her or his perceptual experience more or less *all the time,* and that no evidentiary simulation, limited as it must be in both time and space, can replicate what *that's* like. This opens up the kind of gap between evidence and conclusion of fact that raises the question of how well the evidence supports the fact, and hence demands analysis in terms of the degree of integration of the (propositional) explanatory account. One response to this counterargument might be to characterize the fact to be proved so as to conform to the experiential evidence the simulation makes available; decision makers can *then* be invited to infer what the entirety of the litigant's conscious life is like. That is, the simulation becomes a kind of *direct* evidence with regard to what it's like to experience what the litigant does in the circumstances or for the duration that the simulation depicts, but a kind of *circumstantial* evidence with regard to what it's like to experience that perceptual state more or less all the time. (The litigant's oral testimony would also provide direct evidence of the latter.) A second response might be that at least some simulations so strongly imply that the experiences they purport to replicate extend to the entirety of the litigant's waking life that they effectively constitute the "entire wall" with respect to that fact as well.

The preceding analysis may not be uniquely true of experiential evidence offered in support of experiential facts. Arguably, *any* direct evidence, to the extent it's reliable (or, in a subjectivist account of evidence, to the extent it's believed), establishes the fact it is offered to prove, without the need for any fuller explanatory account or the need to determine how well the item of evidence can be integrated into any such account. To appreciate what makes experiential evidence offered in support of experiential facts a highly unusual, if not sui generis, type of proof, I turn to Haack's (2014) third criterion for evaluating the quality of evidence going to prove a conclusion of fact: how *comprehensively* the evidence has been marshaled. The more potentially relevant evidence that's missing, the less of a warrant for the fact to be proved the evidence in question establishes (presumably because, were that missing evidence to be found, it might turn out to make the fact in question less rather than more likely to be the case). For most kinds of facts, numerous sorts of evidence can readily be imagined and may as a practical matter exist, so it makes good sense to determine how comprehensive the proof is in relation to the total body of possible evidence. With regard to proof of a litigant's phenomenal experience, however, there is typically very little evidence the litigant himself does not marshal that could undermine his claim about what it's like to see or hear as he does. Instead, the comprehensiveness of the simulation of subjectivity is largely folded into the taxonomy of simulations that follow. That is, once the litigant *describes* what his subjective experience is like, we might ask the comprehensiveness question: what further relevant evidence of that experience could there be? One answer is psychophysical testing to confirm and specify with greater precision what the experience is like (thus differentiating the second from the first type of simulation). Another is direct physical measurement of the perceptual apparatus, from which the subjective experience can be determined (thus differentiating the third type of simulation). Only a very limited amount of potentially available "missing evidence" remains: for example, evidence from other witnesses concerning the litigant's behavior that is arguably inconsistent with the severity of the impairments the litigant claims.

In short, because (with these various provisos) the question of how well the simulation supports the fact it's offered to prove collapses into its reliability, and the question of how comprehensive the simulation is largely does so as well, we can meaningfully proceed to evaluate the probative value of simulations of subjectivity as a question of reliability alone, as I have.

2. To be as straightforward and accessible as possible, I have designed my taxonomy in terms of the more or less positivist epistemology generally as-

sumed by the law of evidence. There are certainly other ways of approaching the epistemology of trial evidence. For instance, we could profitably adopt a *constructivist* (e.g., Hacking 1999; Latour 1999) rather than a positivist approach to the fashioning of facts at trial. Constructivism offers more explanatory power in at least two respects. First, based on the principle that facts are partly constituted by how we represent them, constructivism's more capacious sense of knowledge brings within epistemology much of what the traditional positivist approach consigns to psychology, sociology, rhetoric, and aesthetics. Second, to understand the relationship between the forms and objects of knowledge, it replaces the often problematic concept of indexicality with a more articulated and nuanced inquiry into (for instance) the *chains of transformation* (Latour 1999) connecting knowledge to its referents.

I have, nevertheless, adopted the traditional approach. It is (as already noted) the epistemology underlying the law as generally understood and practiced, so it will be more familiar to lawyers, judges, and many legal scholars. Setting out the background theory and method needed to appreciate the virtues of constructivism could be off-putting to some readers. And I don't want to discourage those unwilling to accept a constructivist approach from engaging with the case studies that form the core of the book.

3. William Martin, e-mail message to author, July 22, 2011.
4. At the request of the plaintiff's attorney, the names of the parties have been changed to protect the plaintiff's privacy.
5. These three kinds of simulations comprise a taxonomy of "pure" types. In actual litigation, the types may be combined in various ways. For instance, in *Devadas,* the photo simulations were created by a visual consultant in collaboration with the plaintiff and were not derived from clinical test data, making them "artist's sketch" demonstratives, but an expert neuro-ophthalmologist who examined the plaintiff for purposes of litigation also authenticated the simulations as "consistent" with his wavefront data, arguably making the photos a kind of hybrid of types. A plaintiff's attorney might conceivably use more than one kind of simulation in a case—for instance, both a photo simulation and an objective wavefront-based image simulation to show post-LASIK visual complications—although this does not appear to have been done yet (Todd Krouner, telephone interview by author, August 7, 2013).
6. One could go further. It could be argued that, *in principle,* words are incapable of expressing phenomenal experience adequately, because "perceptual contents are analog. . . . Perceptions of colour, for example, allow us to make an indefinite number of fine-grained discriminations, which far outstrip our powers of categorization and description" (Carruthers 2000, 11; see also Goodman 1976, 229–30) (pictures are a more "replete" symbol system than words). The great nineteenth-century German physiologist and physicist Hermann von Helmholtz, a pioneer in the measurement of human vision

and hearing, remarked on "the impossibility of describing sensations . . . in words" (quoted in Lenoir 1993, 124). It can even be argued that words can get in the way of some experiences. Neuroanatomist Jill Bolte Taylor explained in a 2008 TED talk, "My Stroke of Insight," that when her "brain chatter" stopped after a massive stroke, she was able to experience a completely different type of consciousness, a "beautiful" and "euphori[c] sense of peacefulness" (Taylor 2008).

7. The belief goes back to ancient Greece. Explaining the theory of sensory knowledge held by Empedocles, Democritus, and Epicurus, Boring (1942, 5) writes: "It is natural to attempt to explain representative adequacy by similarity." Or, more recently, art historian Martin Kemp (2014, 344) has observed: "The naturalistic image, which overtly or implicitly claims significant elements of matching with the observer's direct experience of what is being represented, is particularly potent in evoking our trust."
8. I would like to thank my colleague Brad Saxton, professor of law at Quinnipiac University School of Law, for suggesting this example.
9. American Tinnitus Association, www.ata.org/sounds-of-tinnitus (last visited December 27, 2014).
10. Martin e-mail message.
11. When pictures represent more fully than words alone do (see Elkins 1999, 73–74, discussing Goodman 1976), they necessarily *add* to the litigant's verbal account.
12. That is, whatever level of reliability jurors attribute to the litigant's testimony, as long as it's not zero, that same level of reliability attaches to *more information* about the fact of the matter, and thus that additional information adds probative value. Consider also that ordinary police artists' sketches of persons observed by eyewitnesses are regarded as substantive evidence, that is to say, as potentially probative, because they are subject to the hearsay rule, which means that they are tantamount to statements offered to prove the truth of what they assert. (Because they are treated as prior identifications of a person under Federal Rule of Evidence 801(d)(1)(C), these sketches are technically not hearsay, as long as the eyewitness testifies and is subject to cross-examination concerning her prior identification.) By analogy, might not artist's sketches that depict a litigant's subjective perceptions (as opposed to external reality), and that are similarly authenticated by the eyewitness who avers that they fairly and accurately represent those perceptions, be regarded as potentially probative as well?
13. This appears to have been the original understanding of *all* demonstrative evidence when the doctrinal category was created in the late nineteenth century; see Mnookin 1998.
14. There is some authority for an even less stringent standard for admitting purely illustrative evidence: the proponent need only show that the exhibit will help jurors to understand the testimony it illustrates (e.g., *State v. Dontigney* 1990). Arguably, however, there is not much difference between this

test and the one stated in the text, since in order to be helpful, an illustrative exhibit presumably must fairly and accurately represent what it purports to.

15. See Federal Rules of Evidence 2014, 901(b)(9).
16. In federal court and about half of state courts, the admissibility of expert evidence is governed by *Daubert,* which requires the trial judge to assess the reliability of a proffer of expert evidence. The remaining states continue to follow the older test from *Frye v. United States* (1923), which allows the trial judge to admit expert evidence if the principles and methods on which it is based are "generally accepted" in the relevant scientific community. In both law and practice, variations among states are much more complex than this. The scholarly literature discussing the standards for admissibility of scientific and other expert evidence since *Daubert* is immense.
17. Or in settlement negotiations (as in *Smith,* the case of the woman with idiopathic intracranial hypertension).

CHAPTER FOUR

1. If the condition is intermittent, the testifying litigant may have to recall what previous episodes of impairment were like. And if the perception in question occurred only in the past, as in the *Murtha* case discussed below, then of course the accuracy of memory may be an issue.
2. Observers (i.e., neither tappers nor listeners) who were told the name of the tune beforehand overestimated the percentage of listeners who would correctly identify the tune just as tappers did (average estimate 50%), so the overestimation was due not to the act of tapping but to the mental (auditory) imagery associated with knowing the song and the failure to take into account that listeners would not have access to those thoughts.
3. In addition, the plaintiffs called an ink dating analysis expert, who testified that Dr. Niksarli had intentionally and artificially aged a note in his chart concerning his purported conversation with the patient and his wife concerning the risks, benefits, and alternatives to the LASIK surgery.
4. The trial judge in *Devadas,* in rejecting the defendants' posttrial motion for a new trial or judgment notwithstanding the verdict on the ground that the verdict was excessive, explicitly cited *Schiffer* as precedent for the reasonableness of the $5.6 million award (*Devadas v. Niksarli,* Memorandum Decision, July 9, 2010, 14). I discuss *Schiffer* in chapter 6.
5. Todd Krouner, telephone interview by author, June 19, 2012.
6. VisionSimulations.com, www.visionsimulations.com/ (last visited September 14, 2012).
7. Unlike most other crucial testimony and exhibits, however, the photo simulations were hardly subject to any serious criticism or objection from opposing counsel or other witnesses. One of the defendant's experts, Dr. Peter Hersh, an ophthalmologist, did suggest the photo simulations may have overstated how impaired Devadas's visual acuity was (trial transcript,

June 3, 2009, 1801–2). But keratoconus, the effects of which the exhibits were intended to illustrate, is associated with other visual defects besides reduced sharpness of vision. And in his closing argument, defense lawyer Ekblom told jurors that "instead [of direct testimony by Devadas about what he couldn't do because of his impaired eyesight] we got the pictures, which I submit are fanciful indications of what he can see and not see" (*Devadas* transcript, June 8, 2009, 2295). "Fanciful" connotes unreliable, even imaginary, but standing alone it's just an epithet; it's not an argument as to *why* the pictures may not have faithfully replicated Devadas's subjective vision. And in fact, Devadas *did* testify about his impairments and their effects on his life (as discussed later in the chapter).

8. The words *halos* and *starbursts* might not even be fully intelligible apart from the pictures.
9. For instance, nineteenth-century Czech physiologist Jan Purkinje investigated afterimages by using himself as a subject and then meticulously drawing what he observed ([1823] 2001; for discussions of Purkinje's drawings of afterimages, see Canales 2011; Crary 1990). So did other scientists investigating other sorts of subjective visual sensations (e.g., Helmholtz [1867] 1924). In the mid-twentieth century, psychologist Angiola Massuco Costa and neuroscientist John Smythies published drawings of the highly varied patterns their respective experimental subjects saw when exposed to strobe lights (on Costa, see Canales 2011; Smythies 1959; 1960). This method of documenting observational research into subjective visual phenomena continues today (e.g., Allefeld et al. 2011).
10. Early scientific observers of visual phenomena pointed to what they claimed was the great difference between their own observational discipline and those of laypeople. Thus, physiologist Rudolph Wagner (1844, 594): "There is the greatest difference among individuals in point of retinal impressibility. . . . Different eyes seem to have very different capacities to form spectral or after-images. . . . Want of attention and of the faculty of observation, however, seem frequently to be at the bottom of [this]." To the same effect, Helmholtz ([1867] 1924, 3:6):

    > We are not in the habit of observing our sensations accurately, except as they are useful in enabling us to recognize external objects. On the contrary, we are wont to disregard all parts of the sensations that are of no importance so far as external objects are concerned. Thus in most cases some special assistance and training are needed in order to observe these latter subjective sensations. It might seem that nothing could be easier than to be conscious of one's own sensations; and yet experience shows that for the discovery of subjective sensations some special talent is needed, such as Purkinje manifested in the highest degree.

11. For a brief explanation of the concept of just noticeable difference (JND), see chapter 5.

12. Philosopher of mind Michael Tye (2003, 20), in the course of a longer discussion of whether the representational content of perceptual experience must vary if the phenomenal content does, remarks: "It seems obvious that, in principle, an experimental set-up could be devised that would leave one without any way of telling from the phenomenal character of one's visual experience . . . whether one had shifted from seeing a sharp screen image through a blur to seeing clearly a suitably blurred version of that same screen image in at least some cases." This is analogous to the demonstrative strategy in *Devadas*. In principle, there need not be any difference between seeing an object with blurred vision (the plaintiff's condition) and seeing clearly that same object suitably blurred (the simulation presented to the jurors). Yet, as explained in the text, there are several reasons to doubt whether this ideal parallel can be created in the courtroom.
13. It's more complicated than this, of course; "his experience of the world" unfolds over time, including the present of his constant visual saccades and fixations (e.g., Lauwereyns 2012), and is infused with his memories and expectations based on his past visual and other experiences. I return later to some differences between the evidentiary simulations and litigants' lived perceptual experiences.
14. If the tinnitus sound is in only one ear or is different in the other ear, the patient can still make the comparisons between his tinnitus and the external tone needed to determine the "matching" tone. Or, in the *Janson* case (discussed in chapter 5), although the plaintiff could not directly confirm that the external tone of the sound file was as loud as his tinnitus, a match could be indirectly derived by increasing the volume of the tone until he could hear it, and then reducing the volume back down to the (highest) level at which he could not.
15. See Gescheider 1997 on time errors in psychophysical measurement.
16. No photo or video *just* records the imprint of reality, in the way that (to use Charles Sanders Peirce's famous example) the footprint that Robinson Crusoe found in the sand was an indexical sign of the existence of some creature (Sebeok 1994). Every photo or video is deliberately constructed, involving many choices on the part of its maker (regarding camera angle, depth of field, and lighting, among many others), as well as the choices embedded in the design of the equipment (Spiesel 2010), so that what results is not so much a copy or record of the reality in front of the lens as it is a newly fashioned reality of its own. Art historian John Tagg (1988, 2–3) offers a paradigmatic (if somewhat hyperbolic) critique of photographic indexicality: "*Every* photograph is the result of specific and, in every sense, significant distortions which render its relation to any prior reality deeply problematic and raise the question of the determining level of the material apparatus and of the social practices within which photography takes place. . . . The indexical nature of the photograph—the causative link between the pre-photographic referent

and the sign—is therefore highly complex, irreversible, and can guarantee nothing at the level of meaning" (emphasis in original). In a related vein, Peter Galassi, former curator of photography at the Museum of Modern Art in New York, reviewing a retrospective of the work of photographer Garry Winogrand, has written: "Photography inescapably but surreptitiously transforms what it describes. If you want your picture to look the way the scene in front of you feels, you are likely to be disappointed, and no matter how the picture turns out everyone else is likely to assume that the camera simply copied what was there. But along with the probability of failure there is the rare chance of backdoor success: a fortuitous scene that never existed but carries the authority of reality copied by the camera" (2013, 44–45). To treat photos as indexical is also, obviously, not to say that the evidence they provide is necessarily unambiguous or conclusive as to the facts they may be offered to prove, or indeed that they cannot be misleading or simply false. Indeed, to treat photographs as providing factual evidence at all is in part the consequence of institutional and cultural deployments of photography *as evidence*, beginning in the mid-nineteenth century—for instance, in police and medical files and other compendia of information about those on the margins of society (e.g., Tagg 1988).

In *digital* photography and videography, moreover, the physical connection between the photographed object and the image on analog film is disrupted, so that it is often remarked that digital images are not indexical at all. In the words of architect and media theorist William J. Mitchell, "the referent has become unstuck" (1992, 31). On the other hand, ordinary unedited digital images retain their *deictic* or pointing function, providing evidence that *this* event or scene was in front of the lens when the picture was taken. In addition, since the belief that even analog photos and videos constitute indexical evidence for the reality in front of the lens has always been a matter not just of physics but of cultural habits, specifically viewer expectations, to the extent that digital photos and videos are taken or shot and then presented to serve the same functions as their analog precursors (for instance, as documentation of actual events), it's equally plausible to regard digital photos and videos as indexical (Dzenko 2009, 19).

17. To put it another way: when either an artist's sketch or a photo is offered as an accurate depiction of what it purports to depict, there is a *declaration* to this effect. In the case of the artist's sketch, that declaration comes from the litigant himself when he authenticates the exhibit as a "fair and accurate representation" of his perceptual experience. These words function as a sort of caption to the simulation. In the case of the photo, by contrast, the declaration is partly implicit in the photo itself; more specifically, the *act* of having taken the photo is itself a performative gesture that declares what is depicted to have been the case (Green and Lowry 2003, 47). The photo thus makes a claim to depict the real that is *independent* of any witness's statement that the

photo corresponds to what it depicts, although an authenticating witness must still testify that the photo is a fair and accurate representation of what was happening at a particular time and place, to establish its relevance as well as its reliability. Photos and videos are not "self-authenticating" in the technical evidentiary sense of needing no witness to lay a foundation for their admissibility (Federal Rules of Evidence 2014, 902), but photography and videography produce objects with independent probative force (i.e., to prove the existence of what they depict, as they depict it, at the time and place the photo was taken or the video shot) in a way that drawings, analog or digital, do not.

18. More recently, on the presumed veridicality of photography in non-US evidence law, see Torresi 2014, 127–28.
19. See note 16 above.
20. The word "Photoshop" was used by counsel during sidebar conferences but not in front of the jury.
21. See note 16 above.
22. See "How Digital Cameras Work" 2014 (demosaicing algorithms in consumer-level digital cameras).
23. See also Spiesel 2009, 399–400, discussing the work of Alfred Yarbus on individual differences in sequence of eye movements while looking at same picture, depending in part on verbal priming.
24. I discuss these issues in much more detail in chapter 7.
25. The matter is more complicated than this. *Subjectivity* in the sense with which we are concerned in this book has primarily to do with interindividual differences in visual (or other sensory) experience. Art historian Jonathan Crary, in his important work *Techniques of the Observer*, examines "subjective vision" in a different sense: the transition from the Enlightenment conception of human vision as an objective and privileged means of knowing the real, symbolized by the camera obscura's ability to capture external reality transparently, to a modernist conception of vision as embodied and hence opaque, no longer the untroubled "mirror of nature." He places the transition, "the moment when the visible escapes from the timeless order of the camera obscura and becomes lodged in another apparatus, within the unstable physiology and temporality of the human body" (1990, 70), at the beginning of the nineteenth century, when Goethe, in the *Theory of Colors* (1810), describes the experience of seeing transitory colored afterimages when staring at a spot of sunlight admitted into a camera obscura and then continuing to stare at that point after the hole admitting the light is shut. This is subjectivity as opposed to objective vision (and knowledge of the world), but it is a subjectivity that all people have in common; it is not a question of interindividual differences. *This* kind of subjectivity of vision could best be ascertained by paying attention to phenomena such as afterimages, in which sensation is divorced from the perception of external objects.

26. This is precisely how the *personal equation*, referring to differences between individual astronomers' measurements of the times of transit of stars across the meridian, was discovered at the turn of the nineteenth century and measured with increasing precision over the course of that century (Duncombe 1945; Schaffer 1988).
27. See note 25 above.
28. At the motion hearing in *Wilke v. Dudley* (2011), attorney Mark Budzinski, representing the defendant, raised precisely this point: "Let's deal with the control images that depict 20/20 vision that's clear. We know that's not how Mr. Wilke saw before his LASIK. That's why he had LASIK, so we know those are inaccurate by definition" (*Wilke* hearing transcript, December 12, 2013, n.p.). Budzinski has since explained that the argument of Todd Krouner (the plaintiff's attorney) "was to demonstrate to the jury how Mr. Wilke's vision currently was, and what a person with normal vision would see—he's trying to establish a baseline, and asking the jury to award damages based on the difference. But the entire analysis starts with a flawed premise: The baseline is by definition inaccurate" (Mark Budzinski, telephone interview by author, February 6, 2015). At the motion hearing, Krouner attempted to sidestep this point: "We are not offering the control photo to say this is what Mr. Wilke saw prior to 2007. . . . The control photo is simply for the jury's benefit to know this is the Radisson hotel. This is what it looks like without fuzz, without visual distortion; and then when you add glare, halos, and the panoply of visual quality complaints and visual acuity issues, this is how much worse it gets for Mr. Wilke" (*Wilke* transcript, December 12, 2013, n.p.). Trial Judge Mark McGinnis concluded that admitting the photos would "confuse the issues potentially," and he excluded them.
29. Todd Krouner, telephone interview by author, August 7, 2013.
30. Krouner (interview, August 7, 2013) has told me he was "surprised" that Devadas and Davis did not produce a family picture.
31. Krouner interview, August 7, 2013.
32. On viewers' urge to seek narratives behind and around photographic images, see Battye 2014.
33. I elaborate on this theme in chapter 7.
34. See note 7 above.
35. For this reason, the visual experience recreated in *Murtha* could not be anything other than an artist's-sketch type of simulation, because it is not possible, at least given current technology, to measure past conscious states reliably.
36. This discussion is adapted from Feigenson and Spiesel 2009, 92–98.
37. Jeffrey Taylor, telephone interview by author, August 5, 2013.
38. Ibid.
39. Technically, in some systems the dashcam is always recording but the footage is constantly overwritten until the lights go on, in which case the preceding thirty or sixty seconds are also retrieved from the cache and saved.

CHAPTER FIVE

1. In Gustav Fechner's own (translated) words, psychophysics is "an exact theory of the functionally dependent relations of body and soul or, more generally, of the material and the mental, of the physical and the psychological worlds" ([1860] 1966, 7). This basic definition itself was anticipated by, among others, Jan Purkinje, who wrote in 1819: "It is an imperative belief of the natural scientist that each and every modification of a subjective state in the sphere of the senses corresponds to an objective state" (Wade and Brožek 2001, 1). Elsewhere, Wade and Brožek refer to Purkinje's desire to provide physiological accounts of subjective experiences as his "exact subjectivism" (22).
2. To be more precise, since a person's responses to the same stimulus or pairs of stimuli may vary from one exposure to another for any number of reasons, the same stimuli are presented repeatedly, in randomized order, yielding a *curve* that describes the percentage of positive responses (experiencing a sensation, in a test of perceptual threshold, or being able to discriminate between different stimuli, in a test of JND) at each stimulus intensity. The curve is the *psychometric function* for those stimulus intensities. The point at which the person senses the stimulus (or the difference between stimuli) at least 50% of the time defines the subject's perceptual threshold or JND, as the case may be. The steeper the curve, the smaller the difference in intensity needed to prompt a sensation or ability to discriminate at least half the time, hence the greater the subject's *sensitivity*. For a discussion of the basic methods and some of their more recent variations, see Gescheider 1997.
3. For a discussion of precursors of clinical perimetry, including Purkinje's measurements of the range of the normal visual field, see Lloyd 1936.
4. These data are first presented numerically, with a number at each location in *decibels*, ranging from 0 to 50. These numbers are actually the *reciprocal* of stimulus intensity, which is measured in *apostilbs* (see Rowe 2006; Walsh 2011). The decibel readings represent the density of the filter used to reduce the intensity of the maximally emitting bulb, so the denser the filter, the higher the decibel reading, the *lower* the intensity of the light that can be perceived, and thus the *more sensitive* the person's vision at that location. This numerical readout is accompanied by a *greyscale map* that represents those same values as darker squares the higher the stimulus threshold, so that a location at which the person does not perceive even the strongest test stimulus is shown in black. The greyscale map thus provides a roughly iconic picture of the person's visual field: the gradations present a more nuanced picture than the dichotomous isopter map generated by manual kinetic perimetry, which indicates only the boundary between what can be seen and what can't. Other sorts of data are also presented, such as numerical and/or greyscale maps comparing the person's visual sensitivity at each location to age-matched norms (Rowe 2006; see also Budenz 1997).

5. It's worth emphasizing that the measurement of the visual field began and developed as a way of diagnosing neurological disorders, not simply as part of experimental research. The goal was to establish precise correlations between observed visual field impairments and pathologies in the visual pathway in the brain (Simpson and Crompton 2008a; 2008b). That is, perimetry has from its origins been a *clinical* science, although its role in diagnosing neurological problems and planning surgery has been reduced in recent decades owing to the development of noninvasive brain imaging techniques such as CT and MRI.
6. Michael Jainchill, interview by author, Hartford, CT, July 1, 2013.
7. Ibid.
8. Ibid.; video producer and editor Patrick Volk, interview by author, Woodbridge, CT, March 19, 2013.
9. Neuro-ophthalmologist Robert Lesser, telephone interview by author, July 12, 2013.
10. Jainchill interview.
11. Ibid.; Volk interview.
12. Jainchill interview.
13. Robert Silva, telephone interview by author, July 29, 2013.
14. These include age-related loss in sensitivity (which results in a contraction of the isopters when kinetic perimetry is used); refractive error and defocus (changing the perceived luminance of the target and hence the visual threshold for perceiving small stimuli); loss of fixation during the test (increasing the variability of results, since stimuli are more easily perceived the closer to the center of the field they are); experience effects (patients perform better the more experienced they are with that sort of test); fatigue (leading to loss of attention, resulting in more false negatives, slower reaction times, and more fluctuation); and adaptation (patients' eyes need some time to adjust to the level of light in the test environment, so if the test is begun before the eyes have adapted to the background illumination, results during that period will be inaccurate) (Henson 1993, 44–55).
15. A fourth point is that the *examiner* may also introduce variability and imprecision in a kinetic test. For instance, an examiner in a kinetic field test who (inadvertently) varies the speed at which stimuli are moved from outside to inside the visual field will reduce the measured area of the visual field because the faster the movement, the farther the stimulus travels before the patient detects it (Henson 1993). In manual Goldmann perimetry, the recording of the data also introduces a small amount of imprecision (the phrase "margin of error" would be apt) beyond what is already inherent in any sampling technique.
16. The reliability of results can be enhanced in several ways. The clinician can properly calibrate the test machinery (e.g., Anderson 1987); rigorously implement standard test protocols (e.g., Tate and Lynn 1977); provide "catch trials" to spot false positives and false negatives (Henson 1993); scrutinize

test data for internal inconsistencies (Lesser interview); cross-check the data against other relevant measures of vision (Tate and Lynn 1977); and carefully monitor the patient (e.g., for bodily signs of inattention or fatigue) (Frisén 1990). Above all, retesting the patient provides the best measure of reliability (ophthalmologist Aron Rose, e-mail message to author, June 15, 2012; vision scientist Michael Wall, e-mail message to author, September 24, 2014). Concerns that a patient may be malingering, i.e., merely fabricating claimed visual field defects, can be addressed not only by retests (neuro-ophthalmologist Paul Hoffman, telephone interview by author, May 16, 2012) but also by cross-testing (Ali 2011) and various "tricks of the trade" (e.g., tossing a ball around the examination room and seeing if the patient responds self-protectively when the ball approaches the patient within portions of the visual field that his test responses indicate are "blind") (Frisén 1990).

17. Wall e-mail message.
18. Ophthalmologist Janet Serle, telephone interview by author, October 1, 2014.
19. Ibid.
20. Ophthalmologist Janet Serle confirmed during her interview that a patient whose visual field results are "horrible" may swear that she sees just fine, because she has accommodated to her deficit in ways no psychophysical or other test can yet detect.
21. The *Smith* video simulation also differs in this regard from the only other video simulation I have discovered of restricted visual field resulting from idiopathic intracranial hypertension. In the late 1980s or early 1990s, attorney Daniel Schultz, who practices in Washington, DC, represented Bridget Doherty. Doherty suffered from significant absolute contractions, i.e., effective blindness, in all four quadrants of her visual field, leaving vision only in a small, irregularly shaped area straddling the center of vision approximately 30 degrees in each horizontal direction and somewhat less than that above and below the center. Doherty's neuro-ophthalmologist, Dr. Paul Hoffman, formerly associated with Johns Hopkins University in Baltimore, indicated that he "looked for consistency" across "several retests" to assure himself that his mapping of her visual field was reliable (Hoffman interview).

    Doherty brought suit against her neurologist, the hospital, and the radiology department involved in her care for delayed diagnosis of the idiopathic intracranial hypertension. Dan Schultz came up with the idea of creating a video to simulate what Doherty's vision was like. To derive the video simulation from the clinical data, a filmmaker, Peter Ettinger, constructed a mask for the camera lens. Dr. Hoffman agreed that the mask corresponded to the size and shape of Doherty's visual field as measured by the kinetic visual field test (Daniel Schultz, telephone interview by author, May 15, 2012). Ettinger then shot a series of test films using the masked lens, until Dr. Hoffman was prepared to confirm that what was visible through the masked lens conveyed accurately enough what Doherty was able to see. The test films were also shown to Doherty, who said that they captured her visual experience; what's interesting about this, Schultz observed, was that her own severely flawed vision would make it quite difficult for her to tell whether the films matched her visual experience. (See the discussion of this issue in chapter 4.) Two film crews then shot identical walk-throughs of typical scenes from Doherty's daily life—trips to the grocery store, the mall, and the subway—one using a camera with an ordinary, unmasked lens and the other, following immediately behind, with the masked lens. (Schultz explained that "the guy with the filtered lens couldn't see where he was going, so he needed someone to guide him.") The two sets of footage were then combined to give viewers the point-of-view experience of someone with and without the plaintiff's visual impairment. The production "got awfully expensive," according to Schultz, running upward of $20,000.

Schultz gave the simulation to defense counsel before a mediation session. He then showed it to the mediator and included it as part of the required settlement presentation. The case settled favorably for the plaintiff. In retrospect, Schultz recalls that he "had a lot of fun" making the video simulation (Schultz interview).

22. Lesser interview.
23. Dr. Lobarinas is now associate professor in the School of Behavioral and Brain Sciences at the University of Texas at Dallas (http://bbs.utdallas.edu/people/detail.php5?i=1275, last visited February 20, 2016).
24. Edward Lobarinas, telephone interview by author, September 1, 2011. Most of the material in this and the following paragraph is derived from this source.
25. Antonio Ponvert III, telephone interview by author, July 6, 2011.
26. In *State v. Porter* (1997), Connecticut rejected the *Frye* "general acceptance" test (see chapter 3, note 16) but adopted a version of *Daubert* that, at least on the surface, is heavily weighted toward the older test.
27. Ponvert interview.
28. Ibid.
29. This is *pure tone audiometry* (Hirsh 1952), which is the fundamental but not the only technique for measuring hearing ability. The ability to hear speech, for instance, is also very important and is tested using different sorts of stimuli.
30. E.g., Lipin/Dietz Associates 2014.
31. For a general description, see also American Tinnitus Association 2015.
32. The standard testing protocol "alternates systematically among threshold testing, loudness matching, and pitch matching to achieve a pitch match and a loudness match at the pitch match frequency" (Henry 2004, 225).
33. The testing can be much more complicated than this suggests; the procedures (and there are several variations on the basic pitch- and loudness-matching protocols; see Tyler 2000) must be adjusted depending on where the patient reports hearing the tinnitus (one ear, both ears, neither), the

complexity of the reported sound, and other individual variables. As a result, the process can be quite time-consuming (Henry 2004). Since the mid-1990s, some audiologists have developed a computer-automated procedure whereby the patient herself is able to control the pitch and loudness of the external sounds to arrive more efficiently at a match.

34. See note 26 above.
35. MML (minimum masking level, also expressed in dBs) is also used. MML is the loudness of a noise (pure tones, narrow band noise, or white noise) necessary to cover up or mask the tinnitus sound (Henry, Dennis, and Schechter 2005, 1204).
36. William Martin, e-mail message to author, July 22, 2011.
37. There are other reasons why tinnitus measured in dB SL may understate the severity of the condition for the patient. For instance, the patient may also suffer from *hyperacousis*, a heightened sensitivity to sound. Indeed, "there are persons with normal hearing and tinnitus matched to a stimulus one decibel level above threshold who nonetheless tried to commit suicide because of the tinnitus" (Goodwin 1984, 84). (On the problematic relationship between measures of tinnitus loudness and the reported severity of the condition, see note 38 below.)
38. For instance, James A. Henry, research career scientist, National Center for Rehabilitative Auditory Research and research professor in otolaryngology, Oregon Hearing Research Center, states that "a loudness match in dB HL is essentially meaningless. We want to know how many decibels the tinnitus loudness is with respect to the level of hearing, so we use dB SL" (Henry, e-mail message to author, July 26, 2011). Similarly, audiologist Natan Bauman says that measuring tinnitus loudness in HL "should not be done. [It's] not the right way to do it" (interview by author, Hamden, CT, August 15, 2011). Tyler reports several studies finding significant correlations between subjective loudness (in dB SL) and ratings of annoyance (2000). In contrast, Gerhard Andersson found that "correlations between tinnitus loudness in dB HL and annoyance are stronger than when loudness is described in SLs" (2003, 131). Ross Coles sums up the research thus: "Studies have repeatedly shown that although there is a positive correlation between severity and loudness measurements expressed in HL or SL units, it is usually rather poor" (2000, 409).
39. Bauman interview.
40. For one recent example out of hundreds, see Mahmoudian et al. 2015.
41. Henry e-mail message.
42. Richard Tyler, e-mail message to author, September 20, 2011.
43. Lobarinas interview.
44. This oversimplifies DNA proof, of course. DNA identification evidence, including relevant population statistics, can at most show the odds that DNA taken from a person at random would match the sample taken from the victim or the scene (typically, those odds are very low). The probative value

of that evidence depends not only on the reliability of the testing but also on the size of the "reference population"—the number of other persons, matching any eyewitness description given of the perpetrator(s), who might also have been at the scene at the time.

45. Consider also a bit of stagecraft that may have encouraged the *judge*, who had to decide whether the simulation provided good enough knowledge to be admissible, to believe that the plaintiff's own auditory experience could be vicariously experienced in court. At the evidentiary hearing, attorney Ponvert and Dr. Lobarinas told the judge that when the jurors listened to the exhibit, they would use the *same headphones* Janson had used when his tinnitus was measured (*Janson* transcript, March 1, 2011, 10–11). To ensure that the conditions in which the jurors would experience the sounds that Janson had indicated matched his tinnitus would be similar enough to the conditions of Janson's testing, *any* pair of headphones with the same specifications would do. Using the *identical* headphones, though, may well have fostered a kind of sympathetic magic, symbolically linking the listeners with Janson by creating an unbroken chain from his mind to his ears to the headphones, and from the headphones to the ears and the minds of whoever heard the exhibit.

46. We might think of *presence* as having, phenomenologically, at least three features. First, when something is present to one's awareness, it is present *now*—that is, "present" in the temporal sense—and *here*: present in the spatial or locational sense. Second, the perceiver is aware of *being in the presence of* the object or person in question when that object or person is not only part of the perceiver's perceptual field but also a target of the perceiver's conscious attention. Third, the perceiver has a sense of the *immediacy* of the object or person; that is, the object or person seems directly accessible, not merely represented (as in a photograph that the perceiver recognizes as a photograph). All three of these features of presence are made available to legal decision makers by a demonstrative exhibit of a litigant's subjective sensations. We might add a fourth feature: The perceiver feels her consciousness to be narrowed to or focused on the target of attention, the person or thing present, shrinking the range of awareness of other thoughts not related to the target, including memories of the past and anticipations of the future; this is the sense of which we speak when we refer to being "present in the moment."

47. Thus, photographs have paradigmatically been analyzed as conveying simultaneously both a presence and an absence, although either term may be foregrounded: absence as presence (Barthes 1981), or presence as absence (Noë 2012, 85). What is depicted is present in the sense of being in the viewer's perceptual field, here and now, but absent in that the subject matter of the photo is elsewhere, and the picture itself, taken at some point in the past, shows a moment in time forever gone. The same analysis could be extended to drawings, paintings, and other visual works intended to repre-

sent a particular (now absent) person or event; it can also apply to televised events. In the case of simulations of a litigant's ongoing perceptual experience, however, the presence-absence dynamic is differently inflected. This is because what is being made *present* is not just a currently unavailable bit of observable reality but an unseen and, in principle, *unseeable* reality that is (believed to be) ontologically different from observable reality (see discussion in chapter 2).

In an insightful analysis of the concept of presence in photography, communications and media scholar and photographer Greg Battye argues that if "presence occurs during periods of time when cognition (processes such as perception, attention, learning, thought, and affect) is *closely tied to current perceptual stimuli*, . . . then clearly presence is an experience which is likely to be initiated (for example) by closely attending to a photograph—perceiving it, thinking about it, being affected by it—as by anything in the salient physical and sensory environment of the 'real world'" (2014, 86, quoting Heeter 2003, 335, emphasis added). That is, an effective and engrossing representation (such as a photograph, the subject of Battye's work) may not merely asymptotically approximate the sense of presence we ordinarily experience in real life; instead, our experience of the representation may elicit a *stronger* sense of presence than the intermittent and fluctuating senses of it we usually have. Simulations of litigants' subjectivity may thus provide a heightened sense of the presence of litigants' sensory impairments—perhaps even more intense than what the litigants themselves experience. (I return to this possibility in chapter 7, in connection with the possible effects of the *focusing illusion* on the judgments jurors derive from their experiences of simulations.)

48. It's worth pointing out that people's inclination to respond to certain images as if they have a live presence, an animating power, did not end with the Renaissance. It continues to pervade Western culture (Freedberg 1989), and not only in the context of religious belief: consider why teenagers put up posters of popular music performers in their bedrooms, or why their parents keep photos of their spouses and children on their desks at work.

49. "The image [of the dead] was no longer merely compensation for a loss but had, in the very act of representing a body, acquired 'Being' in the name of that body. . . . Through images and their use, the social realm was now expanded to include the realm of the dead" (Belting 2011, 87).

50. Moreover, when listening to recorded sound, people tend not to pay attention to the recording medium (in this case, the digital file on an iPod) in the same way they often do when looking at a photo or a video, so the sound files would not make salient the *pastness* that is always a part of the experience of viewing a photograph. Consequently, jurors would be freer to experience the sounds as a *present* event (which, for the plaintiff, they are). (I would like to thank to Greg Battye for suggesting this point.)

51. A similar effect might be achieved if a litigant's visual experience were

simulated for jurors by having them don goggles or other eyewear, so that wherever they looked, their visual experience would conform to the litigant's impaired vision. To the best of my knowledge, this sort of simulation has not yet been used.

CHAPTER SIX

1. "Corneal topography and wavefront refraction [are] complementary measurement technologies" for the ophthalmologist considering the performance of customized corneal surgery (Campbell 2004, 309). Some devices *combine* topographical and wavefront measurements (e.g., Karpecki 2006, 204–5). "The major difference [between an aberration map produced by wavefront and the corneal topographic map produced by Orbscan] is that a corneal map describes the curvature of a physical surface, whereas an aberration map describes the difference between a wavefront of light and a reference wavefront" (Thibos and Applegate 2004, 55).
2. The Zernike polynomials can be thought of as a series of three-dimensional best-fitting shapes, analogous to the best-fitting lines generated by other statistical formulas to describe two-dimensional relationships among data (Tripoli 2003). The Zernike modes comprise dozens of typical patterns of aberrant wavefronts with clinical significance for the diagnosis and treatment of different ophthalmological conditions, including the lower-order aberrations (LOA) of defocus and astigmatism and the higher-order aberrations (HOA) such as coma, spherical aberration, trefoil, and more complicated variations (Mattioli and Tripoli 2006).
3. This optimally focused spot of light is known as the Airy disk (or disc), named after George Biddell Airy, the noted nineteenth-century British astronomer.
4. For example, experts in vision science often publish image simulations (e.g., Karpecki 2006, 205; Thibos and Applegate 2004, 56) or other "photographic simulations" of patients' degraded views. Brian Barsky (2004) describes a similar process of "*vision-realistic rendering*," which incorporates computation of the point spread function at different depths in the visual field to produce simulations of impaired vision of photographs or synthetic images. In addition, ophthalmic surgeons may use software programs such as IOL Counselor (e.g., *Eyeworld* Staff 2007) and InterWave Visualizer (Carr et al. 2004), which generate image simulations of typical scenes (rather than an eye-chart letter) to give prospective eye surgery patients an idea of the results they can expect.
5. Thus, Raymond Applegate, Gene Hilmantel, and Larry Thibos (2004, 74) write:

> We would like to believe that visual performance tests are a good surrogate measure for the optical quality of the retinal image. . . . Such an

> ideal test is a fantasy. Visual systems vary in their capacity to interpret the retinal image and form a percept. It is unrealistic for such tests to perfectly mimic retinal image quality. . . . Fortunately, the reliance on visual performance tests to serve as a surrogate measure of retinal image quality will likely disappear over the next several years as sensitive new objective tests of retinal image quality make their way to the market. . . . Further, and perhaps more importantly, new metrics will be developed that reflect input from both the optical and neural stages of vision.

6. In addition, Antonio Guirao and David Williams (2003) determined that objective wavefront measurements of patients with corneal aberrations indicated corrections within 0.1 diopters (the standard unit of refraction) of participants' subjective judgment—an error less than half of the smallest step size (0.25 diopters) typically used in prescribing spectacles and contact lenses. The authors conclude that "the best objective image quality closely corresponds to the best subjective image quality in terms of refraction" (41). One might think that by doing away with any conscious contribution from the patient, wavefront technology, and the image simulations it can produce, would achieve objectivity only at the cost of sacrificing subjectivity—which is, after all, the point of introducing evidentiary simulations in the law. By comparing the fruits of objectively derived data with different representations of subjective perception (the self-reported best quality image and the patient's drawing), however, the Guirao and Williams research and the research of Mattioli and Tripoli, respectively, suggest that objective scientific measurement can take us quite far toward knowing what it's like for another person to see as he or she does.
7. Wavefront image simulations have probably been used in other cases addition to *Schiffer*. For instance, textbook illustrations of "starbursting" and "ghosting" as a result of LASIK surgery were reportedly introduced in *Post v. University Physicians, Inc.* (2002), *original judgment reinstated after new trial*, 2004 WL 5030672 (Trial Order) (Ariz. Super., Oct 29, 2004), in which the plaintiff claimed the surgery should not have been performed because the defendants should have determined that given his dim-light pupil size, the surgery would impair his ability to see clearly at night, essential to his job as an airline pilot. Attorney Ted Schmidt has said that he and his expert, Jeffery Machat, went through Machat's textbook and found pictures of what lights at night looked like to someone with the plaintiff's condition (Ted Schmidt, telephone interview by author, May 2, 2012). Schmidt, however, also said the exhibits themselves have been lost, and after contacting Schmidt's cocounsel, Robert Beal, and others, I have been unable to locate either the exhibits or any further information about them (e.g., Robert Beal, e-mail message to author, July 29, 2012). The jury awarded the plaintiff $4 million in damages, which the judge reduced to $3.4 million based on comparative negligence (2002 WL 32832041 (Ariz. Super., May 9, 2002)). Wavefront image simula-

tions may also have been used in another Arizona case, according to the plaintiff's lawyer in that case (attorney Richard Plattner, telephone interview by author, May 1, 2012).

8. The award was affirmed in *Schiffer v. Speaker*, 36 A.D.3d 520 (1st Dept. 2007).
9. That the wavefront measurement, and hence the image simulation, might be affected by the condition of structures in the eye other than the cornea is certainly true (e.g., Artal 2004; Wakil, Padrick, and Molebny 2006). This does not imply that the simulation doesn't accurately capture what the patient sees, however; it just means that any simulated defects in the patient's vision may be due to problems arising elsewhere than in the cornea. Of course, that would be a legally important fact for the defense in this type of case to establish.
10. Had the PSF image been shown as white-on-black, as they sometimes are in the literature (e.g., Roorda 2004, 13), it might well have reminded jurors of an image of (or the experience of seeing) stars in the night sky, which would be fitting, given the original astronomical applications of wavefront technology (Platt and Shack 2001). The actual PSF image, which is a very faint blue as well as gray or black on white, does not have this obvious connotation, although (as noted in the text) it does evoke black-on-white representations of astronomical objects whose very existence may be equivocal (see, e.g., Elkins 2008, 83). (Image simulations of Snellen letters are typically black-on-white, presumably for better legibility.)
11. Not altogether unlike the *vera icon* of Jesus's face that Veronica captured on the cloth or *sudarium* she used to wipe away his sweat and blood (Belting 1994; Kuryluk 1991).
12. Taking the advocate's point of view, we might ask, Why not use both types of simulation, supplementing the scientific image simulation with the photo-realistic evocation of the plaintiff's experience? (See chapter 3, note 5 above.)
13. The defendant's lawyer in a personal injury case, for instance, may be reluctant to cross-examine the litigant himself at length on his claim that the simulation corresponds to his experience, because doing so would enable the litigant to talk even more about his impairments, further emphasizing them for the jurors.
14. To be sure, the efficacy of limiting instructions is disputed (see generally, e.g., Lieberman and Arndt 2000; Sklansky 2013). Research is needed to test whether jurors could understand and properly use instructions explaining the evidentiary status of different types of simulations. As examples of the sorts of instructions that judges might provide, consider the following:

    Artist's sketch: "The plaintiff in this case introduced photographic [videographic] images that were offered to show, according to the plaintiff, what things look like to him. These images are like a drawing or sketch that a witness might make to illustrate his or her spoken testimony. They are not like ordinary photographs; they do not themselves provide any independent proof of what it's like to see as the plaintiff sees. Whether you believe that these images accurately illustrate what the plaintiff's vision is like depends on the extent to which you believe the plaintiff's testimony that they do."

Psychophysical: "The plaintiff in this case introduced photographic [videographic] images that were offered to show, according to the plaintiff and the [neuro-]ophthalmologist who testified as an expert witness, what things look like to the plaintiff. These images are offered to prove what things look like to the plaintiff, much as a computer simulation might be presented in an auto accident case to prove how the accident occurred. As with that sort of computer accident simulation, how much weight you give to the photo [video] simulation[s] depends on the extent to which you believe that the clinical measurements on which the simulation is based are accurate and reliable and that the images you saw reliably correspond to those measurements."

Machine readout: "The plaintiff in this case introduced photographic [videographic] images that were offered to show, according to the plaintiff and the [neuro-]ophthalmologist who testified as an expert witness, what things look like to the plaintiff. These images are offered to prove what things look like to the plaintiff, much as a computer simulation might be presented in an auto accident case to prove how the accident occurred. As with that sort of computer accident simulation, how much weight you give to the photo [video] simulation[s] depends on the extent to which you believe that the wavefront equipment used to measure the distortions in the plaintiff's eyesight and to generate the images you saw produces reliable results. You should consider whether wavefront technology is based on reliable principles and methods, whether the wavefront machine was well calibrated and well maintained, whether it was competently operated, whether any features of the plaintiff or the test may have resulted in inaccurate measurements, and whether the images the machine produced, which were introduced into evidence, reliably correspond to accurate measurements taken of the plaintiff's vision."

CHAPTER SEVEN

1. Some seriously injured tort plaintiffs—for instance, those with severe brain damage—are incapable of speaking for themselves. Their personae must be constructed in other ways: through their presence in court, the testimony of family members and caregivers, and (not least) day-in-the-life movies.
2. Antonio Ponvert III, remarks at Connecticut Trial Lawyers Association 31st Annual College of Evidence, Hamden, CT, September 7, 2013.
3. As Wissler, Kuehn, and Saks (2000, 712n1) observe, "*pain and suffering* often is used synonymously with and as a synecdoche for general damages," but it is in fact only one component of general or noneconomic damages. We might also distinguish pain and suffering from what are sometimes called *hedonic* damages, meaning the opportunity costs of the forgone benefits of life's

enjoyments, or the loss of *capabilities* to enjoy various aspects of life (e.g., Sunstein 2008). Throughout this chapter I'll refer to "pain and suffering" to include hedonic damages as well, unless otherwise noted.

4. The trial judge in *Janson* instructed the jury using this same boilerplate rule: "You must attempt to put the plaintiff in the same position, as far as money can do it, that he would have been in had he not been injured" (*Janson* transcript, March 3, 2011, 13).

5. Wissler, Kuehn, and Saks (2000) argue that some aspects of the jury instructions themselves may increase the variability of awards. On the other hand, noneconomic damage awards, although variable, are hardly as arbitrary as some legal scholars have contended. Experimental studies show that the judged severity and duration of the plaintiff's suffering (mental suffering and disability more than pain) are strong predictors of the size of the awards (Greene and Bornstein 2003; Wissler et al. 1997; see also Vallano 2013). Analyses of actual verdicts show a strong positive correlation between noneconomic and economic damages (Chang et al. 2015; Hans and Reyna 2011). Moreover, jurors' evaluations of injury severity tend to be consistent with those of judges and lawyers, although the dollar figures they assign for pain and suffering are more variable, largely because jurors, unlike judges and lawyers, do not have the reference frame of other, similar cases on which to draw (Wissler, Hart, and Saks 1999). For a contrasting discussion of research emphasizing the variability and unpredictability of these damage awards, along with recommendations for reform, see Chase 1995.

6. Indeed, normative judgments determine what sorts of losses are compensable at all (see L. Meyer 2014). For instance, tortious injuries may deprive people of *capabilities* that we consider essential to a full human life and of the ability to experience a broader and more complex range of life states (see note 3 above), so even if the victims report being no less happy (or even happier) in their newly limited state, the loss of those capabilities and experiences also deserves compensation, and of necessity that loss must be gauged with reference to some norm of human flourishing (e.g., Ubel and Loewenstein 2008).

   The normative character of the pain and suffering award and the jury's discretion in deciding it are connected. According to legal scholar Harry Kalven Jr., it is because "the computing of damages involves a complex value judgment as well as a literal determination of fact" that "the law intends the jury to legislate interstitially. . . . On this view the jury's freedom and discretion is not by default but by preference . . . for the community sense of values as the standard by which to price the personal injury" (1958, 161). Kalven was writing about personal injury damage awards in general, not specifically their pain and suffering component, but his remarks about the vagueness of instructions and the value judgments inherent in the awards apply with special force to pain and suffering.

7. "If injuries diminish people, then juries, in a sense, reconstruct them, at least

to the extent that money is able to do so" (Greene and Bornstein 2003, 3). Perhaps the idea that general damages focus on the whole person is clearest in the allowance of recovery for hedonic damages, the limitations on a person's ability to enjoy life that the injury has caused (110; see note 3 above).

8. To the contrary, see, e.g., Caruth 1996; Madeira 2006.
9. How accurately observers can estimate a person's pain is a difficult question. According to phenomenologists such as Max Scheler ([1912] 1970), perceptions of others' pain are naturally accurate because those perceptions are intuitive and immediate (see discussion in Zahavi 2005). Quantitative experimental research, on the other hand, indicates that observers often underestimate the pain that the person suffering it reports, although some studies indicate overestimation (see Goubert, Craig, and Buysse 2011).
10. That is, even (normal) present consciousness is temporally dynamic, including not only awareness of the immediate present but also of the just-past and the next-to-come, as Husserl and other phenomenologists, as well as other philosophers, cognitive scientists, and neuroscientists, have explained. (On the phenomenological understanding of the experience of time, see, e.g., Gallagher 2012b.)
11. Still images, including photographs and paintings, can *imply* temporal duration (and hence narrative), although they do not *depict* it (see, e.g., Battye 2014; Goodman 1981).
12. See chapter 3, text at note 5.
13. I am grateful to Philip Meyer, professor of law at the University of Vermont Law School, for his comments on an earlier draft of this chapter, in which he suggested this way of framing the analysis of the plaintiff's narratives.
14. Perhaps needless to say, jurors' concepts of what certain persons and forms of personhood are worth are highly contestable. Anthropologist Mary Douglas (1993, 501), has observed: "There is no culture-free theory of the person. . . . A theory of justice devised for a pluralistic culture can never hope to describe the person, or the citizen, in terms that will be agreed." Skillful lawyers try to anticipate what their jurors will value most about personhood (as well as other important values) that can be made relevant to the case at hand.
15. Mark Budzinski, defense counsel in *Wilke v. Dudley* (2011, decided February 12, 2014), has said that he was able to introduce the plaintiff's own unaltered, "control" photo of the plaintiff's workstation, which included small letters and numbers on the equipment Wilke operated, to attack Wilke's credibility on the stand. It was not disputed that the plaintiff could still work. After Wilke had testified about how poor his vision was, the trial judge allowed Budzinski to use that photo to show that Wilke *had* to be able to see those small letters and numbers to do his job. Having thus undermined the plaintiff's credibility, Budzinski explained that had the simulations been introduced, "I would have focused on the real-life things that the plaintiff could still do. For instance, he admitted that he still drove a motorcycle, at night, without a helmet. Given that, the jury would never have believed the

simulations. Same thing with the blurry simulation of his workstation: If Wilke could do his job at all, then the pictures couldn't be accurate" (Mark Budzinski, telephone interview by author, February 6, 2015).

16. Presumably, if the plaintiff's lawyer thinks the plaintiff's and others' testimonial performances (and his own closing argument) by themselves construct a sufficiently persuasive case for pain and suffering, the lawyer would choose not to use a simulation (e.g., Antonio Ponvert III, telephone interview by author, July 6, 2011). For instance, if a simulation of tinnitus is not as loud or otherwise intrusive as jurors would likely imagine from the plaintiff's and the expert audiologist's accounts and the clinical test results, hearing the simulation might lead jurors to evaluate the tinnitus as *less* severe than they otherwise would.
17. I want to thank Dawn Moore of the Department of Law and Legal Studies, Carleton University, for this observation.
18. I am grateful to Linda Meyer, professor of law at Quinnipiac University School of Law, for suggesting this. In addition, Linda points out that replaying the simulation during closing argument could have the further effect of bolstering the plaintiff's credibility and deservingness without her lawyer giving the appearance of vouching for her, which the law of evidence prohibits.
19. Although experienced clinicians today strongly recommend that doctors take the time to listen to their patients' accounts of their symptoms (e.g., Groopman 2007), the financial pressures of modern practice and the spread of electronic medical records (which allow only certain kinds of data, not discursive narratives, to become part of the patient's profile), among other factors, discourage it (e.g., Hartzband and Groopman 2008).
20. Jurors who approach the case with the intuitive belief that the contents of consciousness can't possibly be measured and made available for others to see or hear may be especially interested in expert testimony to the contrary.
21. The extent to which neuroscience can help us understand how minds work, and in particular, how consciousness functions, is a hotly contested topic in psychology, philosophy, law, and elsewhere. For a leading critique of the reductive nature of some neuroscientific explanations, see Bennett and Hacker 2003.
22. Ponvert, remarks at Connecticut Trial Lawyers Association 31st Annual College of Evidence, September 7, 2013.
23. *Do* simulations of plaintiffs' perceptual impairments in fact lead jurors to sympathize with the plaintiffs even more than the testimony and other evidence already does? It's reasonable to assume they often would. All things being equal, simulations' rich, sensory concreteness would be expected to provoke stronger emotional reactions than the relatively abstract verbal descriptions in testimony, and the very unexpectedness of a demonstrative simulation of subjective experience would tend to heighten jurors' emotional responses. The simulation's first-person point of view invites jurors to

adopt the plaintiff's perspective, which would be expected to enhance jurors' empathy (see Önder and Öner-Özkan 2003), an important component of sympathy (e.g., Batson 1991; see Feigenson 1997). Simulations like the video in *Smith* (and in a more attenuated fashion, the photos in *Devadas*) can also elicit jurors' sympathy by casting the plaintiff as the heroine of a dramatic narrative (as discussed earlier in this chapter).

24. Other psychological research shows that emotions lead people to process ambiguous information in a direction consistent with the cognitive structure or *appraisal tendency* of the emotion. For instance, angry people tend to blame more, because the cognitive structure of anger—"disapproving of someone else's blameworthy action and being displeased about the related event" (Ortony, Clore, and Collins 1988, 148)—makes the other person's blameworthiness salient (e.g., Lerner and Tiedens 2006). Since the cognitive structure of sympathy includes the perception that the plaintiff is suffering undeservedly, jurors who feel sympathetic toward the plaintiff may be inclined to construe ambiguous evidence in a way that reduces her responsibility. Again, if simulations make jurors' sympathy for the plaintiff more intense, they would increase the risk of distorting judgment in these ways.

    More generally, any features of a simulation that lead jurors to believe the plaintiff's suffering is more severe than it actually is may also unfairly prejudice the defendant by making jurors more likely to hold the defendant responsible in the first place (the *severity effect*; see Robbennolt 2000).

25. Thus, people asked to estimate whether paraplegics experience more good moods or more bad moods gave answers that depended on whether they knew any paraplegics: those who didn't thought bad moods would predominate, whereas those who did thought the opposite. Respondents who didn't know any paraplegics focused on what to them was the paraplegics' most salient characteristic, and thus they overestimated the (bad) mood associated with paraplegia. Respondents who knew paraplegics also brought to mind other, more positive features of their daily existence and were thus less prone to overvalue that one (admittedly negative) feature in making their overall assessment (Schkade and Kahneman 1998).

26. Indeed, some research has shown a *self-other* bias in affective forecasting (Igou 2008). People generally predict that negative affect will last longer for others than for themselves because thoughts about psychological strategies that would reduce negative affect are more available when they think about their own future suffering. This would be predicted to inflate the judged severity of others' suffering. Thus, the focusing illusion and affective forecasting errors discussed in the text would apply with special force to jurors' evaluations of plaintiffs' future suffering.

27. Recent experimental research confirms that laypeople tend to underestimate hedonic adaptation and thus overestimate sufferers' lost enjoyment of life (Greene, Sturm, and Evelo 2016).

28. Some audiologists go so far as to assert that "for assessment of severity, either

for clinical purposes or for compensation assessment, matching tests of tinnitus loudness are virtually useless" (Baskill, and Coles 1999, 427; see also chapter 5, note 38 above). Similarly, one study of glaucoma patients found little correlation between the extent of the reduction of their visual fields as measured by standard psychophysical testing and their assessments of the effect of their condition on their quality of life (Jampel et al. 2002). Another study, however, using different measures, found a moderate correlation ($r = .55$) between objective measures of participants' visual deficits and their self-reported assessment of the impact of their impairments on their daily lives (Richman et al. 2010).

29. Some courts have held that while Golden Rule arguments should not be allowed, any error in permitting them is rendered harmless by appropriate jury instructions on the elements of the claim and the burden of proof. Other courts have tolerated these arguments on the ground that instructions to jurors not to decide on the basis of emotions, prejudice, or bias were sufficient to purge any taint the arguments may have created (see generally Feigenson 1997).
30. The Golden Rule can be and has been justified as a principle of *impartiality* (e.g., Finnis 1980, 107–8): it commands that people not elevate their self-preferences over the preferences of others by encouraging them to act in a way that equates their treatment of others with self-treatment. In the context of jury decision making, however, Golden Rule arguments are traditionally proscribed because they promote partiality. There's no contradiction here. As a rule of conduct, the Golden Rule *reduces* partiality toward *oneself* at the expense of others. When jurors are deciding damages, Golden Rule arguments *promote* partiality toward the *plaintiff* at the expense of the defendant.
31. See chapter 2, note 14.
32. To put this another way: Decety and Jackson (2004, 84), state that given our default egocentricity in reasoning about others, "the mental flexibility to adopt someone else's point of view is an effortful and controlled process." Experiencing the simulation makes what would otherwise be effortful as easy as looking or listening: jurors simply see or hear what the plaintiff does (assuming that the simulation more or less reliably and accurately reproduces the plaintiff's sensations). So to the extent that adopting the plaintiff's point of view is the judgmental goal in evaluating the plaintiff's pain and suffering, simulations should make it easier for jurors to do that.

    Recent research suggests why this is so important. Rachel Ruttan and colleagues (Ruttan, McDowell, and Nordgren 2015) found that people evaluate another person's failure to endure an emotionally distressing event more negatively if they themselves have previously endured what they believe to be the same emotionally distressing event, compared to those who have not experienced that sort of event. Participants who have had the same experience as the judgment target tended to view the distressing event as less difficult to overcome. Many jurors may imagine, based on the plaintiff's verbal description of his visual or auditory impairments, that they've experienced something similar (e.g., blurred vision) themselves, and would be more likely to judge, "That's not so bad." A vivid simulation can make it emphatically clear that the plaintiff's experience is *not* the same as the jurors,' inclining them to be more empathetic—perhaps to say, as did the members of the focus group in *Janson*, "How could anyone live with that?"

CHAPTER EIGHT

1. The device is also known as an "Active Denial System" (Turner 2012). See also "US Military" 2007.
2. The unreported case is *Stephenson v. Honda Motors Ltd. of Am.* 1992, also discussed in Joseph 1996.
3. See also "Sights and Sounds of Schizophrenia" 2002; Abel 2007.
4. In addition, Rule 704(b) (Federal Rules of Evidence 2014) prohibits an expert witness in a criminal case from offering an opinion whether the defendant did or did not have the mental state or condition that constitutes an element of the crime charged or of a defense; intent or lack thereof may be such an element, and the expert opinion on which a re-creation is based would be subject to this rule.
5. See a video of their data at https://www.youtube.com/watch?v=daY7u00eftA (last visited January 29, 2015).
6. For examples of the test movies juxtaposed with the reconstructed movies, see https://www.youtube.com/watch?v=nsjDnYxJ0bo (last visited January 25, 2015).
7. Marvin Chun, interview by author, Hamden, CT, September 19, 2014.
8. The brain imaging research described in the text aims to establish correspondences between participants' subjective perceptions, as translated from measurements of their brain activity while perceiving a target, and those targets as others would see them. The simulations we've studied throughout this book, in contrast, aim to depict perceptions that *differ* significantly from what people with ordinary perceptual abilities would see or hear. Presumably, however, if and when visual image reconstruction from fMRIs of unimpaired participants can be generally validated by reference to objective measures, it might then be relied on as enabling an accurate simulation of a person's subjective perceptions even when those diverge from what most of the rest of us see.
9. Computational neuroscientists Moran Cerf and colleagues (Cerf et al. 2011), for instance, made single-neuron recordings of participants while perceiving and then thinking about images and showed that many participants were able to change the dominance of one or the other of two superimposed images simply by thinking about it. Presumably, if the validity of the method is established, it would be possible to reconstruct a person's subjective visual experience from measurements of the person's brain activity. Recently, other

researchers have been able to use fMRI to identify, although not yet to recreate, the visual content of imagery during dreams (Horikawa et al. 2013).

10. See Brown and Murphy 2010.
11. Ibid. More importantly, the very nature of recalled long-term memories as active reconstructions from fragments of past perceptions and thoughts, not merely colored but transformed by conscious desires, subconscious drives, and the situation at the time of recall, would limit if not defeat the probative value of the visual memory reconstruction as proof of past facts. It might still, at least in theory, be useful during cross-examination to show that a witness was not accurately describing his or her own present memory.
12. Recall that in *Janson*, plaintiff's attorney Antonio Ponvert III, ostensibly to protect jurors against discomfort from hearing the sound files, advised them to lower the headphones slowly toward their ears and put them on only if comfortable (*Janson*, trial transcript, March 1, 2011, 72; see discussion in chapter 5). That warning, of course, may actually have prompted jurors to evaluate the sound they were hearing as more severe.
13. In *Commonwealth v. Serge* 2006, 696, the Pennsylvania Supreme Court opined that "the relative monetary positions of the parties are relevant for the trial court to consider when ruling on whether or not to admit a [computer generated animation] into evidence" and that a disparity of resources that prevents a defendant from countering the prosecution's animation with one of his own could lead the court not to allow the prosecution's animation to be shown.

References

Abel, Christina. 2007. "Virtual Hallucination Machine Gives User Mental Illness Lesson" (March 28). http://nationalnews.ncmentalhealth.org, accessed June 29, 2011.

Adler, Matthew. 2000. "Expressive Theories of Law: A Skeptical Overview." *University of Pennsylvania Law Review* 148:1363–1501.

Ali, Nadeem. 2011. "Functional Constriction of the Ocular Motor Field: Description and Preliminary Evaluation of a New Technique to Help Distinguish Organic from Nonorganic Visual Field Loss." *Journal of Neuro-Ophthalmology* 31:131–34.

Allefeld, Carsten, Peter Pütz, Kristina Kastner, and Jiří Wackermann. 2011. "Flicker-Light Induced Visual Phenomena: Frequency Dependence and Specificity of Whole Percepts and Percept Features." *Consciousness and Cognition* 20:1344–62.

Alter, Torin. 2008. "Phenomenal Knowledge without Experience." In *The Case for Qualia*, edited by Edmond Wright, 247–67. Cambridge, MA: MIT Press.

American Tinnitus Association. 2015. "Tinnitus Clinic Test Protocol." www.tinnitusarchive.org/dataSets/1/methods/tinnitusClinicTestProtocol/, accessed June 28, 2015.

Amsterdam, Anthony, and Jerome Bruner. 2000. *Minding the Law*. Cambridge, MA: Harvard University Press.

Amsterdam, Anthony, Randy Hertz, and Robin Walker-Sterling. 2005. "Stories Told and Untold: Lawyering Theory Analyses of the First Rodney King Assault Trial: Introduction." *Clinical Law Review* 12:1–32.

Anderson, Douglas. 1987. *Perimetry: With and Without Automation*. St. Louis: C. V. Mosby.

Andersson, Gerhard. 2003. "Tinnitus Loudness Matchings in Relation to Annoyance and Grading of Severity." *Auris Nasus Larynx* 30:129–33.

Ando, Shuntaro, Sarah Clement, Elizabeth Alexandra Barley, and Graham Thornicroft. 2011. "The Simulation of Hallucinations to Reduce the Stigma of Schizophrenia: A Systematic Review." *Schizophrenia Research* 133:8–16.

Angell, Marcia. 2011. "The Illusions of Psychiatry." *New York Review of Books*, July 14, 20–22.

Applegate, Raymond, Gene Hilmantel, and Larry Thibos. 2004. "Assessment of Visual Performance." In Krueger, Applegate, and MacRae 2004, 65–75.

Artal, Pablo. 2004. "Combining Corneal and Ocular Wave Aberrations." In Krueger, Applegate, and MacRae 2004, 311–16.

Balcetis, Emily, and G. Daniel Lassiter, eds. 2010. *The Social Psychology of Visual Perception*. New York: Psychology Press.

Ball, David. 1997. *Theater Tips and Strategies for Jury Trials*. 2nd ed. South Bend, IN: National Institute for Trial Advocacy.

Ball, Milner. 1981. *The Promise of American Law*. Athens: University of Georgia Press.

Bandes, Susan, and Jeremy Blumenthal. 2012. "Emotion and the Law." *Annual Review of Law and Social Science* 8:161–81.

Banks, Jasmine, Geoffrey Ericksson, Kevin Burrage, Peter Yellowlees, Sean Ivermee, and Jennifer Tichon. 2004. "Constructing the Hallucinations of Psychosis in Virtual Reality." *Journal of Network and Computer Applications* 27: 1–11.

Baron-Cohen, Simon, Helen Tager-Flusberg, and Donald Cohen, eds. 2000. *Understanding Other Minds: Perspectives from Autism and Developmental Cognitive Neuroscience*. Oxford: Oxford University Press.

Baron-Cohen, Simon, Sally Wheelwright, John Lawson, Richard Griffin, Chris Ashwin, Jac Billington, and Bhismadev Chakrabarti. 2005. "Empathizing and Systemizing in Autism Spectrum Conditions." In *Handbook of Autism and Pervasive Developmental Disorders*, edited by Fred Volkmar, Rhea Paul, Ami Klin, and Donald Cohen, 1:628–39. 3rd ed. Hoboken, NJ: John Wiley.

Barrett, Lisa Feldman, and Moshe Bar. 2009. "See It with Feeling: Affective Predictions during Object Perception." *Philosophical Transactions of the Royal Society B* 364:1325–34.

Barsky, Brian. 2004. "Vision-Realistic Rendering: Simulation of the Scanned Foveal Image from Wavefront Data of Human Subjects." *Proceedings of the 1st Symposium on Applied Perception in Graphics and Visualization*, 73–81. New York: Association for Computing Machinery.

Barthes, Roland. 1981. *Camera Lucida*. Translated by Richard Howard. New York: Hill and Wang.

Baskill, J. L., and R. R. A. Coles. 1999. "Relationships between Tinnitus Loudness and Severity." In *Proceedings of the Sixth International Tinnitus Seminar*, edited by Jonathan W. P. Hazell and the Tinnitus and Hyperacusis Centre, 424–28. London: The Centre.

Batson, C. Daniel. 1991. *The Altruism Question*. Mahwah, NJ: Lawrence Erlbaum.

Battye, Greg. 2014. *Photography, Narrative, Time*. Bristol, UK: Intellect.

Baudrillard, Jean. 1983. *Simulations*. Translated by Paul Foss, Paul Patton, and Phil Beitchman. N.p.: Semiotext(e).

Baudry, Jean-Louis. 1986. "Ideological Effects of the Basic Cinematographic Apparatus." In *Narrative, Apparatus, Ideology*, edited by Philip Rosen, 286–98. New York: Columbia University Press.

Belting, Hans. 1994. *Likeness and Presence*. Chicago: University of Chicago Press.

———. 2011. *An Anthropology of Images*. Princeton, NJ: Princeton University Press.

Bennett, M. R., and P. M. S. Hacker. 2003. *Philosophical Foundations of Neuroscience*. Malden, MA: Blackwell.

Biocca, Frank, Taeyong Kim, and Mark Levy. 1995. "The Vision of Virtual Reality." In *Communication in the Age of Virtual Reality*, edited by Frank Biocca and Mark Levy, 3–14. Hillsdale, NJ: Lawrence Erlbaum.

Bittner, Ava, Mohammed Ibrahim, Jennifer Haythornthwaite, Marie Diener-West, and Gislin Dagnelie. 2011. "Vision Test Variability in Retinitis Pigmentosa and Psychosocial Factors." *Optometry and Vision Science* 88:1496–1506.

Block, Ned. 1995. "On a Confusion about a Function of Consciousness." *Behavioral and Brain Sciences* 18:227–87.

Block, Ned, Owen Flanagan, and Güven Güzeldere, eds. 1997. *The Nature of Consciousness*. Cambridge, MA: MIT Press.

Blumenthal, Jeremy. 2005. "Law and the Emotions: The Problems of Affective Forecasting." *Indiana Law Journal* 80:155–238.

Bolter, Jay David, and Richard Grusin. 1999. *Remediation*. Cambridge, MA: MIT Press.

Boring, Edwin. 1942. *Sensation and Perception in the History of Experimental Psychology*. New York: Appleton-Century-Crofts.

———. 1950. *A History of Experimental Psychology*. 2nd ed. New York: Appleton-Century-Crofts.

Bornstein, Brian. 1998. "From Compassion to Compensation: The Effect of Injury Severity on Mock Jurors' Liability Judgments." *Journal of Applied Social Psychology* 28:1477–1502.

Breidbach, Olaf. 2011. "Imaging Science: The Pictorial Turn in Bio- and Neurosciences." In *Imagery in the 21st Century*, edited by Oliver Grau, 111–27. Cambridge, MA: MIT Press

Bronsteen, John, Christopher Buccafusco, and Jonathan Masur. 2014. *Happiness and the Law*. Chicago: University of Chicago Press.

Brooks, Peter, and Paul Gewirtz, eds. 1996. *Law's Stories*. New Haven, CT: Yale University Press.

Broun, Kenneth, ed. 2006 *McCormick on Evidence*. 6th ed. St. Paul, MN: Thomson West.

Brown, Kevin. 1984. "Propriety and Prejudicial Effects of Attorney's 'Golden Rule' Argument to Jury in Federal Civil Case." *American Law Reports* (Federal series) 68:333–41.

Brown, Teneille, and Emily Murphy. 2010. "Through a Scanner Darkly: Functional

Neuroimaging as Evidence of a Criminal Defendant's Past Mental States." *Stanford Law Review* 62:1119–1208.

Bruner, Jerome. 1990. *Acts of Meaning*. Cambridge, MA: Harvard University Press.

Budenz, Donald. 1997. *Atlas of Visual Fields*. Philadelphia: Lippincott-Raven.

Burns, Robert. 1999. *A Theory of the Trial*. Princeton, NJ: Princeton University Press.

Byrne, Alex. 2014. "Inverted Qualia." In *The Stanford Encyclopedia of Philosophy*, edited by Edward N. Zalta, http://plato.stanford.edu/archives/sum2014/entries/qualia-inverted, accessed March 11, 2015.

Cameron, C. Daryl, Kristen Lindquist, and Kurt Gray. 2015. "A Constructionist Review of Morality and Emotions: No Evidence for Specific Relationships between Moral Content and Discrete Emotions." *Personality and Social Psychology Review* 19:371–94.

Campbell, Charles. 2004. "Corneal Topography and Customized Ablation." In Krueger, Applegate, and MacRae 2004, 301–10.

Canales, Jimena. 2011. "'A Number of Scenes in a Badly Cut Film': Observation in the Age of Strobe." In *Histories of Scientific Observation*, edited by Lorraine Daston and Elizabeth Lunbeck, 230–54. Chicago: University of Chicago Press.

Carney, Brian, and Neal Feigenson. 2004. "Visual Persuasion in the Michael Skakel Trial: Enhancing Advocacy through Interactive Multimedia Presentations." *Criminal Justice* 19 (1): 22–35.

Carr, Jonathan, Henia Lichter, Jose Garcia, R. Doyle Stulting, Keith Thompson, and P. Randall Staver. 2004. "Spatially Resolved Refractometry: Principles and Application of the Emory Vision InterWave Aberrometer." In Krueger, Applegate, and MacRae 2004, 155–60.

Carr, Nicholas. 2010. *The Shallows*. New York: Norton.

Carruthers, Peter. 2000. *Phenomenal Consciousness: A Naturalistic Theory*. Cambridge: Cambridge University Press.

Carter, Robert Brudenell. 1872. "An Improved Perimeter (for Measuring the Field of Vision)." *Lancet*, July 6, 5–7.

Carter, Robert Brudenell, and William Adams Frost. 1887. *Ophthalmic Surgery*. London: Cassell.

Caruth, Cathy. 1996. *Unclaimed Experience*. Baltimore: Johns Hopkins University Press.

Cerf, Moran, Nikhil Thiruvengadam, Florian Mormann, Alexander Kraskov, Rodrigo Quian Quiroga, Christof Koch, and Itzhak Fried. 2011. "On-line, Voluntary Control of Human Temporal Lobe Neurons." *Nature* 467:1104–10.

Chadwick, Martin, Dennis Hassabis, Nikolas Weiskopf, and Eleanor Maguire. 2010. "Decoding Individual Episodic Memory Traces in the Human Hippocampus." *Current Biology* 20:544–47.

Chang, Yun-chien, Theodore Eisenberg, Tsung Hsien Li, and Martin T. Wells. 2015. "Pain and Suffering Damages in Personal Injury Cases: An Empirical

Study." Unpublished working paper, available at http://ssrn.com/abstract=2406012.

Chase, Oscar. 1995. "Helping Jurors Determine Pain and Suffering Awards." *Hofstra Law Review* 23:763–90.

Chisholm, Roderick. 1957. *Perceiving: A Philosophical Study*. Ithaca, NY: Cornell University Press.

Churchland, Patricia. 2002. *Brain-Wise: Studies in Neurophilosophy*. Cambridge, MA: MIT Press.

Clark, John Greer. 1984. "Tinnitus—an Overview." In *Tinnitus and Its Management*, edited by John Greer Clark and Paul Yanick, 3–14. Springfield, IL: Charles C. Thomas.

Classen, Constance. 2012. *The Deepest Sense: A Cultural History of Touch*. Urbana: University of Illinois Press.

Cleary, Edward, ed. 1984. *McCormick on Evidence*. 3rd ed. St. Paul, MN: West.

Coady, C. A. J. 1992. *Testimony: A Philosophical Study*. Oxford: Oxford University Press.

Cohen, Ilan, Tracy Swartz, Ray-Ann Lin, and Ming Wang. 2006. "Axial, Elevation, and Pachymetric Mapping." In Wang 2006, 41–54.

Coles, Ross. 2000. "Medicolegal Issues." In *Tinnitus Handbook*, edited by Richard Tyler, 399–417. San Diego, CA: Singular.

Collins, Heather. 2006. "Ex-Hartford Officer Acquitted in Shooting; Wants Job Back." *Journal Enquirer*, October 20.

Commonwealth v. Serge. 2006. 586 Pa. 671.

Connecticut General Statutes, 2015.

Cowen, Alan, Marvin Chun, and Brice Kuhl. 2014. "Neural Portraits of Perception: Reconstructing Face Images from Evoked Brain Activity." *Neuroimage* 94:12–22.

Crabb, David, Nicholas Smith, Fiona Glen, Robyn Burton, and David Garway-Heath. 2013. "How Does Glaucoma Look?" *Ophthalmology* 120:1120–26.

Crary, Jonathan. 1990. *Techniques of the Observer*. Cambridge, MA: MIT Press.

Damasio, Antonio. 1994. *Descartes' Error*. New York: Putnam.

Danziger, Kurt. 1990. *Constructing the Subject*. Cambridge: Cambridge University Press.

Daston, Lorraine, and Peter Galison. 2007. *Objectivity*. New York: Zone Books.

Daubert v. Merrell Dow Pharmaceuticals, Inc. 1993. 509 U.S. 579.

Davis, Roger. 2008. "Depression, Suicide, and LASIK Complications." www.lasikcomplications.com/RSSS.pdf, accessed March 11, 2015.

Decety, Jean, and Philip Jackson. 2004. "The Functional Architecture of Human Empathy." *Behavioral and Cognitive Neuroscience Reviews* 3:71–100.

Dennett, Daniel. 1991. *Consciousness Explained*. New York: Back Bay Books.

Devadas v. Niksarli. 2009. No. 107637–07 (N.Y. Sup. Ct., N.Y. County), affirmed, 120 A.D.3d 1000 (1st Department, 2014).

Dormehl, Luke. 2014. *The Formula*. New York: Perigee.

Douglas, Mary. 1993. "Emotion and Culture in Theories of Justice." *Economy and Society* 21:501–15.

Duncombe, Raynor. 1945. "Personal Equation in Astronomy." *Popular Astronomy* 53:63–74.

Dunn, Jeffrey. n.d. "Virtual Reality Evidence." www.lectlaw. com/files/lit04.htm, accessed April 14, 2015.

Dunn, Meghan, Peter Salovey, and Neal Feigenson. 2006. "The Jury Persuaded (and Not): Computer Animation in the Courtroom." *Law and Policy* 28: 228–48.

Durrie, Daniel, and Erin Stahl. 2004. "Comparing Wavefront Devices." In Krueger, Applegate, and MacRae 2004, 161–68.

Dzenko, Corey. 2009. "Analog to Digital: The Indexical Function of Photographic Images." *Afterimage* 39:19–23.

Elkins, James. 1999. *The Domain of Images*. Ithaca, NY: Cornell University Press.

———. 2008. *Six Stories from the End of Representation*. Stanford, CA: Stanford University Press.

Epley, Nicholas. 2014. *Mindwise*. New York: Knopf.

Epley, Nicholas, and Eugene Caruso. 2009. "Perspective Taking: Misstepping into Others' Shoes." In *Handbook of Imagination and Mental Simulation*, edited by Keith Markman, William Klein, and Julie Suhr, 295–309. New York: Psychology Press.

Epley, Nicholas, and Adam Waytz. 2010. "Mind Perception." In *Handbook of Social Psychology*, edited by Susan Fiske, Daniel Gilbert, and Gardner Lindzey, 1: 498–541. 5th ed. Hoboken, NJ: John Wiley.

Eyeworld Staff. 2007. "The IOL Counselor . . . a Cataract Surgeon's New Best Friend?" *American Society of Cataract & Refractive Surgery Eyeworld* (September), www.eyeworld.org/article.php?sid=3628, accessed November 28, 2015.

Fechner, Gustav. (1860) 1966. *Elements of Psychophysics*. Translated by Helmut E. Adler. New York: Holt, Rinehart, and Winston.

Federal Rules of Civil Procedure. 2014.

Federal Rules of Evidence. 2014.

Feigenson, Neal. 1997. "Sympathy and Legal Judgment." *Tennessee Law Review* 65: 1–78.

———. 2000. *Legal Blame: How Jurors Think and Talk about Accidents*. Washington, DC: American Psychological Association.

———. 2011a. "The Brain Sciences in the Courtroom" (symposium remarks). *Mercer Law Review* 62:797–804.

———. 2011b. "The Visual in Law: Some Problems for Legal Theory." *Journal of Law, Culture and the Humanities* 10:13–23.

———. 2014. "Visual Common Sense." In *Law, Culture, and Visual Studies*, edited by Richard Sherwin and Anne Wagner, 105–24. Dordrecht: Springer.

———. 2016. "What It's Like: Demonstrative Evidence of Subjective Experience." In Hamilton et al. 2016.

Feigenson, Neal, and Christina Spiesel. 2009. *Law on Display: The Digital Transformation of Legal Persuasion and Justice*. New York: New York University Press.

Finnis, John. 1980. *Natural Law and Natural Rights*. Oxford: Oxford University Press.

Firestone, Chaz. 2013. "On the Origin and Status of the 'El Greco Fallacy.'" *Perception* 42:672–74.

Firestone, Chaz, and Brian Scholl. 2014. "'Top-Down' Effects Where None Should Be Found: The El Greco Fallacy in Perception Research." *Psychological Science* 25:38–46.

Fowler, Edmund, and R. L. Wegel. 1922. "Audiometric Methods and Their Applications." In *Transactions of the 28th Annual Meeting of the American Laryngological, Rhinological and Otological Society*, 98–132. New York: The Society.

Fox Talbot, William Henry. (1844) 2011. *The Pencil of Nature*. Chicago: KWS

Frederick, Shane, and George Loewenstein. 1999. "Hedonic Adaptation." In *Well-Being: The Foundations of Hedonic Psychology*, edited by Daniel Kahneman, Ed Diener, and Norbert Schwarz, 302–29. New York: Russell Sage.

Freedberg, David. 1989. *The Power of Images*. Chicago: University of Chicago Press.

Frisén, Lars. 1990. *Clinical Tests of Vision*. New York: Raven Press.

Frye v. United States. 1923. 293 F. 1013 (D.C. Cir.).

Galassi, Peter. 2013. "'Bursting with Meaning and Emotions.'" *New York Review of Books*, October 24, 44–45.

Galison, Peter. 1996. "Computer Simulations and the Trading Zone." In *The Disunity of Science*, edited by Peter Galison and David Stump, 118–57. Stanford, CA: Stanford University Press.

———. 1997. *Image and Logic*. Cambridge, MA: Harvard University Press.

Gallagher, Shaun. 2012a. "On the Possibility of Naturalizing Phenomenology." In *Oxford Handbook of Contemporary Phenomenology*, edited by Dan Zahavi, 70–93. Oxford: Oxford University Press.

———. 2012b. *Phenomenology*. Basingstroke, UK: Palgrave Macmillan.

Gallagher, Shaun, and Dan Zahavi. 2012. *The Phenomenological Mind*. 2nd ed. Abingdon, UK: Routledge.

Garry, Maryanne, and Matthew Gerrie. 2005. "When Photographs Create False Memories." *Current Directions in Psychological Science* 14:321–25.

Geistfeld, Mark. 2006. "Due Process and the Determination of Pain and Suffering Tort Damages." *DePaul Law Review* 55:331–77.

Gerrig, Richard, and Deborah Prentice. 1996. "Notes on Audience Response." In *Post-Theory: Reconstructing Film Studies*, edited by David Bordwell and Noël Carroll, 388–403. Madison: University of Wisconsin Press.

Gescheider, George. 1997. *Psychophysics: The Fundamentals*. Mahwah, NJ: Lawrence Erlbaum.

Gibson, James. 1979. *The Ecological Approach to Visual Perception*. Boston: Houghton Mifflin.

Gilbert, Daniel. 1991. "How Mental Systems Believe." *American Psychologist* 46: 107–19.

———. 1998. "Ordinary Personology." In *Handbook of Social Psychology*, edited by Daniel Gilbert, Susan Fiske, and Gardner Lindzey, 2:89–150. 4th ed. Boston: McGraw-Hill.

———. 2006. *Stumbling On Happiness*. New York: Knopf.

Gill, Michael, William Swann, and David Silvera. 1998. "On the Genesis of Confidence." *Journal of Personality and Social Psychology*. 75:1101–14.

Gilovich, Thomas, and Dale Griffin. 2010. "Judgment and Decision Making." In *Handbook of Social Psychology*, edited by Susan Fiske, Daniel Gilbert, and Gardner Lindzey, 1:542–88. 5th ed. Hoboken, NJ: John Wiley.

Gilovich, Thomas, Kenneth Savitsky, and Victoria Husted Medvec. 1998. "The Illusion of Transparency: Biased Assessments of Others' Ability to Read One's Emotional States." *Journal of Personality and Social Psychology* 75:332–46.

Gold, Victor. 1982. "Federal Rule of Evidence 403: Observations on the Nature of Unfairly Prejudicial Evidence." *Washington Law Review* 58:497–533.

Goldman, Alvin. 2006. *Simulating Minds*. New York: Oxford University Press.

Goodman, Nelson. 1966. *The Structure of Appearance*. Indianapolis: Bobbs-Merrill.

———. 1976. *Languages of Art*. Indianapolis: Hackett.

———. 1981. "Twisted Tales: Or Story Study and Symphony." *Synthese* 46:331–49.

Goodwin, Patricia. 1984. "The Tinnitus Evaluation." In *Tinnitus and Its Management*, edited by John Greer Clark and Paul Yanick, 79–84. Springfield, IL: Charles C. Thomas.

Goodwin, Patricia, and Charles Johnson. 1980. "The Loudness of Tinnitus." *Acta Otolaryngolica* 90:353–59.

Goubert, Liesbet, Kenneth D. Craig, and Ann Buysse. 2011. "Perceiving Others in Pain: Experimental and Clinical Evidence on the Role of Empathy." In *The Social Neuroscience of Empathy*, edited by Jean Decety and William Ickes, 153–65. Cambridge, MA: MIT Press.

Graham, Douglas, and Daryl Lapp. 1992. "Day-in-the-Life Videos: Evolving Arguments on Their Making and Use at Trial." *Tort and Insurance Law Journal* 27: 574–94.

Green, David, and Joanna Lowry. 2003. "From Presence to the Performative: Rethinking Photographic Indexicality." In *Where Is the Photograph?*, edited by David Green, 47–60. Brighton, UK: Photoforum and Photoworks.

Greene, Edith. 1989. "On Juries and Damage Awards: The Process of Decision Making." *Law and Contemporary Problems* 52:225–46.

Greene, Edith, and Brian Bornstein. 2003. *Determining Damages*. Washington, DC: American Psychological Association.

Greene, Edith, Kristin Sturm, and Andrew Evelo. 2016. "Affective Forecasting about Hedonic Loss and Adaptation: Implications for Damage Awards." *Law and Human Behavior*.

Gregory, Richard. 1997. *Eye and Brain*. Princeton, NJ: Princeton University Press.

Griffin, Dale, and Lee Ross. 1991. "Subjective Construal, Social Inference, and Human Misunderstanding." In *Advances in Experimental Social Psychology*, edited by Mark P. Zanna, 24:319–59. San Diego, CA: Academic Press.

Groopman, Jerome. 2007. *How Doctors Think*. Boston: Houghton Mifflin.

Guirao, Antonio, and David Williams. 2003. "A Method to Predict Refractive Errors from Wave Aberration Data." *Optometry and Vision Science* 80:36–42.

Gutmark, Ron, and David Guyton. 2010. "Origins of the Keratometer and Its Evolving Role in Ophthalmology." *Survey of Ophthalmology* 55:481–97.

Güzeldere, Güven. 1997. "The Many Faces of Consciousness: A Field Guide." In Block, Flanagan, and Güzeldere 1997, 1–67.

Haack, Susan. 2014. *Evidence Matters: Science, Proof, and Truth in the Law*. New York: Cambridge University Press.

Hacking, Ian. 1990. *The Taming of Chance*. Cambridge, UK: Cambridge University Press.

———. 1999. *The Social Construction of What?* Cambridge, MA: Harvard University Press.

Haidt, Jonathan. 2001. "The Emotional Dog and Its Rational Tail: A Social Intuitionist Approach to Moral Judgment. *Psychological Review* 108:814–34.

———. 2007. "The New Synthesis in Moral Psychology." *Science* 316:998–1001.

Hamilton, Sheryl. 2009. *Impersonations*. Toronto: University of Toronto Press.

Hamilton, Sheryl, Diana Majury, Dawn Moore, Neil Sargent, and Christiane Wilke, eds. 2016. *Sensing Law*. London: Routledge.

Hans, Valerie. 2014. "What's It Worth? Jury Damage Awards as Community Judgments." *William and Mary Law Review* 55:935–69.

Hans, Valerie, and Valerie Reyna. 2011. "To Dollars from Sense: Qualitative to Quantitative Translation in Jury Damage Awards." *Journal of Empirical Legal Studies* 8:120–47.

Hartzband, Pamela, and Jerome Groopman. 2008. "Off the Record—Avoiding the Pitfalls of Going Electronic." *New England Journal of Medicine* 358:1656–58.

Heeter, Carrie. 2003. "Reflections on Real Presence by a Virtual Person." *Presence* 12:335–45.

Heider, Fritz, and Marianne Simmel. 1944. "An Experimental Study of Apparent Behavior." *American Journal of Psychology* 57:243–59.

Helmholtz, Hermann von. (1867) 1924. *Helmholtz's Treatise on Physiological Optics*. Translated by James Southall. 3 vols. Rochester, NY: Optical Society of America. Electronic edition published 2001 by University of Pennsylvania, http://poseidon.sunyopt.edu/helmholtz/OCRVolume3.pdf, accessed February 27, 2016.

Henderson, Lynn. 1988. "The Dialogue of the Heart and Head." *Cardozo Law Review* 10:123–48.

Henkel, Linda. 2012. "Seeing Photos Makes Us Read between the Lines: The Influence of Photos on Memory for Inferences." *Quarterly Journal of Experimental Psychology* 65:773–95.

Henry, James. 2004. "Audiological Assessment." In *Tinnitus: Theory and Management*, edited by James Snow, 220–36. Hamilton, ON: BC Decker.

Henry, James, Kyle Dennis and Martin Schechter. 2005. "General Review of Tinnitus: Prevalence, Mechanisms, Effects, and Management." *Journal of Speech, Language, and Hearing Research* 48:1204–35.

Henson, David. 1993. *Visual Fields*. Oxford: Oxford University Press.

Higgins, E. Tory. 1998. "The Aboutness Principle: A Pervasive Influence on Human Inference." *Social Cognition* 16:173–98.

Hirsh, Ira. 1952. *The Measurement of Hearing*. New York: McGraw-Hill.

Hoffman, Howard, and George Reed. 2004. "Epidemiology of Tinnitus." In *Tinnitus: Theory and Management*, edited by James Snow, 16–41. Hamilton, ON: BC Decker.

Holmes, Oliver Wendell. 1859. "The Stereoscope and the Stereograph." *Atlantic Monthly*, June, www.theatlantic.com/magazine/archive/1859/06/the-stereoscope-and-the-stereograph/303361/, accessed March 12, 2015.

Horberg, Elizabeth, Christopher Oveis, and Dacher Keltner. 2011. "Emotions as Moral Amplifiers: An Appraisal Tendency Approach to the Influences of Distinct Emotions upon Moral Judgment." *Emotion Review* 3:237–44.

Horikawa, T., M. Tamaki, Y. Miyawaki, and Y. Kamitani. 2013. "Neural Decoding of Visual Imagery during Sleep." *Science* 340:639–42.

"How Digital Cameras Work." 2014. In HowStuffWorks, http://electronics.howstuffworks.com/cameras-photography/digital/digital-camera.htm, accessed September 5, 2014.

Howes, David. 2005. "Introduction: Empires of the Senses." In *Empire of the Senses*, edited by David Howes, 1–17. Oxford, UK: Berg.

Howland, Howard. 2004. "Ophthalmic Wavefront Sensing: History and Methods." In Krueger, Applegate, and MacRae 2004, 39–42.

Hughes, Brodie. 1954. *The Visual Fields*. Oxford, UK: Blackwell Scientific.

Hughes, R. I. G. 1999. "The Ising Model, Computer Simulation, and Universal Physics." In *Models as Mediators*, edited by Mary Morgan and Margaret Morrison, 97–145. Cambridge: Cambridge University Press.

Hume, David. (1739) 1896. *A Treatise of Human Nature*. Oxford, UK: Clarendon Press.

Iacoboni, Marco. 2009. *Mirroring People*. New York: Picador.

Igou, Eric. 2008. "'How Long Will I Suffer?' versus 'How Long Will You Suffer?' A Self-Other Effect in Affective Forecasting." *Journal of Personality and Social Psychology* 95:899–917.

"Inner Life of a Cell." 2006. XVIVO. www.xvivo.net/ animation/the-inner-life-of-the-cell/, accessed March 11, 2015.

Jackson, Frank. 1986. "What Mary Didn't Know." *Journal of Philosophy* 83 (5): 291–95.

James, William. (1890) 1950. *The Principles of Psychology*. 2 vols. New York: Dover.

Jampel, Henry, Arthur Schwartz, Irvin Pollack, Donald Abrams, Howard Weiss, and Rhonda Miller. 2002. "Glaucoma Patients' Assessment of Their Visual Function and Quality of Life." *Journal of Glaucoma* 11:154–63.

Janson v. J.D.O.R.A.P., Inc. 2011. No. DBD-CV08-5006215 (Conn. Super. Ct., J.D. Danbury).

Jastreboff, Pawel. 1990. "Phantom Auditory Perception (Tinnitus): Mechanisms of Generation and Perception." *Neuroscience Research* 8:221–54.

Johnson, Chris, Michael Wall, and H. Stanley Thompson. 2011. "A History of Perimetry and Visual Field Testing." *Optometry and Vision Science* 88:E8–E15.

Johnson, Marcia. 1998. "Individual and Cultural Reality Monitoring." *Annals of the American Academy of Political and Social Science* 560:179–93.

Johnson, Marcia, and Carol Raye. 1981. "Reality Monitoring." *Psychological Review* 88:67–85.

Joseph, Gregory. 1996. "Virtual Reality Evidence." *Boston University Journal of Science & Technology Law* 2:212–23.

Kalven, Harry. 1958. "The Jury, the Law, and the Personal Injury Damage Award." *Ohio State Law Journal* 19:158–78.

Kanas, Nick. 2012. *Star Maps: History, Artistry, and Cartography*. 2nd ed. New York: Springer.

Karpecki, Paul. 2006. "Bausch & Lomb Orbscan II/IIz Anterior Segment Analysis System." In Wang 2006, 191–205.

Kay, Kendrick, and Jack Gallant. 2009. "I Can See What You See." *Nature Neuroscience* 12:245–46.

Kemp, Martin. 2014. "A Question of Trust: Old Issues and New Technologies." In *Representation in Scientific Practice Revisited*, edited by Catelijne Coopmans, Janet Vertesi, Michael Lynch, and Steve Woolgar, 343–46. Cambridge, MA: MIT Press.

Kern, Iso. 1997. "Intersubjectivity." In *The Encyclopedia of Phenomenology*, edited by Lester Embree, Elisabeth A. Behnke, David Carr, J. Claude Evans, José Huertas-Jourda, J. J. Kockelmans, W. McKenna, Algis Mickunas, J. N. Mohanty, Thomas Nenon, Thomas M. Seebohm, and Richard M. Zaner, 355–59. Dordrecht: Kluwer Academic.

Kersten, Fred. 1997. "Intentionality." In *The Encyclopedia of Phenomenology*, edited by Lester Embree, Elisabeth A. Behnke, David Carr, J. Claude Evans, José Huertas-Jourda, J. J. Kockelmans, W. McKenna, Algis Mickunas, J. N. Mohanty, Thomas Nenon, Thomas M. Seebohm, and Richard M. Zaner, 350–55. Dordrecht: Kluwer Academic.

Keysers, Christian, Bruno Wicker, Valeria Gazzola, Jean-Luc Anton, Leonardo Fogassi, and Vittorio Gallese. 2004. "A Touching Sight: SII/PV Activation during the Observation and Experience of Touch." *Neuron* 42:335–46.

Kohnen, Thomas, Jens Bühren, Thomas Kasper, and Evdoxia Terzi. 2005. "Quality of Vision after Refractive Surgery." In *Cataract and Refractive Surgery*, edited by Thomas Kohnen and Douglas Koch, 303–14. Berlin: Springer-Verlag Berlin Heidelberg.

Kolber, Adam. 2011. "The Experiential Future of Law." *Emory Law Journal* 60:585–652.

Kranz, Fred. 1963. "Audiometer: Principles and History." *Sound* 2:20–32.

Kronman, Anthony. 1987. "Living in the Law." *University of Chicago Law Review* 54:835–76.

Krueger, Ronald, Raymond Applegate, and Scott MacRae, eds. 2004. *Wavefront Customized Visual Correction*. Thorofare, NJ: Slack.

Kuryluk, Ewa. 1991. *Veronica and Her Cloth*. Cambridge, MA: Basil Blackwell.

Lanier, Jaron. 2011. *You Are Not a Gadget*. New York: Vintage.

LASIK Newswire. 2009. "$5.6 Million LASIK Medical Malpractice Verdict" (June 11). www.lasiknewswire.com/2009/06/56-million-lasik-medical-malpractice-verdict.html, accessed February 19, 2016.

Latour, Bruno. 1988. "Opening One Eye while Closing the Other . . . a Note on Some Religious Paintings." In *Picturing Power: Visual Depiction and Social Relations*, edited by Gordon Fyfe and John Law, 15–38. London: Routledge.

———. 1998. "How to Be Iconophilic in Art, Science and Religion." In *Picturing Science, Producing Art*, edited by Carrie Jones and Peter Galison, 418–40. London: Routledge.

———. 1999. *Pandora's Hope*. Cambridge, MA: Harvard University Press.

Lauwereyns, Jan. 2012. *Brain and the Gaze*. Cambridge, MA: MIT Press.

Lazarus, Richard. 1991. *Emotion and Adaptation*. New York: Oxford University Press.

Lenoir, Timothy. 1993. "The Eye as Mathematician: Clinical Practice, Instrumentation, and Helmholtz's Construction of an Empiricist Theory of Vision." In *Hermann von Helmholtz and the Foundations of Nineteenth-Century Science*, edited by David Cahan, 109–53. Berkeley: University of California Press.

Lerner, Jennifer, and Larissa Tiedens. 2006. "Portrait of the Angry Decision Maker: How Appraisal Tendencies Shape Anger's Influence on Cognition." *Journal of Behavioral Decision Making* 19:115–37.

Levene, John. 1965. "The True Inventors of the Keratoscope and Photo-Keratoscope." *British Journal for the History of Science* 2:324–42.

Levine, Moe. 2009. *Moe Levine on Advocacy*. Portland, OR: Trial Guides LLC.

Levitin, Daniel. 2006. *This Is Your Brain on Music*. New York: Plume.

Lewis, Clarence Irving. 1956. *Mind and the World Order*. Mineola, NY: Dover.

Lewis, David. 1997. "What Experience Teaches." In Block, Flanagan, and Güzeldere 1997, 579–95.

Lieberman, Joel, and Jamie Arndt. 2000. "Understanding the Limits of Limiting Instructions," *Psychology, Public Policy, and Law* 6:677–711.

Lin, Anthony. 2005. "Former Banker Awarded $7M in Damages from LASIK Eye Surgery." *New York Law Journal*, August 1, www.law.com/jsp/article.jsp?id=1122627916703.

Lipin/Dietz Associates, Inc. 2014. "Audiometers." www.lipindietz.com/audiometers.htm, accessed October 4, 2014.

Lloyd, Ralph. 1936. "Evolution of Perimetry." *Archives of Ophthalmology* 15:713–32.

Lodge, David. 2002. *Thinks. . . .* New York: Penguin.

Loftus, Geoffrey, Walter Nelson, and Howard Kallmann. 1983. "Differential Acquisition Rates for Different Types of Information from Pictures." *Quarterly Journal of Experimental Psychology* 35A:187–98.

Lynch, Michael. 1988. "The Externalized Retina: Selection and Mathematization in the Visual Depiction of Objects in the Life Sciences." In *Representation in*

Scientific Practice, edited by Michael Lynch and Steve Woolgar, 153–86. Cambridge, MA: MIT Press.

Lynch, Michael, and Samuel Edgerton. 1988. "Aesthetics and Digital Image Processing: Representational Craft in Contemporary Astronomy." In *Picturing Power: Visual Depiction and Social Relations*, edited by Gordon Fyfe and John Law, 184–220. London: Routledge.

Madeira, Jody Lynée. 2006. "Recognizing Odysseus' Scar: Reconceptualizing Pain and Its Empathic Role in Civil Adjudication." *Florida State University Law Review* 34:41–97.

Mahmoudian, Saied, Mohammad Farhadi, Mehrnaz Mohebbi, Farshid Alaeddini, Mojtaba Najafi-Koopaie, Ehsan Darestani Farahani, Hamidreza Mojallalf, Ronak Omrani, Ahmad Daneshi, and Thomas Lenarz. 2015. "Alterations in Auditory Change Detection Associated with Tinnitus Residual Inhibition Induced by Auditory Electrical Stimulation." *Journal of the American Academy of Audiology* 26:408–22.

Maroney, Terry. 2006. "Law and Emotion: A Proposed Taxonomy of an Emerging Field." *Law and Human Behavior* 30:119–42.

Mattioli, Renzo, and Nancy Tripoli. 2006. "The Keratron and Keratron Scout Corneal Topographers." In Wang 2006, 227–47.

Mauet, Thomas. 2013. *Trial Techniques and Trials*. 9th ed. New York: Wolters Kluwer Law & Business.

Mauet, Thomas, and Warren Wolfson. 2012. *Trial Evidence*. 5th ed. New York: Wolters Kluwer Law & Business.

McKenna, William R. 1997. "Perception in Husserl." *Contributions to Phenomenology* 18:517–21.

Merleau-Ponty, Jean. 1964. "The Primacy of Perception and Its Philosophical Consequences." Translated by James M. Edie. In *The Primacy of Perception*, 12–42. Evanston, IL: Northwestern University Press.

Meyer, Linda. 2010. *The Justice of Mercy*. Ann Arbor: University of Michigan Press.

———. 2014. "Suffering the Loss of Suffering: How Law Shapes and Occludes Pain." In *Knowing the Suffering of Others*, edited by Austin Sarat, Montré Carodine, Cathy Caruth, Alan Durham, and Brian Fair, 14–61. Tuscaloosa: University of Alabama Press.

Meyer, Philip. 2014. *Storytelling for Lawyers*. New York: Oxford University Press.

Miller, Robert. 2011. "Ridgefield Man Awarded $1.5 Million in Accident Suit." *Connecticut Post*, March 4.

Mitchell, William J. 1992. *The Reconfigured Eye*. Cambridge, MA: MIT Press.

Miyawaki, Yoichi, Hajime Uchida, Okito Yamashita, Masa-aki Sato, Yusuke Morito, Hiroki Tanabe, Norihiro Sadato, and Yukiyasu Kamitan. 2008. "Visual Image Reconstruction from Human Brain Activity Using a Combination of Multiscale Local Image Decoders." *Neuron* 60:915–29.

Mnookin, Jennifer. 1998. "The Image of Truth: Photographic Evidence and the Power of Analogy." *Yale Journal of Law and the Humanities* 10:1–74.

———. 2006. "Envisioning Evidence: Expertise and Visual Proof in the American Courtroom." Unpublished manuscript in Feigenson's collection.

———. 2012. "*Semi-Legibility* and Visual Evidence: An Initial Exploration." *Journal of Law, Culture, and the Humanities* 11:1–23.

Mody, Cyrus. 2014. "Essential Tensions and Representational Strategies." In *Representation in Scientific Practice Revisited*, edited by Catelijne Coopmans, Janet Vertesi, Michael Lynch, and Steve Woolgar, 223–48. Cambridge, MA: MIT Press.

Molebny, Vasyl, Ioannis Pallikaris, Sergiy Molebny, and Harilaos Ginis. 2004. "Retinal Imaging Aberrometry: Principles and Applications of the Tracey (Ray Tracing) Aberrometer." In Krueger, Applegate, and MacRae 2004, 145–48.

Møller, Aage. 2011a. "Different Forms of Tinnitus." In *Textbook of Tinnitus*, edited by Aage Møller, Berthhold Langguth, Dirk DeRidder, and Tobias Kleinjung, 9–12. New York: Springer.

———. 2011b. Introduction to *Textbook of Tinnitus*, edited by Aage Møller, Berthhold Langguth, Dirk DeRidder, and Tobias Kleinjung, 3–8. New York: Springer.

Monti, Martin, Audrey Vanhaudenhuyse, Martin Coleman, Melanie Boly, John Pickard, Luaba Tshibanda, Adrian Owen, and Steven Laureys. 2010. "Willful Modulation of Brain Activity in Disorders of Consciousness." *New England Journal of Medicine* 362:579–89.

Mott, Nicole, Valerie Hans, and Lindsay Simpson. 2000. "What's Half a Lung Worth? Civil Jurors' Accounts of Their Award Decision Making." *Law and Human Behavior* 24:401–19.

Mueller, Christopher, and Laird Kirkpatrick. 2012. *Evidence*. 5th ed. New York: Wolters Kluwer Law & Business.

Murdoch, Iris. 1970. *The Sovereignty of Good*. New York: Schocken Books.

Nagel, Thomas. 1974. "What Is It Like to Be a Bat?" *Philosophical Review* 83:435–50.

Nemirow, Lawrence. 2006. "Physicalism and the Cognitive Role of Acquaintance." In *The Philosophy of Mind*, edited by Brian Beakley and Peter Ludlow, 337–45. Cambridge, MA: MIT Press.

Newman, Eryn, Maryanne Garry, Daniel Bernstein, Justin Kantner, and D. Stephen Lindsay. 2012. "Nonprobative Photographs (or Words) Inflate Truthiness." *Psychological Bulletin and Review* 19:969–74.

Newton, Elizabeth. 1990. "The Rocky Road from Actions to Intentions." PhD diss., Stanford University.

Nichols, Bill. 1991. *Representing Reality*. Bloomington: Indiana University Press.

Nickerson, Raymond. 1998. "Confirmation Bias: A Ubiquitous Phenomenon in Many Guises." *Review of General Psychology* 2:175–220.

———. 1999. "How We Know—and Sometimes Misjudge—What Others Know: Imputing One's Own Knowledge to Others." *Psychological Bulletin* 125:735–59.

Nida-Rümelin, Martine. 1996. "Pseudonormal Vision: An Actual Case of Qualia Inversion?" *Philosophical Studies* 82:145–57.

Nishimoto, Shinji, An Vu, Thomas Naselaris, Yuval Benjamini, Bin Yu, and Jack Gallant. 2011. "Reconstructing Visual Experiences from Brain Activity Evoked by Natural Movies." *Current Biology* 21:1641–46.

Noë, Alva. 2004. *Action in Perception*. Cambridge, MA: MIT Press.

———. 2012. *Varieties of Presence* Cambridge, MA: Harvard University Press.

Noë, Alva, and Evan Thompson. 2002. Introduction to *Vision and Mind*, edited by Alva Noë and Evan Thompson, 1–14. Cambridge, MA: MIT Press.

Norden, Lyman C. 1989. "Reliability in Perimetry." *Journal of the American Optometric Association* 60:880–90.

Nussbaum, Martha. 1986. *The Fragility of Goodness*. Cambridge: Cambridge University Press.

———. 1992. "Emotions as Judgments of Value." *Yale Journal of Criticism* 5: 201–12.

Olender, Jack. 1962. "Proof and Evaluation of Pain and Suffering in Personal Injury Litigation." *Duke Law Journal* 1962:344–78.

Önder, Özdem, and Bengi Öner-Özkan. 2003. "Visual Perspective in Causal Attribution, Empathy and Attitude Change." *Psychological Reports* 93:1035–46.

Oppenheimer, Daniel. 2008. "The Secret Life of Fluency." *Trends in Cognitive Sciences* 12:237–41.

Ortony, Andrew, Gerald Clore, and Allan Collins. 1988. *The Cognitive Structure of Emotion*. Cambridge: Cambridge University Press.

Palmer, Stephen. 1999. *Vision Science*. Cambridge, MA: MIT Press.

Pasveer, Bernike. 2006. "Representing or Mediating: A History and Philosophy of X-Ray Images in Medicine." In *Visual Cultures of Science*, edited by Luc Pauwels, 41–62. Hanover, NH: Dartmouth College Press.

Peacocke, Christopher. 1997. "Sensation and the Content of Experience: A Distinction." In Block, Flanagan, and Güzeldere 1997, 341–54.

Phillips, Brian. 2014. "The Dark Room." *Grantland*, December 3, http://grantland.com/features/ray-rice-janay-palmer-elevator-tape/, accessed December 27, 2014.

Plant, Marcus. 1958. "Damages for Pain and Suffering." *Ohio State Law Journal* 19: 200–11.

Platt, Ben C., and Roland Shack. 2001. "History and Principles of Shack-Hartmann Wavefront Sensing." *Journal of Refractive Surgery* 17:S573–S577.

Posner, Eric, and Cass Sunstein, eds. 2010. *Law & Happiness*. Chicago: University of Chicago Press.

Post v. University Physicians Inc. 2002. 2002 WL 32818729 (Ariz. Super. Ct.).

Price, Donald, and James Barrell. 2012. *Inner Experience and Neuroscience*. Cambridge, MA: MIT Press.

Pronin, Emily. 2008. "How We See Ourselves and How We See Others." *Science* 320:1177–80.

Pronin, Emily, Thomas Gilovich, and Lee Ross. 2004. "Objectivity in the Eye of the Beholder: Divergent Perceptions of Bias in Self versus Others." *Psychological Review* 111:781–99.

Propp, Vladimir. 1968. *Morphology of the Folktale*. Translated by Laurence Scott. Austin: University of Texas Press.

Purkinje, Jan. (1823) 2001. "Observations and Experiments on the Physiology of the Senses." In *Purkinje's Vision*, edited and translated by Nicholas Wade and Josef Brozek, 61–102. Mahwah, NJ: Lawrence Erlbaum.

Ramachandran, V. S., and Richard Gregory. 1991. "Perceptual Filling In of Artificially Induced Scotomas in Human Vision." *Nature* 350:699–702.

Reber, Rolf, and Norbert Schwarz. 1999. "Effects of Perceptual Fluency on Judgments of Truth." *Consciousness and Cognition* 8:338–42.

Regalado, Antonio. 2014. "The Thought Experiment." *MIT Technology Review* 117 (4): 53–59.

Reger, Scott. 1950. "Standardization of Pure Tone Audiometer Testing Technique." *Laryngoscope* 60:161–85.

Reiser, Stanley Joel. 1978. *Medicine and the Reign of Technology*. Cambridge: Cambridge University Press.

Revonsuo, Antti. 2006. *Inner Presence*. Cambridge, MA: MIT Press.

Richman, Jessie, Luciano L. Lorenzana, Dara Lankaranian, Jyoti Dugar, Jason R. Mayer, Sheryl S. Wizov, and George L. Spaeth. 2010. "Relationships in Glaucoma Patients between Standard Vision Tests, Quality of Life, and Ability to Perform Daily Activities." *Ophthalmic Epidemiology* 17:144–51.

Rissman, Jesse, Tiffany E. Chow, Nicco Reggente, and Anthony D. Wagner. 2016. "Decoding fMRI Signatures of Real-World Autobiographical Memory Retrieval." *Journal of Cognitive Neuroscience* 28 (4): 1–17.

Rizzolati, Giacomo, and Laila Craighero. 2004. "The Mirror-Neuron System." *Annual Review of Neuroscience* 27:169–92.

Robbennolt, Jennifer. 2000. "Outcome Severity and Judgments of 'Responsibility': A Meta-Analytic Review." *Journal of Applied Social Psychology* 30:2575–2609.

Robinson, Robert, Dacher Keltner, Andrew Ward, and Lee Ross. 1995. "Actual versus Assumed Differences in Construal: 'Naive Realism' in Intergroup Perception and Conflict." *Journal of Personality and Social Psychology* 68:404–17.

Robinson, William. 2008. "Experience and Representation." In *The Case for Qualia*, edited by Edmond Wright, 73–87. Cambridge, MA: MIT Press.

Rock, Irvin. 1966. *The Nature of Perceptual Adaptation*. New York: Basic Books.

Roorda, Austin. 2004. "A Review of Basic Wavefront Optics." In Krueger, Applegate, and MacRae 2004, 9–18.

Ross, Lee, David Greene, and Pamela House. 1977. "The 'False Consensus Effect': An Egocentric Bias in Social Perception and Attribution Processes." *Journal of Experimental Social Psychology* 13:279–301.

Rowe, Fiona. 2006. *Visual Fields via the Visual Pathway*. Oxford, UK: Blackwell.

Rozin, Paul, Laura Lowery, Sumio Imada, and Jonathan Haidt. 1999. "The CAD Triad Hypothesis: A Mapping between Three Moral Emotions (Contempt, Anger, Disgust) and Three Moral Codes (Community, Autonomy, Divinity)." *Journal of Personality and Social Psychology* 76:574–86.

Ruttan, Rachel L., Mary-Hunter McDowell, and Loran F. Nordgren. 2015. "Having 'Been There' Doesn't Mean I Care: When Prior Experience Reduces Compassion for Emotional Distress." *Journal of Personality and Social Psychology* 108: 610–22.

Sacks, Oliver. 2007. *Musicophilia*. New York: Vintage.

Safran, Avinoam, and Theodor Landis. 1999. "From Cortical Plasticity to Unawareness of Visual Field Defects." *Journal of Neuro-Ophthalmology* 19:84–88.

Scarry, Elaine. 1985. *The Body in Pain*. New York: Oxford University Press.

Schafer, R. Murray. 1977. *The Soundscape: Our Sonic Environment and the Tuning of the World*. Rochester, VT: Destiny Books.

Schaffer, Simon. 1988. "Astronomers Mark Time: Discipline and the Personal Equation." *Science in Context* 2:115–45.

Scheler, Max. (1912) 1970. *The Nature of Sympathy*. Translated by Peter Heath. Hamden, CT: Shoe String Press.

Scheppele, Kim Lane. 1998. "The Ground-Zero Theory of Evidence." *Hastings Law Journal* 49:321–34.

Schiffer v. Speaker. 2005. No. 101191–03 (N.Y. Sup. Ct., N.Y. County).

Schkade, David, and Daniel Kahneman. 1998. "Does Living in California Make People Happy? A Focusing Illusion in Judgments of Life Satisfaction." *Psychological Science* 9:340–46.

Schnabel, Julian, dir. 2007. *The Diving Bell and the Butterfly*. Paris: Pathé Renn Productions.

Schofield, Damian, and Stephen Mason. 2012. "Using Graphical Technology to Present Evidence." In *Electronic Evidence*, edited by Stephen Mason, 217–53. London: Lexis-Nexis.

Schwiegerling, Jim. 2004. "Wavefront Information Sampling, Fitting, and Conversion to a Correction." In Krueger, Applegate, and MacRae 2004, 85–90.

Searle, John. 1992. *The Rediscovery of the Mind*. Cambridge, MA: MIT Press.

———. 1997. "Reductionism and the Irreducibility of Consciousness." In Block, Flanagan, and Güzeldere 1997, 451–59.

Sebeok, Thomas. 1994. *Signs: An Introduction to Semiotics*. Toronto: University of Toronto Press.

Shoemaker, Sydney. 1996. *The First-Person Perspective and Other Essays*. Cambridge: Cambridge University Press.

"The Sights and Sounds of Schizophrenia." 2002. NPR, August 29, www.npr.org/templates/story/story.php?storyId=1149147, accessed June 28, 2015.

Simpson, D. A., and J. L. Crompton. 2008a. "The Visual Fields: An Interdisciplinary History: I, The Evolution of Knowledge." *Journal of Clinical Neuroscience* 15:101–10.

———. 2008b. "The Visual Fields: An Interdisciplinary History: II, Neurosurgeons and Quantitative Perimetry." *Journal of Clinical Neuroscience* 15:229–36.

Singer, Tania, Ben Seymour, John O'Doherty, Holger Kaube, Raymond Dolan, and Chris Frith. 2004. "Empathy for Pain Involves the Affective but Not Sensory Components of Pain." *Science* 303:1157–62.

Sklansky, David Alan. 2013. "Evidentiary Instructions and the Jury as Other." *Stanford Law Review* 65:407–56.

Smith, Craig, and Phoebe Ellsworth. 1985. "Patterns of Cognitive Appraisal in Emotion." *Journal of Personality and Social Psychology* 48:813–38.

Smith, David Woodruff. 2013. "Phenomenology." In *The Stanford Encyclopedia of Philosophy*, edited by Edward N. Zalta, http://plato.stanford.edu/archives/win2013/entries/phenomenology, accessed February 19, 2016.

Smith, David Woodruff, and Amie Lynn Thomasson. 2005. *Phenomenology and Philosophy of Mind*. Oxford, UK: Clarendon Press.

Smith, Thomas. 1977. "Corneal Topography." *Documenta Ophthalmologica* 43: 249–76.

Smythies, John. 1959. "The Stroboscopic Patterns: II, The Phenomenology of the Bright Phase and After-Images." *British Journal of Psychology* 50:305–25.

———. 1960. "The Stroboscopic Patterns: III, Further Experiments and Discussion." *British Journal of Psychology* 51:247–55.

Sotomayor, Sonia. 2013. *My Beloved World*. New York: Knopf.

Spiesel, Christina. 2009. "Reflections on Reading: Words and Pictures in the Law." In *Law, Mind, and Brain*, edited by Michael Freeman and Oliver Goodenough, 391–411. Farnham, UK: Ashgate.

———. 2010. "Fate of the Iconic Sign." In *Courting the Media: Contemporary Perspectives on Media and Law*, edited by Geoff Sykes, 51–73. Hauppague, NY: Nova.

———. 2014. "Trial by Ordeal: *CSI* and the Rule of Law." In *Law, Culture, and Visual Studies*, edited by Richard Sherwin and Anne Wagner, 825–47. Dordrecht: Springer.

Spiesel, Christina, Greg Battye, and Neal Feigenson. Forthcoming. "Animating the Bomber: The Sydney Bomber Trial." In *The Sydney Bomber: Juries, Science, and Popular Culture in an Age of Terrorism*, edited by David Tait and Jane Goodman-Delahunty. London: Palgrave Macmillan.

Stafford, Barbara Maria. 1996. *Good Looking: Essays on the Virtue of Images*. Cambridge, MA: MIT Press.

———. 2007. *Echo Objects: The Cognitive Work of Images*. Chicago: University of Chicago Press.

State v. Dontigney. 1990. 215 Conn. 646.

State v. Murtha. 2006. No. CR-03-0568598 S (Conn. Super. Ct., J.D. Hartford).

State v. Porter. 1997. 241 Conn. 57.

State v. Swinton. 2004. 268 Conn. 781.

Steinman, Dolores, and David Steinman. 2011. "Toward New Conventions for Visualizing Blood Flow in the Era of Fascination with Visibility and Imagery." In *Imagery in the 21st Century*, edited by Oliver Grau, 129–48. Cambridge, MA: MIT Press.

Stephenson v. Honda Motors Ltd. of America. 1992. No. 81067 (Cal. Sup. Ct. Placer Co., June 25).

Sunstein, Cass. 2008. "Illusory Losses." *Journal of Legal Studies* 37:S157–S194.

———. 2014. "Who Knows If You're Happy?" *New York Review of Books*, December 4, 20–22.

Swartz, Tracy, Zuguo Liu, Xiao Yang, Mei Zhang, and Ming Wang. 2006. "Topographic Technologies." In Wang 2006, 31–39.

Swartz, Tracy, Renzo Mattioli, Nancy Tripoli, Doug Horner, and Ming Wang. 2006. "History of Topography." In Wang 2006, 3–11.

Tabar, Pamela. 2007. "Mindstorm: Simulating Psychosis." *Behavioral Healthcare*, September 30, www.behavioral.net/article/mindstorm-simulating-psychosis, accessed March 14, 2015.

Tagg, John. 1988. *The Burden of Representation*. Amherst: University of Massachusetts Press.

Tamayo, Gustavo, and Mario Serrano. 2006. "Corneal Topography and Wavefront Sensing: Complementary Tools." In Wang 2006, 131–37.

Tate, George, and John Lynn. 1977. *Principles of Quantitative Perimetry*. New York: Grune & Stratton.

Taylor, Jill Bolte. 2008. "My Stroke of Insight." TED video, www.ted.com/talks/jill_bolte_taylor_s_powerful_stroke_of_insight/transcript?language=en, accessed September 4, 2014.

Tellier, L. S. 1960. "Prejudicial Effect of Counsel's Argument, in Civil Case, Urging Jurors to Place Themselves in the Position of Litigant or to Allow Such Recovery as They Would Wish If in the Same Position." *American Law Reports*, 2nd series, 70:935–56.

Thibos, Larry, and Raymond Applegate. 2004. "Assessment of Optical Quality." In Krueger, Applegate, and MacRae 2004, 55–63.

Tonndorf, Juergen. 1965. "Introduction to Acoustics." In *Audiometry: Principles and Practices*, edited by Aram Glorig, 15–47. Baltimore: Williams & Wilkins.

Torresi, Ira. 2014. "The Photographic Image: Truth or Sign?" In *Law, Culture and Visual Studies*, edited by Anne Wagner and Richard Sherwin, 125–41. Dordrecht: Springer.

Tripoli, Nancy. 2003. "The Zernike Polynomials." *The Aberrometers: Theory, Clinical and Surgical Applications*, edited by Franco Caimi and Rosario Brancato, 15–26. Canelli, IT: Fabiano.

Turkle, Sherry. 1995. *Life on the Screen*. New York: Touchstone.

———. 2009. *Simulation and Its Discontents*. Cambridge, MA: MIT Press.

———. 2011. *Alone Together*. New York: Basic Books.

Turner, Brad. 2012. "Cooking Protesters Alive: The Excessive-Force Implications of the Active Denial System." *Duke Law and Technology Review* 11:332–56.

Tye, Michael. 2003. *Consciousness and Persons*. Cambridge, MA: MIT Press.

Tyler, Richard. 2000. "The Psychoacoustic Measurement of Tinnitus." In *Tinnitus Handbook*, edited by Richard Tyler, 149–79. San Diego: Singular.

Ubel, Peter, and George Loewenstein. 2008. "Pain and Suffering Awards: They Shouldn't Be (Just) about Pain and Suffering." *Journal of Legal Studies* 37: S195–S216.

"US Military Unveils Heat-Ray Gun." 2007. BBC News, http://news.bbc.co.uk/2/hi/6297149.stm, accessed January 31, 2015.

Vallano, Jonathan. 2013. "Psychological Injuries and Legal Decision Making in Civil Cases: What We Know and What We Do Not Know." *Psychological Injury and Law* 6:99–112.

Van Gulick, Robert. 1997. "Understanding the Phenomenal Mind: Are We All Just Armadillos? Part I: Phenomenal Knowledge and Explanatory Gaps." In Block, Flanagan, and Güzeldere 1997, 559–66.

Varela, Francisco, and Jonathan Shear. 1999. *The View from Within*. Thorverton, UK: Imprint Academic.

Vidmar, Neil, and Valerie Hans. 2007. *American Juries*. Amherst, NY: Prometheus Books.

Von Graefe, Albrecht. (1856) 1935. "Examination of the Visual Field in Amblyopic Disease." Translated by Ralph Lloyd. *Eye, Ear, Nose, and Throat Monthly* 14: 117–22.

Wade, Nicholas, and Josef Brozek, eds. and trans. 2001. *Purkinje's Vision*. Mahwah, NJ: Lawrence Erlbaum.

Wagner, Rudolph. 1844. *Elements of Physiology*. London: Sherwood, Gilbert & Piper.

Wakil, Joe, Tom Padrick, and Sergey Molebny. 2006. "The iTrace Combination Corneal Topography and Wavefront System by Tracey Technologies." In Wang 2006, 177–88.

Walsh, Thomas, ed. 2011. *Visual Fields: Examination and Interpretation*. Oxford: Oxford University Press.

Wang, Ming, ed. 2006. *Corneal Topography in the Wavefront Era*. Thorofare, NJ: Slack.

Ward, W. Dixon. 1965. "Psychoacoustics." In *Audiometry: Principles and Practices*, edited by Aram Glorig, 48–71.

Watts, Shelley. 2000. "Technology Creates Winning Visual Evidence." *Trial* 36 (September): 68.

Werth, Barry. 1998. *Damages*. New York: Simon & Schuster.

White, James Boyd. 1973. *The Legal Imagination*. Boston: Little, Brown.

Wilke v. Dudley. 2011. No. 2011CV001897 (Wis. Cir. Ct., Outagamie County).

Williams, David, Raymond Applegate, and Larry Thibos. 2004. "Metrics to Predict the Subjective Impact of the Eye's Wave Aberration." In Krueger, Applegate, and MacRae 2004, 77–84.

Wilson, Timothy. 2002. *Strangers to Ourselves*. Cambridge, MA: Belknap Press.

Wingfield, Nick. 2015. "To Bring Virtual Reality to Market, Furious Efforts to Solve Nausea." *New York Times*, March 4.

Winkielman, Piotr, Norbert Schwarz, Rolf Reber, and Tedra Faziendro. 2003. "Cognitive and Affective Consequences of Visual Fluency: When Seeing Is Easy on the Mind." In *Persuasive Imagery*, edited by Linda Scott and Rajeev Batra, 75–89. Mahwah, NJ: Lawrence Erlbaum.

Winsberg, Eric. 2010. *Science in the Age of Computer Simulation*. Chicago: University of Chicago Press.

Wispé, Lauren. 1991. *The Psychology of Sympathy*. New York: Plenum.

Wissler, Roselle, David Evans, Allen Hart, Marian Morry, and Michael Saks. 1997. "Explaining 'Pain and Suffering' Awards: The Role of Injury Characteristics and Fault Attributions." *Law and Human Behavior* 21:181–207.

Wissler, Roselle, Allen Hart, and Michael Saks. 1999. "Decisionmaking about General Damages: A Comparison of Jurors, Judges, and Lawyers." *Michigan Law Review* 98:751–826.

Wissler, Roselle, Patricia Kuehn and Michael Saks. 2000. "Instructing Jurors on General Damages in Personal Injury Cases." *Psychology, Public Policy, and Law* 6:712–42.

Wolf, Mark. 1999. "Subjunctive Documentary: Computer Imaging and Simulation." In *Collecting Visible Evidence*, edited by Jane Gaines and Michael Renov, 274–91. Minneapolis: University of Minnesota Press.

Wright v. State. 2005. 178 S.W.3d 905 (Tex. App.).

Zahavi, Dan. 2005. *Subjectivity and Selfhood*. Cambridge, MA: MIT Press.

Index

Abel, Christina, 194n3
aberrations (corneal). *See* cornea(s): aberrations of, complex
aboutness principle, 41
accident(s), 1, 4
accuracy, of evidentiary simulation. *See* simulation(s): accuracy of
acoustic trauma, 85
"Active Denial System," 194n1
Adler, Matthew, 118
admissibility or admission of evidence, 2–3, 6, 21, 28–31, 36, 86, 101, 106–9, 131, 146–47, 151–52; ethical constraints on, 152; of expert evidence, 172n16; jurors misled by complacent judicial attitude toward, 29; lack of published judicial opinions about, 114; may be based on relative monetary positions of the parties, 195n13; objections to (*see* evidence: objections); rhetorical constraints on, 152. *See also* evidence: hearing on admissibility of
affective forecasting, 139, 192n26
affective processing, 13
afterimages, 173n9, 176n25
agency, 19
Airy, George Biddell, 185n3
Airy disk, 185n3
algorithms, 19–20, 23, 104, 111, 149–50, 176n22
Ali, Nadeem, 180n16
alienation effect, 143
Allefeld, Carsten, 173n9
Alter, Torin, 165n17
ambivalence (cultural attitude toward simulations), 5, 7, 20
American Society of Trial Consultants, 160n2
American Tinnitus Association, 25, 171n9, 181n31
Amoils, Selig Percy, 106–9
Amsterdam, Anthony, 121–22
anatomical chart, 40–41, 73
anchoring, 4, 44, 116, 128–29, 164n14; and adjustment, 44
Anderson, Douglas, 71, 79, 179n16
Andersson, Gerhard, 182n38
Ando, Shuntaro, 148
Angell, Marcia, 134
anger, 142, 192n24
animation(s), 1, 29, 34, 58–65, 83, 160n2, 195n13; linked to video in *Murtha*, 63–65; normalized by linking to video, 63; scientific, 166n22. *See also* computer animation
anthropology or anthropologist(s), 7, 190n14
anxiety, 57; cultural attitude toward simulations of consciousness, 7, 18; epistemological, 167n26
apostilbs, 178n4
appearance, 9, 163n7; of experience, indistinguishable from its reality, 163n7
Applegate, Raymond, 23, 105, 185nn1, 5

architecture or architects, 16–17
argument from analogy (for understanding other minds), 164n13
Arndt, Jamie, 187n14
Artal, Pablo, 187n9
artificial intelligence, 20
artist's sketch (police), 21, 171n12
artist's sketch (simulation), 5, 21–27, 29–30, 34–66, 69–70, 81, 101, 104, 109, 131, 170n5, 171n12, 175n17, 177n35, 187–88n14. *See also* simulation(s): artist's sketch
astigmatism, 47, 185n2
astronomy, 71, 187n10
attentional focus, 53
attitudes, 12
attorney. *See* lawyers
audio recordings, 1, 97. *See also* sound files
audiologist(s) or audiology, 2, 22–23, 67, 85–86, 88–89, 91–94, 140, 182nn33, 38, 192–93n28
audiometer, 87–89, 95
audiometry, 68–69, 87–91, 95–96, 181–82nn32–33, 35, 37–38. *See also* clinical: exam or testing; clinical: methods or methodology; pure tone audiometry
auditory evidence, 2. *See also* demonstrative evidence; sound files
auditory hallucination. *See* hallucinations: tinnitus as auditory
authentication, 25, 29, 36, 43, 45–51, 101, 147–48; based on litigant's say-so, 4, 22, 26–27, 42, 48–49, 51, 171n12, 175n17; by experts, 147, 170n5; by experts, lacking, 148, 152; of illustrative evidence, authority for less stringent standard, 171–72n14; by plaintiff to visual consultant, 60, 180–81n21; plaintiff's impairment making it difficult for plaintiff to authenticate, 45–51, 181n21
autism or autistic persons, 164n12
automotive-safety experts, 17

Bacon, Francis, 56
bailiff, 143
Balcetis, Emily, 54, 129
Ball, David, 122
Ball, Milner, 143
Bandes, Susan, 142
Banks, Jasmine, 148
Bar, Moshe, 54
Baron-Cohen, Simon, 164n12
Barrell, James, 15, 45, 69
Barrett, Lisa Feldman, 54
Barsky, Brian, 48, 185n4
Barthes, Roland, 49, 98, 183n47
Baskill, J. L., 90, 193n28
Batson, C. Daniel, 192n23
Battye, Greg, 53, 62, 177n32, 184nn47, 50, 190n11
Bauby, Jean-Dominique, 44
Baudrillard, Jean, 20
Baudry, Jean-Louis, 64
Bauman, Natan, 182nn38, 39
Beal, Robert, 186n7
Becker, Bruce, 74
behaviorism, 68
being-in-the-world, 144–45
belief(s) or believing, 4, 12; grounds for, 4; phenomenal, incorrigible or not, 162n5; religious, 98, 184n48; as shaping perceptions, 161n1; in or about simulations, jurors', 29–30, 39–51, 99–100, 109, 113–14, 129
Belting, Hans, 98, 111, 184n49, 187n11
Bennett, M. R., 191n21
bias: in creation of artist's sketch simulations, 50, 70, 80; engendered by Golden Rule arguments, 140; in jurors' judgments, 4, 116, 135–40; jury instructions regarding, 193n29; in litigants' judgments, 50. *See also* confirmation bias; egocentric bias; focusing illusion; salience bias; self-other bias; similarity bias
Biocca, Frank, 18
bioengineers, 3
biology or biologists, 16–17
Bittner, Ava, 79
blame or blameworthiness, 122, 192n24
blind spots, 81
Block, Ned, 8, 162n6
blogger, 161n4
blogs, 147
Blumenthal, Jeremy, 139, 142
body or bodily, 16, 20; injuries, 119; and mind, 70; movements or posture, 13, 15, 54, 120; presence, 15; as represented by images, 184n49; signals sent by emotions, 135; and soul, 178n1
Bolinsky, David, 166n22
Bolter, Jay David, 63, 110
Boring, Edwin, 55, 68, 159n1, 161n2, 171n7

Bornstein, Brian, 117, 137, 189n5, 189–90n7
bots, 19
"bottom-up" information, 26, 162n3
brain(s), 7, 13, 16, 105, 179n5; activity, 9, 149–51, 194–95nn8–9; brain-machine interfaces, 19; conscious, 149; functions, 134; imaging, 19, 149–51, 179n5, 194n8; scans, 3, 19, 149–51
Breidbach, Olaf, 84
Brennan, William, 144
Bronsteen, John, 117
Brooks, Peter, 121
Broun, Kenneth, 28, 168n1
Brown, Kevin, 140
Brown, Teneille, 195n10
Brozek, Josef, 178n1
Bruner, Jerome, 65, 121
Buccafusco, Christopher, 117
Budenz, Donald, 79, 178n4
Budzinski, Mark, 46, 177n28, 190–91n15
Burns, Robert, 122–23, 135, 143
Buysse, Ann, 190n9
Byrne, Alex, 11, 163nn9–10

camera, 49, 52, 63, 104; angle, 82, 174n16; digital, 36, 48, 52, 54, 63; "eye" of, 60; lens, 53, 63, 180n21; surveillance, 64, 160n4; virtual, 60, 64
camera obscura, 176n25
Cameron, C. Daryl, 136
Campbell, Charles, 185n1
Canales, Jimena, 173n9
capabilities, loss of as compensable, 188–89n3, 189n6
Carney, Brian, 73
Carr, Jonathan, 185n4
Carr, Nicholas, 20
Carruthers, Peter, 8, 14, 164n16, 165n17, 170n6
Carter, Robert Brudenell, 71
Caruso, Eugene, 33, 164n14
Caruth, Cathy, 190n8
Catalano, Gallardo, and Petropolous, 108
Catalano, Ralph, 108
Cerf, Moran, 151, 194n9
Chadwick, Martin, 151
chain(s) of transformations, 96, 170n2
Chang, Yun-chien, 189n5
character (plaintiff's), 57, 82–84, 116, 122–23, 127, 130–32, 134
Chase, Oscar, 117, 189n5
chemists, 17
Chisholm, Roderick, 27
Chun, Marvin, 19, 150, 194n7
Churchland, Patricia,11
cinematic narrative, 34, 59, 63–65
Clark, John, 88
Classen, Constance, 7
Clausen Miller PC, 36
Cleary, Edward, 25, 28
clinical: exam or testing, 27, 69–72, 75, 81, 85, 88–89, 94, 96, 104, 147; experts, 109; knowledge, 23, 67–78; measurements, 23, 26, 79, 87–91, 101, 133, 179n5; methods or methodology, 26, 70, 88–89, 93, 104, 133, 181–82nn32–33; practice, alluded to by wavefront image simulation, 112; research, 86, 91; routine practice, wavefront image simulation made in course of, 109; science, 3, 26, 67, 72, 114, 179n5
clone tool, 50
Clore, Gerald, 135–36, 192n24
close-up, 56, 74–75, 82–83, 129
closing argument, 29, 39, 135, 140, 173n7, 191n18
Coady, C. A. J., 119
cognitive inaccessibility, 10, 14
cognitive psychology, 5, 51
Cohen, Donald, 164n12
Cohen, Ilan, 102
Coles, Ross, 90, 182n38, 193n28
Collins, Allan, 135–36, 192n24
Collins, Heather, 65
color, sensations of, 8–9, 11, 53–54
color filtering, 54
coma (corneal aberration), 185n2
common sense, 7, 12, 22, 95, 99, 162n5
Commonwealth v. Serge, 152, 195n13
community norms or values, 118, 142, 189n6
comparative negligence, 186n7
compassion. *See* sympathy
compensation (damages), 4, 57, 116, 121, 124, 128, 193n28
compensation (for perceptual deficits), 54, 80, 105
computer animation, 2, 4, 22, 34, 60, 62–63, 195n13; helping jurors visualize unfamiliar scenarios, 62
computer model, 17–18, 111
computer simulation, 17, 27, 166nn24–25. *See also* simulation(s): computer-generated

computer technology, 3, 102. *See also* digital: technology or tools
cones, 11
confidence, 3, 25, 43; over-, 27
confirmation bias, 42
Connecticut Trial Lawyers Association, 188n2, 191n22
conscious experience(s), 3, 6–8, 10, 14–16, 27; causal account of how it arises from brain states, lack of, 16; fundamentally subjective, 97; as intentional, 14; nonparticipation in wavefront measurement, 186n6; nonpropositional, 97; other people's not directly observable, 150; participation in psychophysical measurement, 69; subtlety and complexity of some making simulation difficult, 149; transcends the subjective, 14–15. *See also* consciousness
consciousness, 2, 7, 9–10, 14–15, 20, 26, 68, 97–99, 120–21, 135; altered by stroke, 171n6; -altering, 167n26; auditory, 99; jurors' intuitive beliefs about, 191n20; may not be digitized, 20; not directly reached by machine readout simulations, 26; perceptual, as false consciousness, 162n3; phenomenal (or "P-consciousness"), 162–63n6; positivist approach to, 135; as presence, 97–98, 183n46; qualia available to, 162n3; temporal dimensions of, 120–21, 190n10
consultant(s), 31, 159n2; visual, 34, 39, 50, 59, 69, 109, 159n2, 170n5
contact lenses, 36, 46–48, 88, 130, 186n6; corrective lenses, 102, 186n6
continuing legal education, 147
convolution, 103
cornea(s), 23, 35, 101–3, 105–6, 110, 112, 187n9; aberrations of, 101–3, 110, 186n6; aberrations of, complex, 103; higher-order aberrations, 48, 105, 130, 185n2; lower-order aberrations, 185n2
corneal topography, 102–3, 185n1; displayed in graphics, 102
Costa, Angiola Massuco, 173n9
court(s) (when not referring to courtroom), 146, 159n2. *See also* judge(s)
court reporter, 143
courtroom, 3, 6–7, 24, 31, 43, 52, 79, 84, 86–87, 92–93, 95, 98, 113, 151
Cowen, Alan, 19, 150
Crabb, David, 80
Craig, Kenneth, 190n9
Craighero, Lalia, 13
Crary, Jonathan, 173n9, 176n25
crimes or criminal case(s), 1, 4, 27, 58, 65, 148, 194n4
Crompton, J. L., 71, 179n5
cross-dissolve, 65, 74
cross-examination, 30, 108, 114, 123, 135, 143, 187n13, 195n11
Crusoe, Robinson, 174n16
"*CSI* effect," 134
CT (brain imaging), 179n5
culture or cultural, 6–7, 20, 134, 153; anthropologists, 7; habits, 175n16; popular, 3; shared, 15; studies, 20; ubiquity of simulations, 19, 62; Western, 184n48
Cushing, Harvey, 71

damage award(s) or damages, 2, 35, 56–58, 85, 106, 116, 118, 137, 186n7, 193n30; based on "gist" judgments, 118, 140; compensatory (*see* compensation); economic (or special), 117, 189n5; noneconomic (or general), 115–16, 189n5; pain and suffering (*see* pain and suffering damages); punitive, 57; simulations may bias, 137–40
Damasio, Antonio, 135
Danziger, Kurt, 68–69
dashboard camera video (dashcam), 1, 58–60, 63–65, 128, 177n39
Daston, Lorraine, 52
Daubert v. Merrell Dow Pharmaceuticals, 3, 86, 108, 152, 172n16, 181n26
Davis, Bill, 73
Davis, Roger, 35–36, 39, 45–46, 49, 56, 80, 159n2, 177n30
day-in-the-life movies, 61, 81–82, 130
deadly force, 58–59
Decety, Jean, 141, 145, 193n32
decibel scale, 88–91, 178n4
decisions (judicial). *See* opinions (judicial)
Deep Blue, 18
defense counsel. *See* lawyers
defocus, 179n14, 185n2
deixis (in photographs), 175n16
deliberations, 25, 29, 42, 87, 96, 129, 142
demand characteristics, 50
Democritus, 171n7
demonstrative evidence, 2, 20–21, 24–25,

28–31, 33, 40, 58, 60–61, 73, 82, 92, 97, 109, 113, 131–35, 138, 142, 146–49, 153, 159n2, 171n13, 183n46; or "aids," 28, 66, 114, 147; law of, 5, 28–31; objections to admission of (*see* evidence: objections); often unavailable online, 147; original doctrinal conception of, 171n13; vividness of, 138. *See also* exhibits (evidentiary); simulation(s)
Dennett, Daniel, 162n5
Dennis, Kyle, 88, 182n35
depth of field, 174n16
deservingness (of plaintiffs). *See* personal injury plaintiff: deservingness of
desire, 19; as shaping perceptions, 161n1
desubstantialization, 19
detachment (as judgmental virtue), 141, 143–44
deterrence, 124
Devadas, Johnson, 34–36, 39–58, 63, 75, 80, 101, 106, 129–30, 172–73n7, 177n30
Devadas, Sara, 34–36, 52, 63
Devadas v. Niksarli, 22, 24, 29, 33–58, 62–63, 69, 75, 80–81, 83, 96, 99, 101, 105, 110, 113, 115, 129–30, 159n2, 170n5, 172n4, 174n12, 192n23
digital or digitization, 3, 5, 7; age, 52; audiometers, 88; camera (*see* camera: digital); of consciousness, 7, 19–20; file (sound), 184n50; images, 22; imagining, 17; life, skeptics of, 19–20; media, 66; mediation, 19; of personhood, 18–20; photograph (*see* photo(s), photograph(s), or photography: digital); simulations of subjectivity, 19; technology, advances in, 149–53; technology or tools, 3, 19, 45, 102, 151; visual field test data, 73
direct access: to fact of the matter, 24; to one's own sensory experiences, 2, 8, 44; to other's sensory experiences, lack of, 2, 8–9, 13, 26, 44–45, 93, 95; by means of photos and videos, to what they depict, 53–54, 83. *See also* knowledge: direct
disability claimants, 2
discipline: in psychophysical measurement, 69–70; in scientific observation, 173n10
discourse: in courtroom, 93–96; scientific, 112
discovery, 147
disgust, 136
Diving Bell and the Butterfly, The, 44
DNA identification (or "fingerprinting"), 95, 182–83n44
doctors, 2, 39
documentary evidence, 1, 32
documentary film or video, 82, 130
Doherty, Bridget, 180–81n21
Donzis, Paul, 39
Dormehl, Luke, 167n27
Douglas, Mary, 190n14
drawing(s): as illustrative evidence, 40–41; by patient of distorted vision, compared to wavefront image simulation, 105, 186n6; of persons, first, 111; as scientific technique, 44–45, 105, 173n9
dreams, 55, 194–95n9; visual content of, identifiable by fMRI, 194–95n9
Duncombe, Raynor, 177n26
Dunn, Jeffrey, 148, 152, 159n2
Dunn, Meghan, 62
Durrie, Daniel, 104
Dzenko, Corey, 52, 175n16

"E" (on eye chart), 103, 106, 108, 110–13
economic damages. *See* damage awards or damages: economic (or special)
economics, 16
ectasia, 35, 105
Edgerton, Samuel, 84
education or educators, 16–17
effigy, 98
egocentric bias, 13, 33, 193n32
egotistical bias: added by simulations, 142; resisted or corrected for by simulations, 129, 144
Ekblom, Neil, 36, 173n7
"El Greco fallacy," 47
electronic medical records, 191n19
Elkins, James, 84, 110–11, 171n11, 187n10
Ellsworth, Phoebe, 135
embodied (experience), 7
emotion(s) or affect, 83, 116, 135–37, 191–92nn23–24, 193n29; appraisal theory of, 135, 192n24; arousal, 137; as central to personal injury case, 116, 135; cognitive content of, 135–36, 192n24; as intuitive moral judgments, 136; jury instruction regarding, 137, 142; as knowledge, 136; moral value of, 135–36; negative, 84; of patient, influencing perimetric test results, 79; prompted by day-in-the-life movies, 82; prompted by

emotion(s) or affect (*continued*)
simulations, 30, 81–84, 113, 116, 135–37, 191–92n23; as shaping perceptions, 161n1; transient, 54
empathy, 13, 15–16, 57–58, 116, 120, 144–45; enhanced by simulations, 191–92n23; in judgment, 144–45; phenomenological, 15–16, 144–45, 166n21
Empedocles, 171n7
engineering or engineers, 17
Enlightenment, 176n25
entertainment, 16
Epicurus, 171n7
episodic memory identification, 151
epistemology or epistemological, 5, 9, 16–18, 20, 26–27, 30, 151; constructivist, 170n2; errors by jurors, 30, 51; positivist, 169–70n2; public space, 113; rationale for admitting simulations, 144; shift in emphasis at trial, 133–34; status or strengths and weaknesses of simulations, 21, 24, 29–30, 39, 67, 101–2, 109, 113–14, 133; of trial evidence, 170n2; value, 21, 26, 28, 34, 109
Epley, Nicholas, 12–13, 33, 164nn11, 13, 14
establishing shot, 83
Ettinger, Peter, 180n21
Evelo, Andrew, 192n27
evidence: argumentative, as grounds for exclusion, 61; auditory, 2, 91–92; circumstantial, 168n1; demeanor, 83; demonstrative (*see* demonstrative evidence); direct, 168–69n1; documentary, 1, 32; experiential, 168–69n1; expert, 4, 86, 152; forensic, 1, 32, 95, 119; "Ground Zero" theory of, 25; hearing on admissibility of, 36, 86, 92–95, 107–9, 114, 177n28; illustrative, 28–29, 33, 39–41, 43, 51, 61–62, 65, 114, 137, 147, 160n2, 171–72n14, 186n7; inaccurate, as grounds for exclusion, 61; independent, 29, 39–44, 49, 51, 104; law of, 25, 28–30; misleading, 4; misleading, as grounds for exclusion, 30; objections, 36, 61, 106–8, 172–73n7; photographic, 41, 48–49, 52, 104; physical, 60; scientific, 3–4, 30, 107, 134; simulations as powerful form of, 24–25; of subjective states, 4; substantive, 28–30, 39–40, 50–51, 63, 137, 171n12; testimonial, 28, 139; trustworthy, 43; videographic, 49, 62; visual, 2, 58. *See also* exhibit(s) (evidentiary); simulation(s); testimony
evidentiary warrant, 2, 24–27, 40
excessive force, 34, 58–59, 160n2
exhibit(s) (evidentiary), 4–5, 21–30, 34, 39, 43, 45, 50–51, 58, 61–62, 65, 67, 74, 79, 81, 84, 86–87, 92, 95–97, 100–102, 106–10, 114, 131, 134–35, 142, 146–48, 159n2, 168n1, 171–72n14, 173n7, 183nn45–46, 186n7; authentication of (*see* authentication); experience-producing, 97; illustrative (*see* evidence: illustrative); misleading, 4; of schizophrenia, generic, 148–49. *See also* demonstrative evidence; simulation(s); sound files
existential, 16, 18–20
experience: aberrant, 11, 14, 83; abilities of memory and imagination enables, 25, 43, 97; always pre-interpreted, according to phenomenology, 165n19; auditory, 33, 125, 183n45; of color, 11, 165n17; conscious, 3, 6–8, 10, 14, 27, 50, 80, 98–99; conscious, essences or types of, 165n20; direct, 9, 13, 84; drawn on in making judgments, 141–42; of emotion, 135–36; extrapolating from, 14; first-person, 10, 15, 99, 105; impaired, 33, 104; inner or internal, 4, 12, 14–15, 23, 108, 131; jurors' attentiveness to plaintiff's, encouraged by simulations, 141, 144–45, 193–94n32; lived, 174n13; of locked-in syndrome, 44; may diverge from what test results indicate, 80–81, 104–5; mental, 3, 100; others' sensory, 5, 8–9; of pain, 8–9, 120, 148; perceptual, 1, 6–7, 14, 21, 24–25, 29, 33, 40, 42, 53–55, 69–70, 83, 99, 105, 114–15, 144–45, 162n3, 165n19, 173nn9–10, 174n13; phenomenal, 6–10, 13–16, 19, 27, 50, 97–98, 112, 120, 149–50, 161–62n3, 162n4, 173nn9–10, 174n12; of plaintiff's consciousness, jurors', 128; plaintiff's, of impaired vision or hearing, 2, 92, 110, 121, 127–28, 138, 187n12, 193–94n32; of pressure, 148; private, 14; representational properties of, 161n2, 174n12; self-reported, 22–23, 32; sensational properties of, 161n2; sensory, 2, 9, 15, 22, 67, 84, 96, 99, 110, 114, 127–28, 131, 141–42, 144, 146, 161n2; of shock, 148; of simulation, jurors', 3–4, 27, 43, 45, 53, 62, 91, 96-100, 110–13, 128–32, 138–40,

142, 144–45, 184n50, 193n32; subjective, 2–4, 6–12, 15–16, 20–22, 25–27, 30, 34, 39–40, 44–46, 48–52, 54–56, 58, 65, 67–70, 73, 81, 91, 93–96, 99, 102–3, 105, 109, 112, 114, 120, 128–29, 134–35, 13[illegible], 153, 173nn9–10, 194n9; of temperature, 148; of time, 190n10; of tinnitus sufferer (*see* tinnitus: subjective experience of); unmediated, 98; verbal conceptualizations of, 15; vicarious, 3–4, 6, 25, 51, 81, 83, 110, 112–13, 116, 130, 132, 138–39, 144, 148, 183n45; visual, 26, 33–34, 40–45, 47–48, 51–53, 55–57, 66, 73, 80–81, 103–5, 112, 149–50, 173nn9–10, 177n35, 180–81n21, 184–85n51, 194n9; visual, neural substrates of, 150; visual, of photograph, 53; vividness of, 109, 116, 142; of the world, unfolding over time and infused by top-down thinking, 174n13. *See also* Golden Rule arguments; presence

experiential (nature of knowledge). *See* knowledge: experiential

experimental psychology, 68

expert(s) or expertise, 153, 186n[illegible]; automotive safety, 17; clinical, 109; disagree about tinnitus loudness scale, 91, 182n38; evidence, 4, 30, 86, 107; ink dating analysis, 172n3; medical, 35, 39–40, 58; scientific, 30, 133–34, 138; testimony (*see* testimony: experts'); witness(es), 2, 6, 30, 39, 106, 114, 134, 147, 194n4

explanatory integration (of item of evidence with fact it is offered to prove), 168n1

expressive value, 118

external phenomena or reality, 1, 3, 9, 16, 27, 49, 52–53, 69, 82, 95

Extreme Vehicle Builders, 85

eye chart, 24, 106, 112, 185n4. *See also* Snellen

eye movements (influenced by verbal priming), 176n23

eyesight. *See* vision

eyewitness testimony, 1, 29, 32, 119, 134, 151, 171n12; in authentication of photos, 49; of single eyewitness as proof, 32

Eyeworld Staff, 185n4

fabula and syuzhet, 64

Facebook, 20

facial expressions, 13

fact(s), 1, 3–4, 24, 32, 50, 52, 98–100, 128, 143; -finding, 4; measurable, scientific simulations representing subjective experience as, 135; phenomenal, 40; phenomenological, objective versus subjective, according to Nagel, 165n18; of subjective experience, may seem malleable if based only on verbal report, 128

"fair and accurate representation" (standard for authentication of demonstrative evidence), 25, 29, 34, 36, 39–40, 43–50, 61, 73–74, 80–81, 86, 93–94, 108, 131, 171n12, 172n14, 175–76n17

fairness (as grounds to exclude simulation), 152

Farkas, Kassalow, Resnick & Associates, 105

fear, 3

Fechner, Gustav, 68, 70, 178n1

Federal Rules of Civil Procedure, 35, 147

Federal Rules of Evidence 403, 30, 136–37, 140, 152; 702, 30; 704(b), 194n4; 801(d)(1)(C), 171n12; 901, 30; 901(b)(9), 172n15; 902, 176n17

feeling(s), 12, 15. *See also* emotion(s) or affect

"feels" (of phenomenal experience), 7–8, 15, 20, 138, 165n20

Feigenson, Neal, 27, 41, 54, 62, 73, 82, 122, 147, 151, 159n2, 177n36, 192n23, 193n29

field of vision. *See* visual field(s)

"filling-in," 80–81

film editing, 64, 82

Finnis, John, 193n30

Firestone, Chaz, 47, 54

first-person: access to one's consciousness, 8; accounts of subjective experience, 112, 128, 133; experience, 10, 15; features of consciousness, 9; perspective on one's conscious experience, 6, 8–10, 14; phenomena, mental states as, 9; point of view in animation or video (*see* point of view: first-person); report, as warrant for accuracy of artist's sketch simulations, 70; visual experience, 105

fixation, 79

focus group, 86, 129, 140, 193–94n32

focusing illusion, 138–39, 184n47, 192nn25–26

folk psychology, 12, 15

folktales, structure of, 121–22

forensic evidence, 1, 32; computerized, 134

forme fruste keratoconus, 35

Foucault, Michel, 167n27
foundation (for admission of evidence). *See* authentication; "fair and accurate representation" (standard for authentication of demonstrative evidence)
Fowler, Edmund, 88
Fox Talbot, William Henry, 52
Frederick, Shane, 139
Freedberg, David, 98, 184n48
Frisén, Lars, 55, 180n16
Frost, William, 71
Frye v. United States, 107–8, 152, 172n16, 181n26
functional MRI (fMRI), 19, 149–52, 179n5, 194–95nn8–9
functionalism, 9

Galassi, Peter, 175n16
Galison, Peter, 17–18, 52
Gallagher, Shaun, 13, 16, 166n21, 190n10
Gallant, Jack, 19, 149
Garry, Maryanne, 42, 50
Gaussian distribution, 55
Geistfeld, Mark, 117
Geomatrix Productions, 73–74
Gerrie, Matthew, 42, 50
Gerrig, Richard, 82
Gescheider, George, 68, 174n15, 178n2
Gewirtz, Paul, 121
Gibson, James, 7
Gilbert, Daniel, 41, 56, 139
Gill, Michael, 43
Gilovich, Thomas, 12, 33, 41, 44
glaucoma, 80–81, 193n28
Goethe, Johann Wolfgang von, 176n25
Gold, Victor, 137
"golden event" (Galison), 18
Golden Rule arguments: law's rule against, 30–31, 116, 140–41, 193nn29–30; as principle of impartiality in ethics, 193n30; and simulations, 116, 140–45
Goldmann perimetry, 71, 79, 179n15
Goodman, Nelson, 15, 170n6, 171n11, 190n11
Goodwin, Patricia, 88, 90–91, 182n37
Goubert, Liesbet, 190n9
graphs (authentication of), 29
Gray, Kurt, 136
Green, David, 49, 52
Greene, David, 141
Greene, Edith, 117, 189n5, 189–90n7, 192n27
Gregory, Richard, 53, 81
greyscale map, 178n4
grid(s), 71, 111
Griffin, Dale, 12, 33, 41, 44
Groopman, Jerome, 191n19
"Ground Zero" theory of evidence, 25
Grusin, Richard, 63, 110
Guirao, Antonio, 186n6
Gutmark, Ron, 102
Guyton, David, 102
Güzeldere, Güven, 8, 149, 163n7

Haack, Susan, 123, 168–69n1
habituation, 70, 139
Hacker, P. M. S., 191n21
Hacking, Ian, 55, 167n27, 170n2
Haidt, Jonathan, 136
halos (after LASIK surgery), 14, 35–36, 43, 46, 50, 56, 129, 173n8
hallucinations, 55; produced by schizophrenia, 3; tinnitus as auditory, 11
Hamilton, Sheryl, 18–19
Hans, Valerie, 117–18, 140, 142, 189n5
Hart, Allen, 189n5
Hartzband, Pamela, 191n19
Harvard University, 166n22
headphones, 2, 86–87, 96, 99, 138, 183n45
hearing, 4, 84; clinical tests of, 23, 87–88, 181–82nn29, 32–33; deficits, 92; distorted, 138; impaired, 2–3, 20, 121, 153, 193–94n32; loss, 85–86, 88, 90–91, 124; normal, 90–91, 182n37; of speech, 181n29; subjective, 24, 93–94; thresholds, 87–88, 90–91, 181n32; as "touching at a distance," 99; as way of being in the world, 126
hearing level (HL), 89–91, 182n38
hearsay rule, 171n12
hedonic adaptation, 139, 192n27; may be underestimated, 192n27
hedonic damages, 188–89n3, 190n7
hedonic value, 117, 139
Heeter, Carrie, 184n47
Heidegger, Martin, 166n21
Heider, Fritz, 111
Helmholtz, Hermann von, 170–71n6, 173nn9–10
Henderson, Lynn, 144
Henkel, Linda, 41–42
Henry, James, 88, 92, 181–82nn32–33, 35, 38, 41
Henson, David, 71, 79, 179nn14–16

Hersh, Peter, 172n7
Hertz, Randy, 121–22
Higgins, E. Tory, 41
higher-order aberrations (HOA) (of cornea), 48, 105–6, 130, 185n2
Hilmantel, Gene, 105
hippocampus, 151
Hirsh, Ira, 87, 91, 181n29
history, 7; of medicine, 133
Hoffman, Howard, 90
Hoffman, Paul, 180nn16, 21
Hollywood movies, 64
Holmes, Oliver Wendell (Sr.), 52–53
Horberg, Elizabeth, 136
Horikawa, T., 195n9
hostile work environment, 3
House, Pamela, 141
Howes, David, 7
Howland, Howard, 103
Hughes, Brodie, 71
Hughes, R. I. G., 166nn24–25
Hume, David, 14, 165n17
Humphrey field analyzer, 71–72, 74, 79, 81
Husserl, Edmund, 14–15, 165n20, 190n10
hydralazine, 57
hydroxyzine, 57
hyperacusis, 85, 124, 162n3, 182n37

Iacoboni, Marco, 13
IBM, 18
iconicity, 18, 49
Identikit, 21
identity, 95, 129
idiopathic intracranial hypertension, 1, 2, 23, 67, 72, 172n17, 180n21
Igou, Eric, 192n26
illusion of transparency, 33
illustrations (simulations as), 20, 25, 28–29, 39–40, 61, 137
illustrative evidence. *See* evidence: illustrative
image(s), 17, 34; of astronomical objects, 110; based on perimetric testing, 71; believed to contain the divine, 98; computer-generated, 29; control or reference, 177n28; of the dead, 184n49; digital, 22, 153; distortions introduced in process of generating, 27; during dreams, identifiable through fMRI, 194–95n9; implying but not depicting temporal duration, 190n11; -making, 98; mental, 25, 129; naturalistic, as evoking trust, 171n7; photographic, 52–53; and presence, 98, 184nn48–49; process of creating, 50, 52–53; of psychophysical simulation, 26; reconstructed via fMRI, 149–51; remembered, as basis for plaintiff's authentication of simulation, 48, 50; retinal, 23, 104–5, 109, 185–86n5; sacred, 98; true (*vera icon*), 111, 187n11
image simulation (wavefront technology), 23, 67, 101, 103–13, 185n4, 186–87nn7, 9, 12; approximates subjective visual experience, 104–5; lacking in immediacy, vividness, and narrativity, 109, 112–13; may differ from subjective visual perception, 105; superior to psychophysical performance tests as measure of optical quality of retinal image, 105
impairment(s), 4, 32, 56, 121, 127–28, 133, 137, 139, 142, 172n1, 187n13, 191n23; atypical, 162n3; judgments of degree of, 45, 121, 127–28, 136–40; plaintiffs' not obvious, 121; may itself prevent plaintiff from authenticating simulation, 46–48; significance of, plaintiffs' efforts to explain, 121, 125–27. *See also* hearing: impaired; vision: impaired or impairments
inattentional blindness, 53. *See also* tunnel vision
indexicality, 17, 49, 52, 61, 80, 104, 111, 150, 166n23; problematic aspects of, 49, 104, 170n2, 174–75n16
industrial design, 16
informed consent, 35
inner experience, 4, 12, 14–15
"Inner Life of a Cell," 17, 166n22
inner lives, 19
inner or internal reality, 7, 43, 61, 95
instructions. *See* jury instructions
intention: as lacking phenomenal features, 149; as shaping perceptions, 161n1
intentional: beings, 15; movements, 15; objects, 14, 166n20
intentionality, 14
intersubjective or intersubjectivity, 15–16, 118; inversion of spectrum, theoretically undetectable, 163n10; knowledge, 15; norms, 118; thinking about plaintiff's pain and suffering, encouraged by simulations, 141, 144–45
Interwave Visualizer, 185n4

introspection or introspective: access or judgment, 8, 15, 23, 25–26, 45, 50, 69, 89; bypassed by wavefront technology, 101
inverted spectrum or qualia, 11, 163n10
IOL Counselor, 185n4
iPod, 86, 96, 184n50
isopter(s), 71, 79–80; map, 178n4
iTrace (wavefront technology), 106, 110, 112

Jackson, Frank, 8–9, 43, 96
Jackson, Philip, 141, 145, 193n32
Jainchill, Michael, 73–75, 179nn5–7, 10–12
James, William, 8–9, 120
Jampel, Henry, 193n28
Janson, Dennis 84–100, 120, 124–27, 131–32, 134–35, 138, 140
Janson v. J.D.O.R.A.P., Inc., 23–24, 67–68, 83–100, 115–17, 119–21, 125, 129, 134, 138–39, 147, 167n25, 174n14, 189n4, 193–94n32, 195n12
Jastreboff, Pawel, 92, 139
J.D.O.R.A.P., Inc., 85
Jeopardy, 18
Johns Hopkins University, 180n21
Johnson, Charles, 91
Johnson, Chris, 71
Johnson, Marcia, 41
Joseph, Gregory, 194n2
judge(s), 1–7, 14, 16, 21, 25–31, 33, 36, 45–48, 51–52, 60–61, 66, 82, 86, 92–95, 106–9, 114, 131, 143, 146–47, 152–53, 170n2, 172nn4, 16, 177n28, 183n45, 186n7, 187n14, 189nn4–5, 190n15; attitude of toward simulations of subjectivity, 4, 29–30, 66, 146–47, 152; instructions (*see* jury instructions). *See also specific judges*
judgment: norms of good legal, 141–45; phenomenological conception of, 144–45; value, in personal injury damage awards, 189n6. *See also* juror(s) or jury: judgments about plaintiffs and their pain and suffering; severity (of plaintiff's injuries or impairments): jurors' appraisal of
jurisprudence or jurisprudential, 116, 140–41
juror(s) or jury, 1–7, 14, 16, 20–21, 25–33, 35, 39–45, 48, 50–53, 56–63, 65–66, 68, 82, 84–87, 91–100, 106, 109–29, 131–45, 148, 152–53, 173n7, 176n20, 177n28, 183n45, 184n50, 186n7, 187nn13–14, 189–90nn4–7, 190–91nn14–15, 20, 191–92nn23–24, 26, 193–94nn29–30, 32, 195n12; cognitive habits of, 122; educating better, 114; judgments about plaintiffs and their pain and suffering, 115–29, 131–45, 192nn24, 26; may misconstrue meaning of wavefront image simulation, 111; may misconstrue probative value of artist's sketch simulations, 28–30, 34, 39–44, 48–49, 51, 62, 137; putting themselves in plaintiff's shoes (*see* Golden Rule arguments); as representatives of community and its norms, 118, 124, 142, 189n6; viewing habits, 110–11. *See also* belief(s): in or about simulations, jurors'; bias: in jurors' judgments; experience: of simulation, jurors'; experience: vicarious; knowledge: provided by simulations
The Jury Expert, 160n2
jury instructions, 28, 30, 39, 61, 114, 116–17, 119, 135, 137, 142, 187n14, 189nn4–5, 193n29; failure to give adequate, 30, 39; form of, 39; in *Janson*, 116–17, 189n4; in *Murtha*, 61; about probative value of simulations, 114; regarding damages, 189n4; regarding pain and suffering damages, 116–17, 119; regarding simulations, examples, 187–88n14; relating to Golden Rule arguments, 193n29
jury room, 25, 29
just noticeable difference (JND), 45, 68–69, 173n11, 178n2
justice, 1, 4, 31, 116–18, 141, 144–45; corrective, 117, 124; empathic, 145; impossibility of achieving perfect, through pain and suffering damages, 117; phenomenological conception of, 144–45
justified true belief, 51; "knowledge" defined as, 27

Kahneman, Daniel, 138, 192n25
Kallmann, Howard, 43
Kalven, Jr., Harry, 189n6
Kanas, Nick, 71
Kantian ethics, 143
Karpecki, Paul, 104, 185nn1, 4
Kasparov, Garry, 18
Kay, Kendrick, 19, 149
Keefe, Hugh, 59–60
Keller, Christine, 61, 66
Keltner, Dacher, 136

Kemp, Martin, 171n7
keratoconus, 35, 105–6, 173n7
keratometry, 101–3
keratoscope, 102
Kern, Iso, 15
Kersten, Fred, 14
Keysers, Christian, 13
Khadafy, Moammar, 39–40, 43
Kim, Taeyong, 18
Kirkpatrick, Laird, 28–29
knowledge: by acquaintance, 9, 15–16; of audiometric data, via sound files, 91; based on perimetric testing, 79; clinical, 23, 67–68; conceptual, 9, 15–16; confidence in, produced by simulations, 43, 99–100; by description, 9; digitally mediated, 17–18; direct, 8–9, 15–16; emotionally based, 135–36; empathic, 144–45, 166n21; empirical validation of, 17; experiential, 9, 15–16, 96–97; experiential provided by sound files, 96–97, 138, 140; of external reality or events, 1, 4, 17–18, 26–27; of how to imagine having an experience, 14; intersubjective, 15–16; as justified true belief, 27; of litigant's or others' conscious experiences or sensations, or of what it's like to experience another's sensations or qualia, 2, 4–6, 8–16, 25–28, 41, 43–44, 50–51, 58, 67–68, 82–83, 87, 96–101, 113–14, 138, 144, 161n2, 163–64n10, 186n6; of manipulability of simulations, 17–18; objective, 9–10, 16, 93, 100–101, 108, 163n7, 165n17, 186n6; objective, closely aligned with subjective, 186n6; of one's own pain, 9–10; of other minds, 10–16, 101, 114, 153, 164nn11–14; of others' pain, 8–10, 120; of others' sensory experiences as less intense than one's own, 13; performative aspect, 99; of persons, digitized, 19–20; phenomenological, 14–16, 144–45, 165–66n21; photos and videos presumed to provide reliable, 41, 49, 53–54, 63; of plaintiff's experience, for purposes of judging pain and suffering damages, 115–16; as presence, 97–99; propositional, 8, 15, 97; provided by simulations, 7, 21, 28–29, 34, 39–41, 43–44, 50–52, 54, 67, 83–84, 87, 92–94, 96–100, 104–5, 109, 114, 128–29, 138, 144–45, 153, 183n45; provided by simulations, affected by stagecraft, 183n45; provided by simulations, less malleable, 128–29; provided by simulations, making difference between knowing and merely knowing about plaintiff's sensory experience, 2, 129; provided by simulations, not reducible to verbal description, 43, 97; provided by simulations, supplementing plaintiff's verbal account, 44; quality of, 21; reliable or reliability of, 3–5, 10, 16–18, 22, 25–27, 29–30, 41–44, 54, 58, 63, 67–68, 70, 79, 91, 101, 112–13; richness of, provided by simulations, 25, 145; scientific, 4, 67–72, 75–76, 79–80, 87–94, 101–5; subjective, 10, 93, 100, 165n17, 186n6; technologically mediated, 26; of tinnitus, imperfect, 92–93, 138; trustworthiness of, provided by simulations, 27, 68, 70, 83; of what it's like to have a perceptual or phenomenal experience ourselves, 8–12, 14, 97, 161–62n3; world, 141. *See also* direct access; epistemology or epistemological; probative value; proof; simulation(s); testimony
knowledge claims, 4–5, 21–22, 25–28, 31, 51, 113–14
Kohnen, Thomas, 105
Kolber, Adam, 3, 153
Koskoff, Koskoff, and Bieder, 85
Koskoff, Ted, 120
Kranz, Fred, 88
Kronman, Anthony, 144
Krouner, Todd, 35–36, 39, 43, 46, 48, 56, 106, 159n2, 170n5, 172n5, 177nn28–31
Kuehn, Patricia, 117–18, 188n3, 189n5
Kuhl, Brice, 19, 150
Kuryluk, Ewa, 187n11

lack, tale or story of, 122, 127, 132
Landis, Theodor, 81
language(s), 15, 120, 129; suitability for conveying meaning of pain and suffering, 120–23; trial as consciously structured hybrid of, 135
Lanier, Jaron, 19–20
laryngoscope, 133
LASIK, 1, 2, 14, 22–23, 25, 33–35, 46, 56, 67, 101, 105–6, 109, 115, 159n2, 170n5, 172n3, 177n28, 186n7
Lassiter, G. Daniel, 54, 129
Latour, Bruno, 96, 98, 170n2

Lauwereyns, Jan, 7, 53, 174n13
law: of demonstrative evidence, 5; of evidence (*see* rules of evidence); public's faith in, 3
lawyering, creative, 3
lawyers, 2–4, 6, 20, 30–31, 50, 93, 95–96, 109, 114, 140, 143, 146–48, 151–53, 159n2, 170nn2, 5, 176n20, 189n5, 190n14, 191n16; advocate(s), 187n12; defense counsel, 92, 106–8, 147, 173n7, 177n28, 187n13, 190–91n15; opposing counsel, 30, 94–95, 114, 136, 172n7; trial, 73, 147. *See also specific attorneys*
Lazarus, Richard, 135
legal decision making, 5
Lenoir, Timothy, 171n6
Lerner, Jennifer, 192n24
Lesser, Robert, 72–74, 79–80, 84, 179n9, 180n16, 181n22
Levene, John, 102
Levinas, Emmanuel, 145
Levine, Moe, 119
Levitin, Daniel, 126
Levy, Mark, 18
Lewis, Clarence Irving, 161n2
Lewis, David, 25, 43
liability, 57–58, 117
Lieberman, Joel, 187n14
Life on the Screen (Turkle), 167n27
Lin, Anthony, 105–6
Lindquist, Kristen, 136
Ling-Cohan, Doris, 36, 39
Lipin/Dietz Associates, 181n30
litigant(s): collaborating in creating artist's sketch simulations, 22, 34–36, 50, 69, 80; cross-examination of, constrained by trial strategy, 187n13; illustrating words with demonstrative displays, 33; offering more simulations in future, 153; participation by in psychophysical measurement, 69–70, 93; perceptual apparatus of, 5; probative value of words of, 26; proving subjective experiences of, 2, 32; reconstructing memories of, 151; responses of to test stimuli, 67; say-so or "that's what I see" by (as foundation for simulation), 4, 22, 26–27, 42, 48–51, 61, 67, 69, 74, 112, 175n17; self-report by, not part of wavefront image simulation, 103; sensations of, 4–5, 21, 23, 97; sensations of as basis for persuasiveness of simulation, 25; subjective experiences or states of, 3, 21, 25–26, 67, 97, 102, 112–13, 168n1; verbal reports by, 1, 32, 43–44, 51, 69–70, 80. *See also* personal injury plaintiff
litigation, 5–6, 109
litigators. *See* lawyers
Liu, Zuguo, 103
Lloyd, Ralph, 178n3
Lobarinas, Edward, 85–86, 88–89, 91–97, 99, 181nn23–24, 182n43, 183n45
Locke, John, 11
locked-in syndrome, 44
Lodge, David, 10
Loewenstein, George, 139, 189n6
Loftus, Geoffrey, 43
loudness, 86, 88–92, 125–26, 139–40, 147, 181–82nn32–33, 35, 37–38; correlation with severity of tinnitus, 182n38, 192–93n28; matching, 88–93, 174n14, 181–82nn32–33, 38, 192–93n28; scales (*see* hearing level (HL); minimum masking level (MML); sensation level (SL)); of simulation or sound files, 96, 140; subjective, 90–91
loudness growth, 90
lower-order aberrations (LOA), 185n2
Lowry, Joanna, 49, 52
luminance values, 72
Lynch, Michael, 84, 111
Lynch, Traub, Keefe & Errante, 59
Lynn, John, 70, 79, 179–80n16

Machat, Jeffrey, 186n7
machine readout (simulation), 21, 23–24, 26–27, 30, 67, 101–14, 152, 188n14. *See also* image simulation (wavefront technology); simulation(s): machine readout
Madeira, Jody, 190n8
Mahmoudian, Saied, 182n40
malingering, 180n16
malpractice (medical), 1, 22–23, 25, 35, 40, 57, 73, 105, 115, 152
maps, 71, 80, 110–12; aberration (wavefront), 185n1; corneal topographic, 185n1; data, 110; diagrammatic, 111; elevation (of corneal curvature), 102; greyscale, 178n4; numerical, 178n4; visual field, 71, 80, 178n4, 180n21
margin of error, 18, 79, 179n15
Maroney, Terry, 142
Maronich, Michael, 86, 92

Martin, William, 160n2, 170n3, 171n10, 182n36
Mary (philosophical problem), 8–9, 96–97
mask (of camera lens, to simulate constricted visual field), 180–81n21. *See also* matte(s)
masking (of tinnitus), 47, 182n35. *See also* minimum masking level (MML)
Mason, Stephen, 17
Masur, Jonathan, 117
match or matching (in tinnitus testing), 88–95, 181–82nn32–33, 38, 192–93n28; "perfect," 94–95. *See also* loudness: matching; pitch: match
MATLAB, 91
matte(s), 74, 76, 80, 82
Mattioli, Renzo, 23, 102–3, 105, 135n2, 186n6
Mauet, Thomas, 28–29, 140
McCormick, Charles, 168n1
McDowell, Mary, 193–94n32
McGinnis, Mark, 177n28
McKenna, William, 166n20
measurement(s), 2–3, 5, 16; accuracy and reliability of, 70, 87–91, 104, 112; in audiometry, 87–92, 181n29; of brain activity, 149–51, 194–95nn3–9; clinical, 23, 25, 68, 72, 84, 88–91; of cornea, 101–3; errors, 79; fully automated, in wavefront, 101, 103; in keratometry, 101–4, 185–86nn5–6; in medicine, 133; objective, 112, 133, 185–86n5, 193n28; in perimetry, 72, 76, 79–80, 178n4, 179–80nn5, 14–16, 193n28; personal equation, 177n26; physical, 23, 61, 67, 169n1; precise, of corneal condition, 23; professionally disciplined, 23, 88–89, 99; psychophysical, 81; psychophysical, partial subjectivity of, 23, 26, 69–70; psychophysical, time errors in, 174n15; of suffering, 117; of tinnitus, 88–90; tools and protocols, 67, 87–89; of vision, alluded to by wavefront image simulation, 112; of vision and hearing, pioneered by Helmholtz, 170–71n6; of visual field (*see* in perimetry); wavefront, 185n1, 187n9; wavefront, accuracy of, 186n6, 187n9; wavefront, variability of, 104, 108–9
Med-Art & Legal Graphics, 160n2
media studies, 5, 51
medicine or medical: brain imaging, 19; history of, 133; illustration, 19
Medved, Victoria, 33
memory, 42; accuracy of at issue, 172n1; inducing false, with photographs, 42, 50; intuitively believed to track reality, 42; long-term, 195n11; reconstructed via fMRI, 151; as shaping experiences, 174n13; as shaping perceptions, 161n1; of witness, in course of authentication, 48
mental experience. *See* experience: mental
mental imagery. *See* image(s): mental
mental life, 2, 7, 149. *See also* conscious experience(s); consciousness; experience: mental; experience: sensory; mind; perception(s); qualia; sensation(s)
mental or physical examination (court-ordered), 147
mental phenomena, 10–11; caused by physiological, including neurophysiological, states, 11
mental simulation. *See* mirror neurons
mental states, 3, 9, 11–13, 163n8; altered, 167n26; defendant's, as subject of expert testimony, 194n4; inferences about others', 164n14; people's reports of their own, 128; supervenience on neurophysiological states, 163n8; "theory theory" of mind perception and, 164n11
Merleau-Ponty, Jean, 144–45, 166n21
meteorology, 16
method of limits, 68, 71, 87
method or methodology (of making evidentiary simulations), 21–22, 35–36
Meyer, Linda, 118, 145, 189n6, 191n18
Meyer, Philip, 121, 190n13
Miller, Robert, 85
mimicry, 13
mind, 2, 7; and body, in psychophysics, 70, 178n1
mind perception, 12; "theory theory" of, 164n11, 166n21
mind reading, 6, 12–13, 15
mindblindness, 164n12
minimum masking level (MML), 182n35
mirror neurons, 6, 13–14, 130, 166n21
Mitchell, William J., 175n16
Miyawaki, Yoichi, 149
Mnookin, Jennifer, 113, 119, 171n13
model(s), 17–18, 138. *See also* computer model
Mody, Cyrus, 84
Molebny, Sergey, 106, 187n9
Molebny, Vasyl, 110

Møller, Aage, 85, 91
monkeys, 13
montage, 63, 65
Monti, Martin, 19
moods, 192n25
Moore, Dawn, 191n17
moral or morality: evaluation, by jurors at trial, 31, 123–24, 141, 144–45; judgment, 143; of jurors' evaluation of damages based on sympathy for plaintiff, 116, 135–36; significance, accorded by jurors to plaintiff's otherness, 145
motion in limine, 46
Mott, Nicole, 117
Mueller, Christopher, 28–29
Munsell color solid, 163n9
Murdoch, Iris, 143, 145
Murphy, Emily, 195n10
Murtha, Robert, 58–66, 128
Museum of Modern Art (New York), 175n16
"My Stroke of Insight" (Taylor), 171n6

Nagel, Thomas, 9–10, 163n7, 165n17
naïve realism, 12; naïve viewer, 41
narrative, 57, 64–65, 68, 81, 83, 113, 121–22, 132, 135; anti-, 134; cinematic (*see* cinematic narrative); holistic, 132; patients', 133, 191n19; plaintiff's, 122–23, 132, 134–35, 190n13; structure, 65, 121–22; verbal, 64
negligence, 56
Nelson, Walter, 43
Nemirow, Lawrence, 14, 43
Neolithic, 98
neurologist(s) or neurology, 71–72
neuron(al), 9
neuro-ophthalmologist(s), 67, 72, 75, 84, 170n5, 179n9, 180nn16, 21
neuroscience or neuroscientists, 3, 7, 9–10, 13, 19, 97, 134, 149–51, 190n10, 191n21, 194–95n9; reductive nature of explanations of mind by, 191n21; research, advances in, 149–53
New York Post, 39–40, 43
Newman, Eryn, 42
news, 16
Newton, Elizabeth, 33
Nichols, Bill, 82
Nickerson, Raymond, 42, 141
Nida-Rümelin, Martine, 163n10
Niksarli, Kevin, 34, 56–57, 172n3
Nishimoto, Shinji, 159
Noë, Alva, 7, 53, 98, 162n3, 183n47
nomos, 124
noneconomic damages. *See* damage award(s) or damages: noneconomic (or general)
nonprobative: items of evidence, 29; some illustrative evidence as, 39–40
Norden, Lyman, 79
Nordgren, Loran, 193–94n32
normal: person, statistically, 55; sight or vision, 9, 55–56
normative or normativity: fact-finding at trial as, 4; goal of liability judgments, 117; judgments about compensable losses as, 189n6; jurors' judgments as, 116, 132; pain and suffering awards as, 118, 142, 189n6; simulation (*see* simulation(s): normatively charged)
not guilty by reason of insanity, 148
novelists, 10
Nussbaum, Martha, 135–36

objective or objectivity: data underlying psychophysical simulation as partly, 67, 69–70; description of causes or correlates of consciousness, absence of, 9, 16; description of external reality, 9; documentary film presumed to be, 130; event, 12; experience, inapplicable to, 163n7; fact, processing of electromagnetic wavelengths producing sensations of color as, 11; features of experience, 9; judgment, promoted by detachment or psychological distance, 143; image quality, 185–86nn5–6; knowledge (*see* knowledge: objective); machine readout more so than other types of simulation, 26–27, 101, 109; measurement, as ground for machine readout simulation, 112; measurement of medical patients' internal functions, 133; measurement of sensation in psychophysics, 68, 178n1; of methods for converting sensations into a simulation, 101; patients' narratives not, 133; phenomenological facts as, 165n17; photos presumed to be, 41, 49, 52; picture resulting from wavefront analysis as, 23, 101; point of view (camera), 64–65; psychophysical simulation more so than artist's sketch, 26, 67, 69–70; re-creation of phenomenal experience, most closely

achieved by visual image reconstruction, 150; representation(s), 16, 105, 150; reproduction, 108; technological, of photos, 49, 52; technology, 95; viewpoint, 10; vision, 55, 176n25; visual deficits, 80, 193n28; of wavefront, compared to visual performance (psychophysical) tests, 185–86n5; world, 12, 65
O'Brien, Tanski, and Young, 75
occipito-temporal visual cortex, 149
"off-screen," 41
Olender, Jack, 117, 119
Önder, Özdem, 192n23
Öner-Özkan, Bengi, 192n23
ontology, 9, 163n10
opening statements, 135
ophthalmologist(s), 22–23, 25, 39, 43, 47, 72, 80, 102, 106–10, 172n7, 180nn16, 18–20, 185n1; neuro- (*see* neuro-ophthalmologist(s)); ophthalmic surgeons, 185n4
ophthalmometer, 102
ophthalmoscope, 133
opinions (judicial), 114, 147, 159n2
Oppenheimer, Daniel, 42
optic nerve, 1, 72, 105
optics or optical, 23, 27, 101, 103–4, 107; of the eye, simulated by computer, 107; phenomena, 54
optometrist(s), 22, 88; tests, 34
Orbscan, 103, 185n1
Oregon Health and Science University Tinnitus Clinic, 160n2
Oregon Hearing Research Center, 182n38
Ortony, Andrew, 135–36, 192n24
ostensive definition, 162n6
other minds, 5, 10–16
other minds problem, 12
Oveis, Christopher, 136
overconfidence, 27

pachymetry, 35, 102
Padrick, Tom, 106, 187n9
pain: accuracy of assessing others', 190n9; communicability of experience of, 120; experience or feeling of, 8–9, 13; knowledge of, 8–10, 13; "pain matrix," 13; physical, 3; sensory qualities of, 13; simulation of, 148; simulation of, ethical constraints on admissibility of, 152; subjective, first-person character of, 9; testimony about (*see* testimony: regarding pain)
pain and suffering (plaintiffs'), 4, 82, 98, 115–21, 123–24, 127–28, 130, 132–36, 140–41, 145, 189n5, 192n26; differentiated, 120; plaintiff as both source of information about and target of judgment, 123; temporal dimensions of, 120–21, 139
pain and suffering damages, 4–5, 34–35, 51, 54, 57–58, 82, 106, 115–20, 135, 140, 142, 188n3, 189n6; affected by jurors' emotional responses, 135–37; affected by jurors' self-relevant thinking, 142; distinguished from general damages, 188n3; distinguished from hedonic damages, 188–89n3; imprecise and arguably unprincipled, 117; justified, 117–18; lack of guidance for jurors in determining, 117; may be assessed more justly on basis of simulations, 144–45, 193n32; not unpredictable, 189n5; variable, 117
painting, 110
Palmer, Janay, 160–61n4
Palmer, Stephen, 11, 53–54, 163n9
papilloedema, 72
paraplegics, 121, 192n25
Pasveer, Bernike, 133
Peacocke, Christopher, 161n2
Peirce, Charles Sanders, 174n16
perception(s), 7, 12, 20, 43, 120, 161n2; aberrant, 11; active, 53; of color, 53; compared to photography, 53–54; direct, 40; fallible, 56; impaired, 161n2; mis-, 59, 63, 65, 161n2; norms of good, 55, 99; phenomenal, 55; present, 50, 69; reconstruction of subjective contents of, 19, 149; remembered, 69, 46; sense, 7; sensorimotor, 7; significance of as intentionality, 14; subjective, 4–5, 7, 25, 34, 50, 59–61, 63–65, 93–94, 105, 108–9, 113, 148–50, 171n12, 173nn9–10, 194n8; subjective, scientific study of, 173nn9–10; subjective, upon exposure to strobe lights, 173n9; visual, 23, 43, 53–54, 60, 75, 104–5, 148, 149–50, 162n3, 185n4. *See also* hearing; vision; visual field(s)
perceptual: abilities, 50; acts, 129; apparatus, 5, 25, 169n1; capacities, 22; contents as analog, 170n6; experience (*see* experience: perceptual); impairments (*see* hearing: impaired; vision: impaired or

perceptual (*continued*)
impairments); judgments, 45; modality, 24; phenomena, 54; psychology, 51; threshold, 69, 72, 178n2

performance: of plaintiff's character, 122–23; of simulation, 84, 93, 96, 99; testimonial, 123–24, 134–35, 137; trial as dramatic, 123, 143

perimetry, 67–69, 70–72, 76, 79–81, 178–80nn3–5, 14–16; automated, 73–74, 79; as clinical science, 179n5; computerized, 71–72; Goldmann, 71, 79, 179n15; kinetic, 71, 178n4, 179nn14–15, 180n21; manual, 71, 178n4; precursors of, 178n3; quantitative, 71; reliability of, 76, 79–81, 179–80nn16, 21; static, 71; test results, 71–72, 74, 76, 79–80, 180n21; variability of test results, 179nn14–15

personal equation (in astronomy), 177n26

personal injury cases or trials, 4–5, 30, 82, 85, 115–16, 119, 132–35, 143, 147, 187n13

personal injury plaintiff, 1–4, 11, 25, 33, 45, 81, 114–45, 151, 188n1; cast by simulations as protagonists in own life stories, 129–31; credibility of testimony by, influenced by simulation, 131–32; deservingness of, 118–19, 121–23, 125, 127, 129–32, 134, 137; experience of (*see* experience: subjective); as heroic character in day-in-the-life movie, 82–83, 130–31; as heroic character in "lack" story, 122, 132; impairments of not obvious, 121; impossibility of making whole through damages, 117; incentive to exaggerate severity of perceptual impairments, 45; otherness of, as basis for jurors' judgment, 141, 144–45; making whole insofar as damages can, 189–90n7; self-observations less precise than those of disciplined researcher, 45; simulation may counter concern about exaggeration of impairments by, 131; some incapable of speaking for themselves, 188n1; suffering of (*see* pain and suffering); sympathy toward, heightened by simulations, 136–37; testifying under oath, 123; testimony by (*see* testimony: plaintiffs'); as unique person, 143–44. *See also* character (plaintiff's); experience: subjective; litigant(s)

personhood: digitization of, 18–20; jurors' concepts of, 190n14; no culture-free theory of, 190n14; respect for plaintiffs', encouraged by simulations, 145; simulations as connecting plaintiffs to their own, 129

pharmacology, 134

phenomenal experience: litigant not trained observer of his own, 45, 173n10; qualities, 2, 7. *See also* experience: phenomenal; perception(s); qualia; sensation(s)

phenomenology, 6, 14–16, 68, 144–45, 165n19–166n21, 190nn9–10; conception of judgment under, 144–45; data, 69; methodological presumptions of, 15; of presence, 183n46; research, 15

Phillips, Brian, 161n4

photo(s), photograph(s), or photography, 1–3, 24, 28–29, 35–36, 39–41, 46, 48–49, 51–57, 81, 83, 110, 129–30; as absence, 183n47; altered or edited, 46, 53–54; always deliberately constructed, 174n16; analog, 104, 175n16; authentication of, 29, 45, 48–49, 175–76n17; basis of artist's sketch simulation, 35; basis of image simulations (wavefront), 185n4; believed to depict reality directly, 41; color, 53–54; constructing plaintiff as perceiving subject, 129–30; control or reference, 52, 54–55, 190n15; as data, 22; digital, 48, 53–55, 104, 175n16; ease and immediacy of understanding, 42; events depicted in as absent, 98; as evidence, 175n16; iconicity of, 49; implying but not depicting temporal duration, 190n11; implying narratives, 177n32; as independent proof of reality depicted, 175–76n17; indexicality of, 17, 49, 52, 61, 104; indexicality, problematic aspects of, 174–75n16; "inescapably but surreptitiously transforms what it describes" (Galassi), 175n16; may be misleading or false, 175n16; mediation of reality by, 53; as "mirror with a memory" (Holmes), 52; as newly fashioned reality of its own, 174–75n16; as not just recordings, 174–75n16; pastness of, 184n50; as "pencil of nature" (Fox Talbot), 52; performative gesture in act of taking as authenticating, 175–76n17; photorealism, 187n12; as presence, 183–84n47; presumed objective, 41, 52; presumed veridicality of, 17, 41, 49, 52, 55–56, 176n18; as recordings, 27, 41, 95;

simulation(s) (*see* simulation(s): photo or photographic); unaltered or unedited, 46, 48, 54–55
Photoshop, 22, 33, 39, 48, 51, 57, 74, 80, 110, 176n20
physicists, 17; nuclear, 17
physics, 6, 10–12, 16
physiology, 6, 10–12, 68
physionotrace, 111
picture(s), 22, 35, 40, 43, 50, 104, 129; conversion of psychophysical data into, 23; criticized by defense counsel in *Devadas* as "fanciful," 173n7; culturally familiar, 110; of family, not used in *Devadas*, 177n30; as more "replete" symbol system than words, 170n6; Photoshopped, 33, 57; represent more fully than words, 171n11; retouched, 40; sense of conscious experience matched to, 50; of what world looks like to person with corneal aberration, objectivity of, 23. *See also* drawing(s); image(s); photo(s), photograph(s), or photography
pitch, 88–89, 91–92, 94, 125–26, 181–82nn32–33; match, 88, 92, 94, 181–82nn32–33
plaintiffs (civil), 2. *See also* litigants; personal injury plaintiff; testimony: plaintiffs'
Plant, Marcus, 117, 119
Platt, Ben, 187n10
Plattner, Richard, 187n7
plot structure, 121
point of view: camera's, 53, 63, 181n21; dashboard camera's, 60, 63–64; defendant's, 63–65; first-person, 14, 65, 75, 83, 112, 121, 130, 132, 137, 163n7, 181n21, 191–92n23; flexibility needed to adopt another person's, 193n32; inherent in experience, 9–10; objective, 10, 64; scientific analog of, 112; subjective, 10, 14, 53, 64, 163n7; third-person, 65, 83, 112, 130, 132; third-person, absent from sound files in *Janson*, 99; third-person limited, 63–64; third-person omniscient, 64; virtual camera's, 60, 64
point spread function (PSF), 103–6, 110–12, 185n4, 187n10
police: investigator, 22; officer(s), 1–2, 34, 58–60, 62–63
polynomials, 107, 109. *See also* Zernike polynomials
Ponvert, Antonio, 85–87, 93, 95–96, 116, 124, 135, 181nn25, 27–28, 183n45, 188n2, 191nn16, 22, 195n12
positivism, 134–35, 169–70n2
Posner, Eric, 117
Post v. University Physicians, Inc., 186n7
postmodernism, 20
predictive shopping, 19
preferences, 12, 19–20
Prentice, Deborah, 82
pre-Renaissance, 98
presence, 97–99, 183–84nn46–50; bodily, 15; of litigant's subjectivity, 97–99; online, 20; phenomenological understanding of, 183n46; and photographs, 183–84n47
Price, Donald, 15, 45, 69
"primordial communication" (Merleau-Ponty), 144
principle component analysis (PCA), 150
The Principles of Psychology (James), 8
probative value, 5, 21–22, 25–26, 28–30, 39, 41, 61, 136, 152, 167–69n1, 195n11; balanced against risk of unfair prejudice, 136, 152; based largely on reliability, 167–69n1; components of, 167–69n1; of DNA evidence, 182–83n44; independent, 26, 28–29, 39, 175–76n17; lacking independent, artist's sketch simulation as, 26, 29, 39, 61–62; of simulations (*see* simulation(s): probative value of). *See also* evidence: illustrative; evidence: independent; evidence: substantive
processing fluency, 42
products liability, 152–53
Pronin, Emily, 12, 141
proof: artist's sketch not independent, 28–29, 39–44, 51, 61; cross-examination of plaintiff as, 123; DNA, 95, 182–83n44; of facts by eyewitness testimony, 32, 119; forensic, 95; methods of, 2; of reality, picture as, 18; simulations as tangible, 128; as verbally framed, 135; of what it's like for litigant to experience what he or she does, simulations as, 20, 22, 25, 34, 39–40, 51, 134; of what it's like for litigant to experience what he or she does, testimony about, 119, 134
"propositional proxies" (Haack), 168n1
Propp, Vladimir, 121, 132
prosecutor(s) or prosecution, 3, 58–59, 61, 195n13

"pseudoevidence," 42
pseudotumor cerebri. *See* idiopathic intracranial hypertension
psychiatry, 134
psychoacoustics, 88
psychological distance (between jurors and plaintiff), 142–43. *See also* detachment
psychometric function, 178n2
psychophysical (simulation), 5, 21–24, 26, 30, 67–101, 104, 114, 188n14; more probative value than artist's sketch simulation, 26, 67, 169n1. *See also* simulation(s): psychophysical
psychophysics, 22, 61, 68–72, 81, 87, 93, 105, 178nn1–2, 180n20. *See also* audiometry; perimetry; visual performance tests
psychophysiology, 162n3
pure tone audiometry, 181n29
Purkinje, Jan, 173nn9–10, 178nn1, 3

qualia, 2, 7–9, 11–12, 161n2, 162n3, 162n4, 163–64n10; of color, 11; inverted, 11; jurors' own, 99; ontological independence from physicalism or functionalism dependent on undetectability of inversion, 163–64n10

Ramachandran, V. S., 81
ray tracing, 106, 108, 111
Raye, Carol, 41
real evidence, 24, 28
realism, 143
reality: of experience, indistinguishable from its appearance, 163n7; external (*see* external phenomena or reality); higher order of, 98; internal (*see* inner or internal reality); objective (*see* objective or objectivity: event; objective or objectivity: world); subjective (*see* experience: subjective; subjective reality); unseen, 98
reality monitoring, 41
reasonableness (of police officer's belief and conduct), 59–60, 63–65
Reber, Rolf, 42
recognition principle (for knowing what it's like), 164–65n16
reconstruction(s), 16, 62; of accidents or events by computer animation, 63; of subjective contents of perception from fMRI data, 19, 149–51, 194–95n9; of subjective perception of faces, 150; of visual memories, 151; of visual perception of moving images, 149–50; of perception of faces, 150
recording(s), 16; audio, 97, 184n50; devices, in perimetry, 72; persuasive force of, 24; photos and videos as, 27, 52, 63; simulations distinguished, 27, 137–38; single-neuron, 194n9; sound files mischaracterized as, 95, 167n25; sound files not, 95; visual, 97
re-creation(s). *See* simulation(s)
recruitment effects, 90
red-green inversion, 163n9
Reed, George, 90
Reese, Cathie, 73–74
reference population (in DNA proof), 182–83n44
refractive error, 101–2, 111–12, 179n14
refractive power, 102, 106, 110
Regalado, Antonio, 19
Reger, Scott, 87
Reiser, Stanley Joel, 133
reliability, 3–5, 10, 22, 49, 63, 87, 179–80nn16, 21; attributed to testimony, 171n12; of automated measurement, 112; as basis for analyzing probative value, 167–69n1; of clinical measurements, 23, 76, 79–80; of evidence, assessed by judge to determine admissibility under *Daubert*, 172n16; jurors misled about, 29–30; of knowledge (*see* knowledge: reliable or reliability of); lack of, for new simulation technologies, 151–52; patients' narratives less so as guide to their physical symptoms, 133; of perimetry (*see* perimetry: reliability of); of photographs, 52; and probative value, 167–69n1; of scientifically based simulations, 134, 147; of simulations generally, 16–18, 25–27, 41, 49; of simulations to come, 151–52; of sound files, 86–87, 91–93; test-retest, 88; of tinnitus testing, 88; of video (dashcam), 63; of wavefront technology, 103–5, 107–8, 112
remediation, 63
representation(s), 17, 47, 73, 80, 184n47; adequacy of often explained by similarity, 171n7; aestheticized, 84; distinguished from presence, 98, 183n46; eliciting stronger sense of presence than does ordinary life, 184n47; fair and accurate

(*see* "fair and accurate representation"); familiar, 18; guided by conventions of older media, 110; mental, 43–44, 164n15; objective, 150; order (or level) of representation, 53, 63; photo as two-dimensional, 53; of reality, 49, 82; of subjective perception, 186n6; wavefront image simulation as objective, 105, 186n6. *See also* simulation(s)

representational properties (of experience), 161n2, 162n4

reproductions, 16, 88

resemblance, 18, 24, 41, 49. *See also* iconicity

retina, 11, 23, 26, 103–5, 109, 148. *See also* image: retinal

Revonsuo, Antti, 97

Reyna, Valerie, 118, 140, 189n5

rhetoric or rhetorical, 52, 54, 56, 114, 119; of animation-video in *Murthc*, 63–65; constraints on new types of simulations, 151–52; of image simulation in *Schiffer*, 109–13; lawyers' goals, 34, 54, 59, 65, 167n28; of photo simulations in *Devadas*, 52–57; of plaintiff's testimony, 119–23; "of the real" (Feigenson and Spiesel), 54; self-reports, virtues of, 24; of video in *Smith*, 81–84; visual, 51–52, 84, 101, 110

Rice, Ray, 160–61n4

Richman, Jessie, 193n28

RisCassi and Davis, 73

Rissman, Jesse, 151

Rizzolati, Giacomo, 13

Robbennolt, Jennifer, 192n24

Robinson, Robert, 12

Robinson, William, 7

robotic arms, 19

Rock, Irvin, 47

Rohrlich, Fritz, 166n25

Roorda, Austin, 23, 103, 187n10

Rose, Aron, 180n16

Ross, Lee, 12, 33, 141

Rowe, Fiona, 71, 79, 178n4

Rozin, Paul, 136

rules of evidence, 2–3, 21–22, 28–30, 136. *See also* Federal Rules of Evidence

Ruttan, Rachel, 193–94n32

Sacks, Oliver, 126

Safran, Avinoam, 81

Saks, Michael, 117–18, 188n3, 189n5

salience bias, 137

Salovey, Peter, 62

Salvi, Richard, 85, 92

Savitsky, Kenneth, 33

Saxton, Brad, 171n8

Scarry, Elaine, 119–20

Schafer, R. Murray, 99

Schaffer, Simon, 177n26

Schechter, Martin, 88, 182n35

Scheler, Max, 15, 190n9

Scheppele, Kim, 25

Schiffer, Mark, 101, 105–6, 108–9, 111

Schiffer v. Speaker, 24, 35, 67, 101, 105–13, 115, 172n4, 186n7, 187n8

schizophrenia, 3, 148–49, 194n3; simulations of, 148–49

Schkade, David, 138, 192n25

Schlesinger, Alice, 106–7

Schmidt, Ted, 186n7

Schnabel, Julian, 44

Schofield, Damian, 17

Scholl, Brian, 54

Schultz, Daniel, 180–81n21

Schwarz, Norbert, 42

Schwiegerling, Jim, 104

scientific: authority or warrant, 2, 4, 67, 106, 108, 113, 133; evidence, 3; expertise, 134; expertise, none needed to make artist's sketch simulation, 22; factors shaping knowledge of other minds that simulations can offer, 153; findings, 94; method, 112; norms, 93; principles and methodologies, 23, 138; research and research subjects, 44–45; simulation, displacing plaintiff's testimony as main warrant for believing her impairments are what she claims, 133–34. *See also* epistemology or epistemological: status or strengths and weaknesses of simulations; knowledge: scientific; simulation(s): scientifically based

scotomas. *See* blind spots

screen: courtroom, 3, 43; versions of reality, 18; video, 74, 84

Searle, John, 9–11, 163nn7–8

Sebeok, Thomas, 49, 174n16

second-person interaction (and phenomenological knowledge), 166n21

seeing, 4, 129–30; is believing, 4; photo simulations of Devadas' acts of, 129–30

self or selves: digitization of, 18–20; as distributable data, 167n27; sense of, 126; as unitary, self-conscious, embodied, and shaped by a subconscious, 167n27; windows on computer screens as metaphor for distributed self, 167n27. *See also* personhood
self-defense, 1, 59–61, 65
self-other bias, 192n26
self-relevant or self-oriented thinking, 141–42, 144
semiotics, 18
sensation(s), 2, 4–7, 21, 23–25, 27, 32, 45, 67–69, 81, 93, 97, 101, 116, 120, 129, 161n2; auditory, 97; of color, 8–9, 11, 53–54; as measured by psychophysics, 68–70; as properties of experience, 161n2; scientific investigations of, 173nn9–10; subjective, 173n10; visual (*see* vision). *See also* experience: perceptual; experience: phenomenal; experience: sensory; experience: visual; hearing; perception(s)
sensation level (SL), 89–91, 182nn37–38
sense impression (first-hand), 28
sense perception. *See* perception: sense
senses, 9
sensorimotor perception. *See* perception: sensorimotor
sensory experience(s): litigant's, 22, 32, 34; others', 5. *See also* experience: sensory
sensory impairment(s), 27, 32, 138. *See also* hearing: impaired; impairment(s); vision: impaired or impairments
Serle, Janet, 180nn18–20
Serrano, Mario, 103
settlement or settlement negotiations, 2–3, 20, 75, 80, 172n17
severity (of plaintiff's injuries or impairments), 50, 54, 115, 119–20, 136–40, 182n37; jurors' appraisal of, 118, 123, 127–28, 132–33, 136–42, 144–45, 195n12; jurors' possible overestimation of, based on simulations, 116, 136–40; perceptions of, relation to damage awards, 189n5
severity effect, 192n24
sexual harassment, 3
Shack, Roland, 187n10
shadow, 110–11
Shear, Jonathan, 45, 161n2
Shoemaker, Sydney, 162n5, 163n10
shooting (police), 1, 2, 22, 29, 59, 65
sidebar conference, 176n20
"Sights and Sounds of Schizophrenia," 194n3
Silva, Robert, 75, 179n13
Silvera, David, 43
similarity bias, 137
Simmel, Marianne, 111
Simpson, D. A., 71, 179n5
Simpson, Lindsay, 117
simulation(s): accuracy of, 22, 27, 39–40, 42, 44–51, 58, 70, 81, 89–93, 108, 113, 131, 138, 144, 147, 180–81n21, 187n9; anchoring jurors' knowledge, 128–29, 144; as approximation, 43; argumentative, according to opponent, 61; artist's sketch, 5, 21–27, 29–30, 35–36, 39–51, 61, 69–70, 80–81, 101, 104, 109, 131, 170n5, 171n12, 175n17, 177n35, 187n14; of atomic interactions, 166n25; of atomic weapons, 17; auditory (*see* sound files); of auto crashes, 17; of buildings and bridges, 17; as cartoon, 58, 83; challenge to by opposing lawyer and/or by opponent's simulation, 147, 190–91n15; computer-generated, 106–7, 112, 166nn24–25; created by consultant, 35–36, 59–60, 69, 74, 80, 91, 170n5, 180–81n21; credibility of, 128; credibility of, influenced by jurors' view of plaintiff's credibility, 131; educational, 62, 84; effect on damage awards, 115, 128; efforts to make more accurate, 92; enabling more empathic judgment, 144–45, 193–94n32; enabling richer mental representations, 43; engendering sympathy, 135–37, 191–92nn23–24; epistemological value or warrant of, 34, 39–51, 133; exaggerating plaintiff's symptoms, according to opponent, 58, 172n7; expense of, 152; of external reality, 4, 17; facilitating adoption of other person's point of view, 193n32; and focusing illusion, 138; fostering sympathetic magic, 183n45; gap between clinical basis of and litigant's subjective experience, 94; generic, 22, 25, 186n7; and Golden Rule arguments, 140–44; helpful only if lawyer thinks it makes litigant more credible and sympathetic, 167n28, 191n16; hybrid of types of, 170n5; as illustration of plaintiff's words, 25, 29, 39–40, 43, 61, 67, 128; image (wavefront), 103–13, 170n5, 185n4, 186–87nn7, 9, 12; immersive,

18, 113, 132, 145, 184–85n51, 187n9; of impaired vision, 160n2, 177n28, 187n9; inaccurate, according to opponent, 36, 61; likely to increase in number, 146–51; interacting with plaintiff's testimony, 116, 128, 131–35; knowledge offered by, 2–4, 21–28, 31, 39–51, 82–83, 87–93, 116, 129, 136, 144, 167n27; machine readout, 21, 23–24, 26–27, 67, 101–14, 150, 152, 188n14; made in course of routine clinical scientific practice, 109; making litigant's experience seem real, 57; making litigant's phenomenal experience seem present, 97–99, 184n47; manipulability of, 17–18; may be misconstrued, 111; may bias judgments, 136–40, 192nn24–26; may bolster plaintiff's credibility, 191n18; may compensate for perceived deficits in plaintiff's testimony, 132; may confuse jurors' judgments of how bad it is for plaintiff to endure her impairments, 116, 136–42; may correct for tendency to underestimate suffering from tinnitus, 139; may counter concerns about exaggeration of impairments, 13_; may lead to overestimation of severity of plaintiff's pain and suffering, 136–40; might not be challenged, 187n13; misleading, according to opponent, 36; as models of reality, 16–18; as narratives, 57, 63–65, 82–84, 132; normatively charged, 128–31; not independent proof, 61; not photographs, 166n25; not seriously challenged by opposing counsel in *Devadas*, 172–73n7; number used to date, 159–60n2; objections to admissibility of, 36, 61, 92, 107–8, 151–52; offering vicarious experience (*see* experience: vicarious); of other minds, 13, 167n27; overcoming distance between litigant's conscious experience and ours, 98, 144–45; of past experience, 58, 61, 151, 177n35; as persuasive or powerful form of evidence, 24–25, 27, 43, 56–57, 74, 81–84, 130, 132, 146; as persuasive evidence, image simulations arguably less effective than other types of, 102, 109–10, 112–13; phenomenal detail of, 40; photo or photographic, 27, 35–36, 39–58, 62, 69, 75, 96, 99, 113, 129–30, 159n2, 170n5, 172n7, 185n4, 187n12, 192n23; of physical pain, 148; plaintiff's impairment may prevent plaintiff from authenticating, 46–48, 181n21; and presence-absence dynamic, 184n47; preserves particularity or strangeness of plaintiff's experience, 129, 144–45, 193–94n32; probative value of, 28–30, 34, 39–40, 44, 51, 167–69n1; prompting emotional responses, 30, 81–84, 135–37, 191–92n23; psychophysical, 5, 21–24, 26, 67–100, 104, 114, 150, 152, 180–81n21, 188n14; recordings, distinguished from, 95, 109, 138; reliability of, 16–18, 22–27, 29–30, 39, 41–42, 49, 52, 58, 70, 75, 86–87, 91–93, 107–8, 113, 131, 134, 138, 162n3, 168n1, 180–81n21; reliability of new types of may be lacking, 152; of schizophrenia, 148–49; scientifically based, 4, 17, 22–24, 27, 30, 67–114, 132–35, 147, 150, 152, 187n12; as second-best epistemological option, 16, 150; as shifting moral focus of trial, 128, 132–35; and subjective experience, gap between, 95, 105, 150; of subjective experience or subjectivity, 2–6, 16, 18–20, 41–42, 48–50, 58–59, 67, 81–84, 87, 93–95, 112–14, 130, 135, 140, 142, 144–45, 150–51, 153, 159n2, 167–69n1, 180–81n21, 184n47, 184–85n51, 194–95nn8–9; subjunctive nature of, 17; of subtle phenomenal features, less likely, 149; as tangible proof, 128; in time-based media, 120–21; of tinnitus, 2, 22–23, 86–87, 91–100, 183n45; trustworthiness of, 22–23, 53, 92, 108; trustworthiness of method of converting information into exhibit, 22, 76, 80–81, 91, 101, 150; video, 23, 68, 73–75, 80–84, 99, 113, 121, 130–31, 134, 151, 180–81n21, 192n23; videolike, 151; visual (*see* photo(s), photograph(s), or photography); vividness of, 137–38, 193–94n32. *See also* computer simulation; image simulation; reconstruction(s); sound files

simulation theory (of mind perception), 164n11, 166n21

Singer, Tania, 13

Sklansky, David, 187n14

Smith, Craig, 135

Smith, David Woodruff, 165n20

Smith v. Jones, 23–24, 67–68, 70, 72–84, 99, 112–13, 121, 129–30, 134, 172n17, 180n21, 192n23

Smith, Rosalind (pseudonym), 72–75, 79–84, 130
Smith, Thomas, 102
Smythies, John, 173n9
Snellen ("E" or eye chart), 103, 106, 108, 187n10
social networking, 19
social proof, 100
somatic markers, 135
Sotomayor, Sonia, 144
sound(s), 22, 99; conversion of psychophysical data into, 23, 91; of psychophysical simulation, 26; synthesized, 92, 95. *See also* sound files
sound files, 2, 22, 24, 47, 67–68, 83, 86–87, 91–99, 121, 132, 138–40, 147, 160n2, 167n25, 174n14, 184n50, 195n12; allowing experience of sound as present event, 184n50; competing, based on measurements using different loudness scales, 147; computer-generated, 99; distortions introduced in process of generating, 27; made for research, 85; may exacerbate focusing illusion, 138. See also *Janson v. J.D.O.R.A.P., Inc.*
"Sounds of Tinnitus," 25
Speaker, Mark, 105–6
spherical aberration (of cornea), 185n2
Spiesel, Christina, 41, 54, 62, 82, 134, 174n16, 176n23, 177n36
Stafford, Barbara Maria, 19, 167n26
Stahl, Erin, 104
starbursts (after LASIK surgery), 14, 34–36, 43, 51, 56, 173n8, 186n7
State v. Dontigney, 171n14
State v. Murtha, 22, 29, 33, 58–66, 69, 80, 83, 112–13, 151, 160n2, 172n1, 177n35
State v. Porter, 181n26
State v. Swinton, 28
state of mind. *See* mental states
statistical significance, 94
Steinman, David, 84
Steinman, Dolores, 84
Stephenson v. Honda Motors Ltd. of America, 194n2
stimulus: intensity, 71, 178n2; threshold, 68. *See also* test stimuli
storyboard, 60
storytelling: as central to personal injury trial, 121–22; as moral enterprise, 122; visual, 64–65, 113. *See also* narrative
Sturm, Kristin, 192n27
subconscious, 20
subjective experience(s). *See* experience: subjective; tinnitus: subjective; vision: subjective
subjective knowledge. *See* knowledge: subjective
subjective perception(s). *See* perception(s): subjective
subjective reality, 3, 24, 42–43, 95
subjective states, 4, 178n1; transitory, impossible to capture given current technology, 151
subjectivity: aligned with objectivity in wavefront measurement, 186n6; in contrast to objective vision, 176n25; "exact," 178n1; litigant's or plaintiff's, 53, 97, 116, 144–45; of phenomenal perception, 55, 176n25; and presence, 97–99; simulation of, 3, 5, 18–20, 83; of visual experience, history of, 176n25. *See also* conscious experience(s); consciousness; experience: phenomenal; experience: sensory; experience: subjective; perception(s): subjective; point of view: first-person; sensation(s); subjective reality
subjunctive, or subjunctivity (of simulations), 17
substantive evidence. *See* evidence: substantive
sudarium, 187n11
suffering. *See* pain and suffering
summation. *See* closing argument
Sunstein, Cass, 19, 117, 139, 189n3
supervenience, 11, 163n8
Supreme Court (United States), 3; Justices of, 144
surveillance camera. *See* camera: surveillance
Swann, William, 43
Swartz, Tracy, 102
sympathetic magic, 183n45
sympathy, 56–57, 65, 83, 116, 127, 135–37, 142, 144–45, 192n24; balanced against detachment in good legal judgment, 141, 143–44; as potential source of bias in judgment, 136–37, 192n24

Tabar, Pamela, 148
Tager-Flusberg, Helen, 164n12
Tagg, John, 111, 174–75n16
Tamayo, Gustavo, 103

tapping experiment, 33, 172n2
Tate, George, 70, 79, 179–80n16
Taylor, Jeffrey, 59–60, 159n2, 177nn37–38
Taylor, Jill Bolte, 171n6
Techniques of the Observer (Crary), 175n25
Tellier, L. S., 140
test stimuli, 23, 67, 71, 79–80, 179nn14–15
test-retest reliability, 88, 180n16
testimonial infirmities, 32
testimony, 1–2, 24, 28; credibility of, 58, 61–62, 128; credibility of plaintiffs', as influencing uptake of simulation, 131; doctors', 2, 35, 80, 85; earwitness, 29, 32; experts', 1, 35, 39–40, 43, 62–63, 80, 85–86, 93, 95–96, 100, 106–8, 119, 134, 147, 170n5; eyewitness, 1, 29, 32, 100, 119, 134, 151, 171n12; eyewitness, flaws in, 32; interacting with simulations (*see* simulation(s): interacting with plaintiff's testimony); litigants', 29, 32, 34, 44, 61–62, 168–69n1, 171n12; medical, 36; other witnesses', 2, 36, 39, 119; regarding pain, 119; as performance, 122–24, 134–35, 191n16; plaintiffs', 2, 4–5, 35–36, 39–40, 43, 56–57, 73, 82, 94, 115–16, 119–29, 131–35, 191n16; plaintiffs', as moral focus of personal injury trial, 123–24, 128, 132–35; police officers', 2; regarding what it's like to live with plaintiff's pain, 119; simulations may compensate for perceived deficits in, 132
Theory of Colors (Goethe), 176n25
thermometer, 133
Thibos, Larry, 23, 105, 185nn1, 5
thinking, 12
Thinks . . . (Lodge), 10
third-person: accounts of subjective experience, 112; features of experience, 9; observation, 166n21; observation, as warrant for accuracy of psychophysical simulations, 70; point of view in animation or video (*see* point of view: third-person); reality, 9; representations, cannot generate for conscious experience, 16
Thomas, James, 61
Thomasson, Amie Lynn, 165n20
Thompson, Evan, 162n3
Thompson, H. Stanley, 71
Tiedens, Larissa, 192n24
time: in pain and suffering, 120–21; shifts in narrative, 64; in trials, condensed, 123; in video, 81–82
tinnitus, 1–3, 14, 22–23, 25, 47, 68, 85–96, 99, 124–27, 138, 140, 142, 148, 160n2, 174n14, 181–82nn33, 35, 37–38, 183n45, 191n16; as phantom injury, 85; severity of not well correlated with loudness, 182n38, 192–93n28; subjective, 11, 161n2; subjective experience of, 92–93, 96, 140
TLC Laser Eye Center, 105–6
Tonndorf, Juergen, 90
"top-down" cognition or processing, 26, 54, 162n3
Torresi, Ira, 176n18
trace, 110–11
Tracey Technologies, 106, 110
trefoil (corneal aberration), 185n2
Trial, 160n2
trial(s), 4, 6, 20, 31, 114, 119, 123; evidentiary phase of, 29; as intersubjective experience, 123; lawyers (*see* lawyers: trial); moral dimensions of, 123–24; about more than determining facts, 31; as performance, 123; practice, 3, 142; as theater, 143
trial judge. *See* judge(s); *and particular judges*
trier(s) of fact, 20, 28, 50
Tripoli, Nancy, 23, 103, 105, 185n2, 186n6
trust: in plaintiff's other testimony, as affected by jurors' belief in credibility of plaintiff's description of her sensory experience, 131; in plaintiff's words, as basis for jurors' judgments, 123, 133
trustworthy or trustworthiness: of evidence, 3; of method of converting information about subjective experience into exhibit, 22; of photographic evidence, 49; of simulation (*see* simulation(s): trustworthiness of); of witness, 131
truth, 3; intuitive beliefs about, 41; performed at trial, 143; -seeking, 31
tunnel vision, 60, 63. *See also* inattentional blindness
Turing test, 20
Turkle, Sherry, 17–20, 167n27
Turner, Brad, 148, 194n1
20/20 vision, 46–47, 55, 177n28
two-alternative forced choice method (of measuring tinnitus), 88
Tye, Michael, 174n12
Tyler, Richard, 88, 92, 181n33, 182nn38, 42

Ubel, Peter, 189n6
uncertainty, 18
unfair prejudice, 30, 136–37, 140, 192n24. *See also* Federal Rules of Evidence 403
U.S. Army, 148
University of Buffalo, Department of Communicative Disorders and Sciences, 85
University of Connecticut Health Center, 72
University of Texas at Dallas, School of Behavioral and Brain Sciences, 181n23

Vallano, Jonathan, 189n5
van Gulick, Robert, 10
Varela, Francisco, 45, 161n2
vegetative (patients), 19
verbal: conceptualizations of experience, 15; description or self-reports of subjective experience, 1, 10, 24–26, 32–33, 42–43, 45, 69, 80, 131, 137, 193n28, 193–94n32; framing, 43; priming, 176n23; reports, imprecision of, 24, 128; reports of subjective experience, compared with psychophysical data, 69
verdict(s), 3, 65, 87, 106, 115, 172n4, 189n5
Veterans Administration, 89
vicarious experience. *See* experience: vicarious
video(s), 1–3, 24, 28–29, 73–74, 80–84; always deliberately constructed, 174n16; animation, 29, 59, 61, 65; authentication of, 29; dashboard camera, 1, 58–60, 63–65, 128, 177n39; eliciting emotional responses, 81–82; events depicted in as absent, 98; as independent proof of reality depicted, 175–76n17; indexicality of, 17, 49, 61; as not just recordings, 174n16; presumed truthfulness of, 17, 63; as recordings, 27, 63, 95; reenactments, 61; simulation (*see* simulation(s): video); as time-based medium, 81, 121; surveillance, 29, 119, 160–61n4
Vidmar, Neil, 118
viewpoint. *See* point of view
villainy, tale of, 121
virtual camera. *See* camera: virtual
virtual reality display, 148, 167n26
vision: blurred, 1–3, 27, 34–36, 43, 46, 50, 72, 105–6, 129, 142, 148, 193–94n32; of color, 163n9; constricted, 2, 142, 148, 162n3; as different from photography, 53–54; diminished, 138; distorted, 2, 14, 25, 105–6, 112; doubled, 1, 34–35, 43, 46, 56, 142; flashers, 148; floaters, 72, 148; impaired or impairments, 2–3, 20, 22, 25, 35–36, 39, 51–52, 57, 68, 81, 84, 101–2, 109, 121, 130, 139, 148, 153, 177n28, 179n5, 180–81n21, 185n4, 187n9, 193–94n32; normal or unimpaired, 2, 46, 48, 55–56, 73, 84, 177n28; subjective, 24, 48–49, 55–56, 80, 173n7. *See also* halos (after LASIK surgery); starbursts (after LASIK surgery)
"vision-realistic rendering" (wavefront), 185n4
Vision Simulations, 35, 172n6
visual apparatus, 11–12
visual consultant. *See* consultant(s): visual
visual cortex, 11, 149
visual evidence. *See* evidence: visual. *See also* demonstrative evidence
visual experience. *See* experience: visual
visual field(s), 1, 53, 67–68, 70–84, 178–79nn3–5, 15, 180–81nn20–21, 185n4, 193n28; deficit in, 180n20; examination of, 72; impairments of, 179n5; loss, 72–73, 80; maps of, 71, 80, 178n4, 180n21; restricted, 180n21, 193n28; test(s) of (*see* perimetry)
visual image reconstruction, 149–50, 152, 194n8
visual memory reconstruction, 151, 195n11; probative value of, 195n11
visual pathway, 11, 105, 179n5
visual performance tests, 185–86n5
visual rhetoric. *See* rhetoric or rhetorical: visual
visual storytelling. *See* storytelling: visual
visual studies, 5
visuomotor neurons, 13
Volk, Patrick, 74, 80, 179nn8, 11
von Grafe, Albrecht, 71

Wade, Nicholas, 178n1
Wagner, Rudolph, 173n10
Wakil, Joe, 106, 187n9
Walker-Sterling, Robin, 121–22
Wall, Michael, 71, 180nn16–17
Walsh, Thomas, 178n4
Ward, W. Dixon, 89–91
Watson (IBM computer), 18
Watts, Shelley, 159n2, 160n2
wavefront (technology), 23, 26–27, 39, 101, 103–9, 185n1, 186n6, 187n9; accuracy

of, 104, 108; as complementing corneal topography, 185n1; as complex intervention in eye's optics, 103–4; data, 170n5; generating more objective knowledge of retinal image, 185–86nn5–6; origins of in astronomy, 107, 109, 187n10; procedure for testing, 108; reliability of, 108, 185–86n5; summary display, 109–12
wavefront (optics), 103, 112; aberrated, 103–4. *See also* cornea(s): aberrations of
Waytz, Adam, 12–13, 164n11
Wegel, R. L., 88
wergild, 118
Werth, Barry, 120
"What Is It Like to Be a Bat?" (Nagel), 9–10
White, James Boyd, 121
whiteboard, 40
whole person (value of plaintiff's life), 119
Wilke v. Dudley, 46–47, 160n3, 177n28, 190–91n15
Wilke, Travis, 177n28, 190–91n15
Williams, David, 23, 186n6
Wilson, Timothy, 7
Wingfield, Nick, 148
Winkielman, Piotr, 42
Winogrand, Garry, 175n16
Winsberg, Eric, 17
Wispé, Lauren, 135
Wissler, Roselle, 117–18, 188n3, 189n5
witnesses, 2, 6, 106, 114, 143, 194n4; perspective of, 60. *See also* testimony
Wolf, Mark, 17
Wolfson, Warren, 28–29
words: ambiguity and vagueness of, 24, 131; as basis for collective moral judgments, 123–24; inadequacy in conveying sensory phenomena, 24, 32–33, 170–71n6; Janson's, 124–27, 131; litigant's, 26, 51; patients', as personal statement, 133; plaintiff's, importance of in describing pain and suffering, 115, 119–27; used in court to describe sensory experience, 43; used in court to describe simulations, 34, 42

Yale University, 72
Yarbus, Alfred, 176n23

Zahavi, Dan, 13, 15–16, 166n21, 190n9
Zernike polynomials, 103, 185n2
Zyszkowski, Regina, 105